America's
TEST KITCHEN

Cook's Country
BEST LOST
SUPPERS

Old-Fashioned, Home-Cooked Recipes
Too Good to Forget

FROM THE EDITORS AT AMERICA'S TEST KITCHEN

COLOR PHOTOGRAPHY Keller + Keller
FOOD STYLING Mary Jane Sawyer
BLACK AND WHITE PHOTOGRAPHY Daniel J. van Ackere

America's
TEST KITCHEN

America's Test Kitchen
17 Station Street
Brookline, MA 02445

ISBN-13: 978-1-933615-44-8
ISBN-10: 1-933615-44-3
Library of Congress Cataloging-in-Publication Data
The Editors at America's Test Kitchen

Cook's Country Best Lost Suppers
Old-Fashioned, Home-Cooked Recipes
Too Good to Forget

(hardcover): U.S. $29.95/ Can. $38.99
1. Cooking. 1. Title
2009

Manufactured in Thailand
10 9 8 7 6 5 4 3 2 1

Distributed by America's Test Kitchen,
17 Station Street, Brookline, MA 02445

Editorial Director: Jack Bishop
Executive Editor: Elizabeth Carduff
Food Editor: Julia Collin Davison
Senior Editor: Rachel Toomey
Associate Editor: Louise Flaig
Test Cooks: Suzannah McFerran, Adelaide Parker, Dan Souza, Megan Wycoff, Dan Zuccarello
Assistant Test Cooks: Dana Ehrlich, Jennifer Lalime
Editorial Assistant: Elizabeth Pohm
Design Director: Amy Klee
Art Director: Greg Galvan
Designer: Matthew Warnick
Photography: Keller + Keller, Daniel J. van Ackere
Food Styling: Mary Jane Sawyer
Illustration: © Greg Stevenson/www.i2iart.com
Production Director: Guy Rochford
Senior Production Manager: Jessica Lindheimer Quirk
Senior Project Manager: Alice Carpenter
Color and Imaging Specialist: Andrew Mannone
Production and Imaging Specialists: Judy Blomquist, Lauren Pettapiece
Copy Editor: Cheryl Redmond
Proofreader: Christine Corcoran Cox
Indexer: Elizabeth Parson

The Staff of *Cook's Country* Magazine:
Executive Editor: Peggy Grodinsky
Deputy Editor: Bridget Lancaster
Senior Editors: Scott Kathan, Lisa McManus, Jeremy Sauer
Test Kitchen Director: Erin McMurrer
Associate Editors: Cali Rich, Diane Unger
Test Cooks: Lynn Clark, Kris Widican
Assistant Editors: Meredith Butcher, Peggy Chung Collier
Assistant Test Cooks: Meghan Erwin, María del Mar Sacasa
Assistant Test Kitchen Director: Matthew Herron
Copy Editor: Amy Graves
Editorial Assistant: Abbey Becker

Pictured on the front cover: Aunt Fanny's Pasta Soup with Little Meatballs (page 116)
Pictured opposite title page: Traditional Upper Peninsula Pasties (page 108)

Contents

WELCOME TO AMERICA'S TEST KITCHEN **vi**

INTRODUCTION BY CHRISTOPHER KIMBALL **vii**

CHAPTER 1: Potluck Classics **1**

CHAPTER 2: Sunday Night Suppers **31**

CHAPTER 3: From a Storied Past **73**

CHAPTER 4: Easy Family Favorites **89**

CHAPTER 5: Recipes from the Old Country **107**

CHAPTER 6: Dinner on a Dime **135**

CHAPTER 7: American Regional Specialties **153**

CHAPTER 8: Sweet Endings **183**

CONVERSIONS & EQUIVALENCIES **200**

INDEX **203**

Welcome to America's Test Kitchen

THIS BOOK HAS BEEN TESTED, WRITTEN, AND EDITED BY THE FOLKS at America's Test Kitchen, a very real 2,500-square-foot kitchen located just outside of Boston. It is the home of *Cook's Country* magazine and *Cook's Illustrated* magazine and is the Monday-through-Friday destination for more than three dozen test cooks, editors, food scientists, tasters, and cookware specialists. Our mission is to test recipes over and over again until we understand how and why they work and until we arrive at the "best" version.

We start the process of testing a recipe with a complete lack of conviction, which means that we accept no claim, no theory, no technique, and no recipe at face value. We simply assemble as many variations as possible, test a half dozen of the most promising, and taste the results blind. We then construct our own hybrid recipe and continue to test it, varying ingredients, techniques, and cooking times until we reach a consensus. The result, we hope, is the best version of a particular recipe, but we realize that only you can be the final judge of our success (or failure). As we like to say in the test kitchen, "We make the mistakes, so you don't have to."

All of this would not be possible without a belief that good cooking, much like good music, is indeed based on a foundation of objective technique. Some people like spicy foods and others don't, but there is a right way to sauté, there is a best way to cook a pot roast, and there are measurable scientific principles involved in producing perfectly beaten, stable egg whites. This is our ultimate goal: to investigate the fundamental principles of cooking so that you become a better cook. It is as simple as that.

You can watch us work (in our actual test kitchen) by tuning in to *Cook's Country from America's Test Kitchen* (www.cookscountrytv.com) or *America's Test Kitchen* (www.americastestkitchen.com) on public television, or by subscribing to *Cook's Country* magazine (www.cookscountry.com) or *Cook's Illustrated* magazine (www.cooksillustrated.com), which are each published every other month. We welcome you into our kitchen, where you can stand by our side as we test our way to the "best" recipes in America.

Introduction

IN THE GREEN MOUNTAINS OF VERMONT, I HAVE COME ACROSS DOZENS OF THINGS that were lost: cellar holes, in-the-weeds corn cribs, rotted hunting camps, rusted pocket knives, caves up in Beartown, even an entire farm on the top of Red Mountain with a farm-house and three barns, two of which were still standing; well, sort of. In a shed on the top of a ridge behind our farmhouse, there are the makings of a horse-drawn wagon from a time before World War II, and outhouses dot the landscape, usually behind old churches, whose purpose is lost to modern generations.

Some of the lost things I have found are simply signposts to another era, items that are steeped in nostalgia—the outhouses for example—but that are perhaps best left to history. Other lost objects, however, are great finds when dusted off and restored to their original luster. Tom, a neighbor, once found an over/under 22/410 in a river during a flood in Pownal. He brought it home, had a friend fix it up, and now it is one of his favorite guns.

For the most part, we can't re-create the past with hope of success, but recipes do offer us a unique time machine; imperfect perhaps, but "lost" suppers are an easy means of experiencing the lives and foods of those who have gone before us. They have left a rich record of who they were and how they lived through their food, and that is the charm and promise of this volume. A recipe gem from the past can be a revelation, something as startlingly fresh as a muskmelon picked on a late August afternoon, chilled at the bottom of an old well, sliced, and served with a wedge of lemon. While selecting recipes for *Best Lost Suppers,* I tasted a past richer than the present with a large spoonful of Granny's Tamale Pie, Tia's Coffee Pot Roast, Green Mountain Surprise, Corn Pie, Aunt Fanny's Pasta Soup with Little Meatballs (see cover), Grandma's Enchiladas (made with cubes of tender chuck), and French Silk Chocolate Pie.

I spend a lot of time perusing old cookbooks, looking for culinary inspiration (as well as dinner), and although I have developed a pretty good sense of what is likely to work, there are no guarantees—old recipes are about as hit or miss as it gets. I have made dozens of recipes from Boston in the 1890s while researching Fannie Farmer, and most were so bad that it was no wonder that newspapers of the era were chock-full of ads offering cures for dyspepsia and other digestive complaints. Just dig into Prune Pudding or Brain Balls and you willingly divest yourself of the culinary past.

That's why *Best Lost Suppers* is something special. America's Test Kitchen has combed through more than 1,000 submissions and tested hundreds of recipes to come up with the selection in this carefully edited volume. The recipes that finally did make it between these covers have been tested and retested so that you won't have to worry "Will this recipe really work?" If you wish to taste our culinary past, this guide is well worth the small investment.

I recently came across a bit of history that still has me enthralled. In Paris during the 1930s, street fairs were common during winter months and offered fried potatoes, hurdy-gurdies, dodge 'em cars, shooting galleries, roller coasters, wild animals, boxing, and dancing girls. One reporter made the acquaintance of Loie Fuller, who danced every evening for the price of milk and bread. But her husband, Torgue, a former stuntman for Douglas Fairbanks, was the real find. He billed himself as the "Human Gorilla," dressed in full monkey suit, climbing factory chimneys, church steeples, and viaducts, and tumbling from planes, cars, and locomotives. The couple lived in a cheap hotel with their blond, blue-eyed son, along with magicians, snake charmers, and trapeze artists. And then I discovered the photo: Torgue dressed in full gorilla costume complete with checked suit and derby hat, bent over his young son, helping him to get ready for school.

That picture haunts me. It offers clues to an extraordinary, otherworldly existence, one as rich as Jersey cream. One can taste the life captured in the photograph as if one were sitting down to dinner.

Tonight, however, I am going to dine on something more substantial. I intend to travel back in time with Granny's Tamale Pie from Bozeman, Montana. Betty Hesterberg writes about her mother who was given the recipe by the wife of a sheep rancher. She warmed the tamale casserole over a fire and served it at herding camps. Originally, the recipe was made with pheasants, birds that were plentiful in the area long ago, but now the recipe simply calls for chicken. When I first tasted it, I was reminded of a family trip to Bozeman a few years ago: the snap of cold mornings, the piney smell of wood smoke, the sharp, clear air, and the endless horizon. I could taste the place in the food, and that is what *Best Lost Suppers* offers—a taste of another life and another place, and, of course, just plain delicious home cooking. As a nation, we knew the secrets of transforming simple, local ingredients into a lifetime of memories. *Best Lost Suppers* is a celebration of what we used to know and a call to never forget.

I hope that you enjoy *Best Lost Suppers* as much as we did.

Christopher Kimball
Founder and Editor, *Cook's Country* and *Cook's Illustrated*
Host, *Cook's Country from America's Test Kitchen* and *America's Test Kitchen*

HOME RANCH CHICKEN AND DUMPLINGS CASSEROLE

Potluck Classics

Home Ranch Chicken and Dumplings Casserole **2**

Creamy Chicken Pan Pie **4**

Granny's Tamale Pie **7**

Chicken Tetrazzini (à la Aunt Leah) **9**

Preacher's Delight **12**

Salmagundi Bake **13**

Grandma's Enchiladas **14**

Funeral Potatoes with Ham **17**

Fluffy Ham and Grits **18**

Mom's Hominy **19**

Baked Eggplant Casserole **20**

Papa's Lasagna **21**

Martini Mac and Cheese **24**

Mighty Good Shrimp Salad **26**

Corn Pie **27**

Home Ranch Chicken and Dumplings Casserole

TABI LAWRENCE FARNSWORTH | BEVERLY HILLS, CALIFORNIA

"I was raised on a seventeen-thousand-acre hay ranch where we had three cuttings per season. This meant about twenty-six big-appetite field hands for dinner three times per day. Every ranch cook had a recipe for chicken and dumplings, and each one took pride in their individual twist." Tabi's is a sturdy casserole-style version topped with great big fluffy biscuits, perfect for soaking up the hearty filling, and with the inclusion of carrots, celery, peas, and potatoes, this is truly a one-dish meal. Though you'll still find a fair number of working ranches around the country, there's something about this recipe that beckons a bygone era, one where folks spent long days working the land and tilling the soil, building up a huge appetite for a big, satisfying meal. Even if you don't have to serve dozens of hungry ranch hands, this comforting casserole is sure to be gobbled up at your next gathering with family, friends, or neighbors.

SERVES 6 TO 8

FILLING

- 3 pounds bone-in, skin-on chicken pieces (split breasts cut in half, drumsticks, and/or thighs), trimmed
- Salt and pepper
- 1 tablespoon vegetable oil
- 2 tablespoons unsalted butter
- 4 carrots, peeled, halved, and cut into ¼-inch pieces
- 3 celery ribs, sliced ¼ inch thick
- 1 onion, minced
- 3 cups low-sodium chicken broth
- ¾ cup heavy cream
- 1 pound russet potatoes, peeled and cut into 1-inch chunks
- 2 bay leaves
- 1½ cups frozen peas
- ¼ cup chopped fresh parsley

DUMPLINGS

- 2 cups all-purpose flour
- 1 tablespoon baking powder
- ¾ teaspoon salt
- ½ teaspoon baking soda
- ¾ cup whole milk, warm
- ¼ cup buttermilk, warm
- 1 tablespoon unsalted butter, melted

1. **FOR THE FILLING:** Adjust an oven rack to the middle position and heat the oven to 375 degrees. Grease a 13 by 9-inch baking dish and set aside.

2. Pat the chicken dry with paper towels and season with salt and pepper. Heat 1½ teaspoons of the oil in a large Dutch oven over medium-high heat until just smoking. Add half of the chicken and cook until golden brown on both sides, about 10 minutes, flipping halfway through. Transfer the chicken to a plate and remove the skin. Return the pot to medium-high heat and repeat with the remaining 1½ teaspoons oil and the remaining chicken.

3. Melt the butter in the Dutch oven over medium heat. Add the carrots, celery, onion, and ½ teaspoon salt and cook, stirring occasionally, until softened, 5 to 7 minutes. Whisk in the broth, cream, potatoes, and bay leaves, scraping up any browned bits.

4. Return the chicken, along with any accumulated juices, to the pot. Bring to a simmer, cover, and cook until the chicken is fully cooked and tender, about 20 minutes for breasts (160 to 165 degrees on an instant-read thermometer) or 1 hour for thighs and drumsticks (175 degrees on an instant-read thermometer). (If using both white and dark meat, simmer the thighs and drumsticks for 40 minutes before adding the breasts.)

5. Transfer the chicken to a plate. Discard the bay leaves, then skim the fat off the surface of the sauce with a wide spoon. Using a potato masher, gently mash half of the potatoes. When the chicken is cool enough to handle, shred the meat into bite-sized pieces and return it to the sauce with the peas and parsley. Season with salt and pepper to taste. Pour the mixture into the prepared baking dish and set aside.

6. **FOR THE DUMPLINGS:** Whisk the flour, baking powder, salt, and baking soda together in a bowl. Stir in the milk and buttermilk until incorporated and smooth. Using two soup-spoons, drop eight generous ¼-cup dumplings onto the filling about 1 inch apart. Brush the tops of the dumplings with the melted butter.

7. Place the baking dish on a foil-lined rimmed baking sheet and bake until the filling is bubbling and the dumplings are golden brown, 20 to 30 minutes. Cool for 10 minutes before serving.

Notes from the Test Kitchen

Tabi uses potatoes rather than flour to bind her filling, a technique we liked for the texture and pure flavor it provided. Her original recipe relied on stewing chickens and homemade bouillon; we simplified things by switching to chicken pieces and store-bought broth. Even though this revision makes the recipe a bit less old-fashioned, our filling still offers a great amount of rich chicken flavor.

Creamy Chicken Pan Pie

ROSEY ROSSITER | SAN CLEMENTE, CALIFORNIA

Chicken pot pie has long stood as an American classic—it was a standard dish as of the mid-1800s, and it likely existed earlier in concept if not in name. This comforting version of a chicken pot pie features a cheddar cheese crust, which makes this recipe a real standout. You would think that Rosey was an expert pot pie maker given how tasty her recipe is, but surprisingly, before attending a charity potluck many years ago, Rosey's pot pie experiences were limited to the double-crusted, single-serving versions found in the grocer's freezer aisle. Her first encounter with a homemade single-crusted chicken pan pie—as she called it, a "one-crust wonder"—was a revelation. When Rosey tried to find a recipe similar to the one she'd had at that potluck, she came up empty-handed. That was when she began her "personal quest to create the pie I craved." Here are the results of her hard work. You are likely to find it just as Rosey describes—"pure bliss."

SERVES 6 TO 8

CRUST
1¼ cups all-purpose flour
½ teaspoon salt
10 tablespoons (1¼ sticks) unsalted butter, cut into ¼-inch pieces and chilled
½ cup shredded sharp cheddar cheese
4–6 tablespoons ice water

FILLING
1½ pounds boneless, skinless chicken breasts, trimmed
Salt and pepper
1 tablespoon vegetable oil
4 tablespoons (½ stick) unsalted butter
3 carrots, peeled and sliced ¼ inch thick
2 celery ribs, sliced ¼ inch thick
2 cups frozen pearl onions, thawed
½ cup all-purpose flour
2½ cups low-sodium chicken broth
1 cup heavy cream
1½ teaspoons minced fresh thyme
1 cup frozen peas
3 tablespoons chopped fresh parsley
1 large egg, lightly beaten

1. FOR THE CRUST: Process the flour and salt in a food processor until combined. Scatter the butter pieces over the top and pulse the mixture until it resembles coarse crumbs, about 10 pulses. Add the cheese and pulse until just combined, about 5 pulses. Transfer the mixture to a bowl.

2. Sprinkle 4 tablespoons of the ice water over the mixture. Stir and press the dough together using a stiff rubber spatula, until the dough sticks together. If the dough does not come together, stir in the remaining water, 1 tablespoon at a time, until it does.

3. Turn the dough onto a sheet of plastic wrap and flatten into a 5 by 4-inch rectangle. Wrap the dough tightly in the plastic wrap and refrigerate for at least 1 hour, or up to 2 days. Before rolling out the dough, let it sit on the counter to soften slightly, about 10 minutes.

4. FOR THE FILLING: Meanwhile, adjust an oven rack to the lower-middle position and heat the oven to 400 degrees. Grease a 13 by 9-inch baking dish and set aside.

5. Pat the chicken dry with paper towels and season with salt and pepper. Heat the oil in a large Dutch oven over medium-high heat until just smoking. Cook the chicken until golden brown on both sides, about 5 minutes, flipping halfway through. Transfer the chicken to a plate.

6. Melt the butter in the Dutch oven over medium heat. Add the carrots, celery, onions, and ½ teaspoon salt and cook, stirring occasionally, until softened, 5 to 7 minutes. Stir in the flour and cook for 1 minute. Whisk in the broth, cream, and thyme, scraping up any browned bits. Return the chicken, along with any accumulated juices, to the pot. Bring to a simmer, cover, and cook until the thickest part of the breasts registers 160 to 165 degrees on an instant-read thermometer, 10 to 15 minutes.

7. Transfer the chicken to a plate. When the chicken is cool enough to handle, shred the meat into bite-sized pieces and return it to the sauce with the peas and parsley. Season with salt and pepper to taste. Pour the mixture into the prepared baking dish and set aside.

8. Roll out the dough on a lightly floured counter to a 15 by 11-inch rectangle, about ⅛ inch thick. Roll the dough loosely over the rolling pin and unroll it evenly over the baking dish. Trim the dough, leaving ½ inch hanging over the pan lip. Press the dough firmly to seal it to the lip of the pan. (For a decorative border, press the edges of the pie with the tines of a fork.) Cut four oval-shaped vents, about 1 inch long and ½ inch wide, in the top of the pie dough. Brush the dough with the egg.

9. Place the baking dish on a foil-lined rimmed baking sheet and bake until the filling is bubbling and the crust is golden brown, 35 to 45 minutes. Cool for 10 minutes before serving.

Notes from the Test Kitchen

We found ourselves shamelessly devouring this pie, particularly for its flavorful crust (though we were also fans of its ultra-creamy sauce and unusual addition of pearl onions). There wasn't need to change much in Rosey's recipe, aside from making the crust a tad less gummy by rolling it thinner, and streamlining the method to ensure more evenly cooked vegetables.

Granny's Tamale Pie

BETTY HESTERBERG | BOZEMAN, MONTANA

"My mother got this recipe from the elderly wife of a sheep rancher, who would make this dish and heat it up over the fire at herding camps. We always made it with pheasants, which were plentiful in the area when I was a child, but as the pheasant population grew slim we turned to duck or geese; now we use chicken, ideally dark meat for more flavorful broth. This dish was always made on my father's birthday in November, a tradition started in the late 1930s and continued until his death in 1990. Now, I serve it on special occasions and whenever I get to see my brothers." We were immediately drawn to the recipe because it is a far cry from the typical cheesy casserole-style versions we usually come across. First and foremost, this old-fashioned tamale pie is baked in a Dutch oven set in a roasting pan filled with simmering water, a method that mimics how tamales are steamed. And rather than mixing in some sort of sauce before baking, Betty makes a flavorful, spicy tomato sauce to serve on the side. Lastly, you won't find a single shred of cheese in this recipe—don't worry, you won't miss it. You'll need a large roasting pan, ideally one that's 16 by 13 inches, to accommodate the water bath.

SERVES 6 TO 8

PIE

- 3 pounds bone-in, skin-on chicken thighs, trimmed
  Salt and pepper
- ½ cup vegetable oil
- 3 cups low-sodium chicken broth
- 8 slices bacon, chopped
- 1 onion, minced
- 2 garlic cloves, minced
- 2 (14.5-ounce) cans diced tomatoes, drained
- 1 (14.75-ounce) can creamed corn
- 1 (6-ounce) can pitted ripe black olives, drained and chopped
- 1 cup whole milk
- 3 large eggs
- 2 cups yellow cornmeal

SAUCE

- 3 tablespoons all-purpose flour
- 1 tablespoon chili powder
- 1 teaspoon ground cumin
- 1 teaspoon ground coriander
- 1½ cups enriched chicken broth (reserved from making the pie filling)
- 1 (8-ounce) can tomato sauce
  Salt and pepper
- ¼ cup chopped fresh cilantro, for serving

1. FOR THE PIE: Adjust an oven rack to the lower-middle position and heat the oven to 325 degrees.

2. Pat the chicken dry with paper towels and season with salt and pepper. Heat 1½ teaspoons of the oil in a large Dutch oven over

(Continued on page 8)

medium-high heat until just smoking. Add half of the chicken and cook until golden brown on both sides, about 10 minutes, flipping halfway through. Transfer the chicken to a plate and remove the skin. Return the pot to medium-high heat and repeat with 1½ teaspoons more oil and the remaining chicken.

3. Stir the broth into the pot, scraping up any browned bits. Return the chicken, along with any accumulated juices, to the pot. Bring to a simmer, cover, and cook until the thickest part of the thighs registers 175 degrees on an instant-read thermometer, about 1 hour.

4. Transfer the chicken to a plate. Measure out and reserve 1½ cups of the broth for the sauce. (Discard any remaining broth or save for another use.) When the chicken is cool enough to handle, shred the meat into bite-sized pieces and set aside.

5. Bring a kettle of water to a boil. Meanwhile, cook the bacon in the Dutch oven over medium-low heat until crisp, about 10 minutes. Using a slotted spoon, transfer the bacon to a paper towel–lined plate.

6. Increase the heat to medium and heat the bacon fat until shimmering. Add the onion and ½ teaspoon salt and cook, stirring occasionally, until softened, 5 to 7 minutes. Stir in the garlic and cook until fragrant, about 30 seconds. Stir in the remaining 7 tablespoons oil, the tomatoes, corn, olives, and ½ teaspoon pepper and bring to a simmer.

7. Meanwhile, whisk the milk and eggs together in a bowl. Whisk in the cornmeal until incorporated and smooth. Slowly pour the cornmeal mixture into the pot while stirring constantly in a circular motion to prevent clumping, and cook until the mixture thickens slightly, about 1 minute. Off the heat, stir in the reserved bacon.

8. Measure out and reserve half (about 4 cups) of the cornmeal mixture. Smooth the cornmeal mixture left in the pot into an even layer, then top with the shredded chicken. Pour the reserved cornmeal mixture over the chicken and smooth into an even layer, covering the meat completely.

9. Cover the pot and place it inside a large roasting pan. Place the roasting pan in the oven and carefully pour enough boiling water into the pan to reach one-third of the way up the sides of the Dutch oven. Bake until the cornmeal mixture is dry to the touch and lightly browned, 1½ to 2 hours. Cool for 10 minutes.

10. FOR THE SAUCE: While the pie bakes, cook the flour in a medium dry skillet over medium heat, stirring frequently, until light golden brown, 3 to 5 minutes. Stir in the chili powder, cumin, and coriander and cook until fragrant, about 30 seconds. Stir in the reserved broth and tomato sauce, bring to a simmer, and cook until thickened, about 2 minutes. Season with salt and pepper to taste.

11. When the pie has cooled, sprinkle it with the cilantro and serve, passing the sauce separately.

Notes from the Test Kitchen

Our test cooks agreed that this recipe beat out any tamale pie casserole we'd had—it has a genuine flavor and texture that is just like taking a bite of a tamale, and an authentic sauce as well. The water bath was a clever technique, as it was a gentle cooking method that kept the sides from drying out and kept the rest of the pie moist and fluffy. We did, however, make a few changes to the original for the sake of convenience. We swapped out the salt pork called for in the original recipe for bacon, since the latter is easier to find for most of us, and we liked the smoky flavor bacon added (though you can certainly use salt pork if you prefer). This recipe calls for bone-in, skin-on chicken thighs, which provide excellent richness, but it will work with white meat chicken too. We recommend using bone-in, skin-on split breasts for the best flavor; just reduce the cooking time in step 3 to 20 minutes.

Chicken Tetrazzini (à la Aunt Leah)

DEBRA KEIL | OWASSO, OKLAHOMA

The cheesy, creamy, chicken-spaghetti casserole known as tetrazzini is quintessential rich comfort food, so it isn't all that surprising that it is said to have been named for an equally "rich" personality, the early twentieth-century Italian opera diva Luisa Tetrazzini. This particular recipe puts a colorful spin on the original. Debra notes that even though family gatherings always offered a bounty of comfort food, "When Aunt Leah married my favorite uncle, she brought her own special flair to our family's holiday dinners." That included this creative casserole that quickly became a family tradition. Aunt Leah traded in tetrazzini's traditional Parmesan–sherry cream sauce for a cheddar cheese sauce, and she added green peppers, black olives, and roasted red peppers to the usual mushrooms and onions. "I remember a family friend witnessing the magical making of Aunt Leah's tetrazzini. He says that she kept adding and adding ingredients to a huge mixing bowl. Laughing, he watched her add and add, more and more, to the bowl. He knew that with the next ingredient, it would overflow, but it never did. It must have been a bottomless bowl!" While Debra has updated her aunt's original version, which stewed a whole hen and relied on homemade broth, to make it a bit more manageable, "it still makes me nostalgic for those family dinners with all of the aunts, uncles, grandparents, and cousins. This is truly one of my comfort foods."

SERVES 6 TO 8

- 1 **pound spaghetti**
  Salt
- ¼ **cup vegetable oil**
- 1½ **pounds boneless, skinless chicken breasts, trimmed**
  Pepper
- 8 **ounces white mushrooms, sliced thin**
- 1 **onion, minced**
- 1 **green bell pepper, stemmed, seeded, and chopped fine**

- ¼ **cup all-purpose flour**
- 2½ **cups low-sodium chicken broth**
- 2 **cups half-and-half**
- 2 **cups shredded Co-Jack cheese**
- 2 **cups shredded sharp cheddar cheese**
- 1 **(6-ounce) can pitted ripe black olives, drained and chopped**
- ½ **cup drained jarred roasted red peppers, chopped**

(Continued on page 10)

1. Adjust an oven rack to the middle position and heat the oven to 350 degrees. Bring 4 quarts water to a boil in a large Dutch oven. Add the pasta and 1 tablespoon salt and cook, stirring often, until just shy of al dente. Drain the pasta, toss with 1 tablespoon of the oil, and set aside. Wipe the pot dry with paper towels.

2. Pat the chicken dry with paper towels and season with salt and pepper. Add 1 tablespoon more oil to the pot and return to medium-high heat until just smoking. Cook the chicken until golden brown on both sides, about 5 minutes, flipping halfway through. Transfer the chicken to a plate.

3. Heat the remaining 2 tablespoons oil in the Dutch oven over medium heat until shimmering. Add the mushrooms and ¾ teaspoon salt and cook until the mushrooms have released their juices and are brown around the edges, 7 to 10 minutes. Add the onion and bell pepper and cook, stirring occasionally, until softened, 5 to 7 minutes. Stir in the flour and cook for 1 minute.

4. Whisk in the broth and half-and-half, scraping up any browned bits. Return the chicken, along with any accumulated juices, to the pot. Bring to a simmer, cover, and cook until the thickest part of the breasts registers 160 to 165 degrees on an instant-read thermometer, 10 to 15 minutes.

5. Transfer the chicken to a plate. When the chicken is cool enough to handle, shred the meat into bite-sized pieces and return it to the sauce along with the pasta, both cheeses, the olives, and roasted peppers. Season with salt and pepper to taste. Pour the mixture into a 13 by 9-inch baking dish.

6. Place the baking dish on a foil-lined rimmed baking sheet and bake until the sauce is bubbling and the top is golden brown, 15 to 20 minutes. Cool for 10 minutes before serving.

Notes from the Test Kitchen

Debra's original recipe called for Velveeta, but we found using Co-Jack (a combination of Colby and Monterey Jack cheeses) resulted in a much better cheese flavor, and it still melted easily into the sauce. To help remove excess moisture from the vegetables and ensure that they were perfectly tender by the end of baking, we cooked them on the stovetop until they were softened before combining them with the other ingredients.

Preacher's Delight

LEE NEWLIN | GREENSBORO, NORTH CAROLINA

We had no idea what to expect when we first saw Lee's recipe, but after making this indulgent, layered egg noodle casserole with hearty meat sauce and rich cream cheese sauce, we knew we had a keeper. And the name? "I love saying it with a Southern drawl: 'Preachurs Deeelight,'" jokes Lee, who discovered this recipe in a cookbook by the women and friends of the Berea Baptist Church in Mooresville, North Carolina. There are actually a surprising number of recipes out there for Preacher's Delight, from savory casseroles to cookies and cakes. The title likely came out of nineteenth-century community events held to raise a minister's salary. Women would prepare their best dishes for a gathering held in a church member's home, where they hoped good food would lead to good spirits—and a little cash generosity. "I use this recipe whenever I prepare a dish for a church gathering, funeral, or a good ol' Southern-style gathering."

SERVES 6 TO 8

- 1 (12-ounce) package egg noodles
  Salt
- 1 tablespoon vegetable oil
- 1 onion, minced
- 1 green bell pepper, stemmed, seeded, and chopped
- 2½ pounds 85 percent lean ground beef
- 2 (15-ounce) cans tomato sauce
- 1 tablespoon sugar
- ½ teaspoon pepper
- 1 (8-ounce) package cream cheese, softened
- 1½ cups sour cream
- 1 cup shredded sharp cheddar cheese

1. Adjust an oven rack to the middle position and heat the oven to 350 degrees. Grease a 13 by 9-inch baking dish and set aside.

2. Bring 4 quarts water to a boil in a large Dutch oven. Add the noodles and 1 tablespoon salt and cook, stirring often, until just shy of al dente. Drain the noodles and set aside.

3. Wipe the pot dry with paper towels. Add the oil to the pot and return to medium heat until shimmering. Add the onion and bell pepper and cook, stirring occasionally, until softened, 5 to 7 minutes. Add the beef, increase the heat to medium-high, and cook, breaking up any large clumps with a wooden spoon, until no longer pink, about 5 minutes. Stir in the tomato sauce, sugar, 1 teaspoon salt, and pepper, bring to a simmer, then set aside off the heat.

4. Mix the cream cheese and sour cream together in a bowl. Spread half of the meat sauce (about 3½ cups) over the bottom of the prepared baking dish. Scatter the noodles over the sauce in an even layer. Drop dollops of the cream cheese mixture on top of the noodles, then spread it into an even thickness. Spoon the remaining sauce evenly over the cream cheese mixture, then sprinkle evenly with the cheddar.

5. Place the baking dish on a foil-lined rimmed baking sheet and bake until the sauce is bubbling and the top starts to brown, 25 to 30 minutes. Cool for 10 minutes before serving.

Notes from the Test Kitchen

To bring the rich meat sauce and cream cheese mixture into better balance, we increased the amount of noodles and green bell pepper and lessened the amount of cream cheese originally called for. Take care to ensure that each distinct layer is preserved—they are a big part of the dish's appeal.

Salmagundi Bake

CAROL BOWEN | JACKSON, MICHIGAN

When plain ground beef is turned into a saucy, warm-spiced mixture with bell pepper, onion, and corn and baked over a bed of rice, it becomes a casserole sure to appeal to old and young alike. Carol is a grandmother who has been making this recipe for more than 45 years for her family, so she can certainly vouch for its popularity. Carol got her recipe from the 1961 *Better Homes and Gardens Casserole Cook Book*, but salmagundi's culinary history actually goes back to the seventeenth century. Recipes we found run the gamut as far as ingredients go, and the oldest recipes were something completely different from Carol's casserole, closer to a cold chef's salad with all sorts of meats and vegetables. Nevertheless, old and new share in a common theme: the word *salmagundi* means "a hodgepodge" or "a mishmash," and they all seem to qualify in that regard. You'll find Carol's recipe simple, flavorful, and an all-around crowd-pleaser.

SERVES 4 TO 6

- ¾ cup long-grain white rice
- 1 tablespoon vegetable oil
- 1 onion, minced
- 1 green bell pepper, stemmed, seeded, and chopped
- ¾ teaspoon salt
- 1 tablespoon chili powder
- 1 teaspoon ground cumin
- 1 teaspoon ground coriander
- ½ teaspoon pepper
- 2 garlic cloves, minced
- 1 pound 85 percent lean ground beef
- 2 (8-ounce) cans tomato sauce
- 1½ cups frozen corn, thawed
- 1 cup low-sodium chicken broth

1. Adjust an oven rack to the middle position and heat the oven to 375 degrees. Grease an 11 by 7-inch baking dish. Spread the rice over the bottom of the dish and set aside.

2. Heat the oil in a large Dutch oven over medium heat until shimmering. Add the onion, bell pepper, and salt and cook, stirring occasionally, until softened, 5 to 7 minutes. Stir in the chili powder, cumin, coriander, and pepper and cook until the spices darken slightly and are fragrant, about 2 minutes. Stir in the garlic and cook until fragrant, about 30 seconds.

3. Add the beef, increase the heat to medium-high, and cook, breaking up any large clumps with a wooden spoon, until no longer pink, about 5 minutes. Stir in the tomato sauce, corn, and broth, bring to a simmer, and set aside off the heat.

4. Pour the beef mixture evenly over the rice. Place the baking dish on a foil-lined rimmed baking sheet, cover with foil, and bake until the sauce is bubbling and the rice is tender, 35 to 40 minutes. Cool for 10 minutes before serving.

Notes from the Test Kitchen

Rather than layer ingredients raw as the original recipe directed, we gave several ingredients a jump start on the stovetop, shortening the baking time and ensuring everything cooked through. Carol topped her casserole with bacon, and she started with the dish covered and finished uncovered. This allowed the bacon to crisp, but uncovering the dish made the rice's texture suffer. We had the best results with our rice when we covered the dish for the duration, so we had to omit the bacon since it wouldn't crisp properly covered.

Grandma's Enchiladas

JOSIE LANDON | IDAHO FALLS, IDAHO

This recipe, created by the grandmother of one of Josie's good childhood friends, is a classic American adaptation of a favorite Mexican cuisine staple. So many American-style enchiladas today are made with ground meat, so Josie's filling of deliciously tender, slow-cooked shredded chuck roast made her recipe an immediate standout. The combination of a smoky-spicy sauce that coats the enchiladas inside and out and a topping of melted cheese won over the test kitchen at first bite. Though we think they'd make a good hearty meal any time of year, Josie says she loves her enchiladas best "on cold winter nights, when there is plenty of snow outside to play in and I need something warm and gooey in my tummy."

SERVES 6

- 3 pounds boneless beef chuck-eye roast, trimmed and cut into 1½-inch cubes
  Salt and pepper
- 2 tablespoons vegetable oil
- 2 onions, minced
- 3 tablespoons chili powder
- 2 teaspoons ground cumin
- 2 teaspoons ground coriander
- ¼ teaspoon cayenne pepper
- 4 garlic cloves, minced
- 2 (15-ounce) cans tomato sauce
- ¼ cup dry red wine
- 2 cups shredded cheddar cheese
- 12 (6-inch) corn tortillas
- ¼ cup chopped fresh cilantro, for serving
  Lime wedges, for serving

1. Adjust an oven rack to the lower-middle position and heat the oven to 300 degrees. Pat the beef dry with paper towels and season with salt and pepper. Heat 1 tablespoon of the oil in a large Dutch oven over medium-high heat until just smoking. Add half of the beef and cook until well browned on all sides, about 8 minutes, turning as needed. Transfer the beef to a bowl. Repeat with the remaining 1 table-spoon oil and the remaining beef.

2. Pour off all but 1 tablespoon fat from the pot. Add the onions and ½ teaspoon salt and cook, stirring occasionally, until softened, 5 to 7 minutes. Stir in the chili powder, cumin, coriander, cayenne, and ¼ teaspoon pepper and cook until the spices darken slightly and are fragrant, about 2 minutes. Stir in the garlic and cook until fragrant, about 30 seconds. Stir in the tomato sauce and wine and bring to a simmer, scraping up any browned bits.

3. Return the beef, along with any accumulated juices, to the sauce. Bring to a simmer, then cover the pot and place it in the oven. Cook until the meat is tender, 2 to 2½ hours.

(Continued on page 16)

Transfer the beef to a plate. Pour the sauce through a fine-mesh strainer, discarding the solids, and set aside. (You should have about 2 cups sauce.)

4. Adjust an oven rack to the middle position and increase the temperature to 375 degrees. Grease a 13 by 9-inch baking dish. Spread ¾ cup of the sauce over the bottom of the dish and set aside.

5. When the meat is cool enough to handle, shred it into bite-sized pieces and place it in a bowl. Add ¼ cup of the sauce and 1 cup of the cheese and toss to combine.

6. Spray the tortillas on both sides with vegetable oil spray and arrange on a rimmed baking sheet. Bake until the tortillas are warm and pliable, about 1 minute. Spread the tortillas out over a clean counter. Place ⅓ cup of the beef mixture evenly down the center of each tortilla. Tightly roll the tortillas around the filling, then lay them seam-side down in the baking dish.

7. Pour the remaining 1 cup sauce over the enchiladas to coat evenly. Sprinkle with the remaining 1 cup cheese and cover tightly with foil. Bake until the enchiladas are heated through and the cheese is melted, 20 to 25 minutes. Serve with the cilantro and lime wedges.

Notes from the Test Kitchen

Our test cooks were sold on these authentically flavored enchiladas, and particularly on the slow-cooked beef that fills them. While Josie's recipe called for cooking the beef in a slow cooker, we opted to save a few hours by cooking it in the oven. We also substituted store-bought tomato sauce for homemade for the sake of efficiency. The difference in flavor was slight since these enchiladas get a bold boost from the spices. Finally, we found that spraying the tortillas with vegetable oil spray kept them from cracking and drying out while they baked.

ASSEMBLING ENCHILADAS

1. Grease a 13 by 9-inch baking dish, then spread ¾ cup of the sauce over the bottom of the dish.

2. Place ⅓ cup of the beef mixture evenly down the center of each warmed tortilla. Tightly roll the tortillas and place them seam-side down in the baking dish.

3. Pour the remaining 1 cup sauce over the enchiladas to coat evenly.

4. Sprinkle the enchiladas with the remaining 1 cup cheese and cover the baking dish tightly with foil before baking.

Funeral Potatoes with Ham

JACQUELINE GORBUTT | SPRINGFIELD, VIRGINIA

Although this recipe has a gloomy name, once you taste it, you'll realize just how comforting a scoop of this starchy, creamy casserole is. Funeral potatoes are practically the state dish of Utah (they were featured on pins for the 2002 Olympics), but this particular recipe came from a Southern cook who noted that "funeral potatoes with ham are often found at the homes of deceased members of my church. When the family is in need of comfort, funeral potatoes with ham fit the bill. This tasty recipe may also be found at luncheons after baptisms, church parties, and potluck suppers. There are never leftovers to bring home!"

SERVES 8 TO 10

4	pounds russet potatoes, scrubbed
2	tablespoons vegetable oil
1	pound white mushrooms, sliced thin
	Salt
1	onion, minced
2	tablespoons all-purpose flour
1½	cups whole milk
½	teaspoon minced fresh thyme
½	teaspoon pepper
1½	cups shredded sharp cheddar cheese
8	tablespoons (1 stick) unsalted butter
1	pound ham steak, cut into 2-inch matchsticks
1	cup sour cream
1½	cups cornflakes, crushed fine

1. Adjust an oven rack to the middle position and heat the oven to 350 degrees. Grease a 13 by 9-inch baking dish and set aside.

2. Bring the potatoes and 4 quarts water to a simmer in a large pot and cook until just shy of tender (a paring knife should glide through the flesh with slight resistance), 10 to 15 minutes. Drain the potatoes and set aside. When the potatoes are cool enough to handle, peel them, then grate the flesh lengthwise on the large holes of a box grater. Return the grated potatoes to the pot.

3. While the potatoes cook, heat the oil in a large skillet over medium heat until shimmering. Add the mushrooms and ¾ teaspoon salt and cook until the mushrooms have released their juices and are brown around the edges, 7 to 10 minutes. Add the onion and cook, stirring occasionally, until softened, 5 to 7 minutes. Stir in the flour and cook for 1 minute.

4. Whisk in the milk, thyme, and pepper, bring to a simmer, and cook, stirring frequently, until thickened slightly, about 1 minute. Stir in the cheese and 6 tablespoons of the butter and cook until melted, about 1 minute.

5. Off the heat, stir in the ham and sour cream. Pour the mixture over the potatoes and toss to combine. Transfer the mixture to the prepared baking dish. Melt the remaining 2 tablespoons butter in a bowl in the microwave. Stir in the cornflakes, then sprinkle them evenly over the top of the potato mixture.

6. Place the baking dish on a foil-lined rimmed baking sheet and bake until potatoes are bubbling and the top is golden brown, 35 to 45 minutes. Cool for 10 minutes before serving.

Notes from the Test Kitchen

To balance the starchiness of this recipe, we increased the amount of ham and mushrooms, and we added fresh thyme for a little more depth of flavor. Boiling the potatoes until they are barely tender (the flesh should resist only slightly when pierced with a knife) is key to ensuring the proper final texture, one that isn't too crunchy or too mushy.

Fluffy Ham and Grits

JANICE ELDER | CHARLOTTE, NORTH CAROLINA

"Growing up in the South, grits were always a staple and we adored them. Hot, comforting, and satisfying." Our country's familiarity with grits, made by cooking dried corn or hominy in water or milk, can be credited to the Native Americans, who passed their cooking technique on to European settlers. Janice's recipe is indeed fluffy, relying on whipped egg whites for extra lift. "While this dish was sometimes prepared for Christmas morning breakfast, more often it was served as a quick evening meal. It was a great use for leftover country ham, though we sometimes used bacon or regular ham."

SERVES 4 TO 6

4 tablespoons (½ stick) unsalted butter
1 onion, minced
½ teaspoon salt
2 garlic cloves, minced
4 cups water
1 cup old-fashioned grits
2 cups shredded sharp cheddar cheese
5 ounces ham steak, minced
½ teaspoon Worcestershire sauce
¼ teaspoon pepper
⅛ teaspoon cayenne pepper
2 large egg whites
  Pinch cream of tartar
2 scallions, sliced thin

1. Adjust an oven rack to the middle position and heat the oven to 350 degrees. Grease an 11 by 7-inch baking dish and set aside.

2. Melt 2 tablespoons of the butter in a medium saucepan over medium heat. Add the onion and salt and cook, stirring occasionally, until softened, 5 to 7 minutes. Stir in the garlic and cook until fragrant, about 30 seconds. Add the water and bring to a boil.

3. Pour the grits into the boiling water in a slow stream while whisking constantly in a circular motion to prevent clumping. Reduce the heat to low and cook, stirring often, until thick and creamy, 10 to 15 minutes.

4. Off the heat, stir in the remaining 2 tablespoons butter, 1 cup of the cheese, the ham, Worcestershire sauce, pepper, and cayenne. Transfer the mixture to a medium bowl and cool slightly, about 5 minutes.

5. In a large bowl, whip the egg whites and cream of tartar with an electric mixer on medium-low speed until foamy, about 1 minute. Increase the mixer speed to medium-high and continue to whip until the whites are glossy and form stiff peaks, 2 to 4 minutes.

6. Stir about one-third of the whipped egg whites into the grits to lighten the mixture, then fold in the remaining whites until just incorporated. Gently pour the mixture into the prepared baking dish and sprinkle the remaining 1 cup cheese evenly over the top.

7. Place the baking dish on a foil-lined rimmed baking sheet and bake until the grits are puffed and bubbling and the top is golden brown, 35 to 40 minutes. Sprinkle the grits with the scallions and serve immediately.

Notes from the Test Kitchen

Beaten egg whites give these grits the lightness of a soufflé. The original recipe called for country ham; we opted for more readily available ham steak. If you prefer country ham, decrease or omit the additional salt, as country hams are often quite salty. Don't use quick-cooking or instant grits; they will be too gluey. This casserole tastes great anytime, but it does lose a bit of its attractive height after sitting.

Mom's Hominy

TRICIA ROBINSON | PORTSMOUTH, NEW HAMPSHIRE

A lot of folks, particularly Northerners, are not all that familiar with hominy, dried white or yellow corn kernels that have had the hull and germ removed. Like grits, which are actually made from hominy, it's a foodstuff that was a staple in the Native American diet and was passed on to the colonists. Often hominy is served as a side or as part of a casserole. Here in Tricia's mother's recipe, it is the latter, prepared with cheddar and green chiles. "Her dishes are perfect," says Tricia of her mother's cooking, "not because they are flawless, but because they are tailored to us out of love!" She adds that this recipe is the perfect summer complement to marinated, grilled chicken or barbecued ribs and a nice, crisp salad. "Wash down with a cold ale and you will definitely have some happy bellies and a delightful evening!"

SERVES 4 TO 6

- 2 tablespoons olive oil
- 1 onion, minced
- 1 (4-ounce) can chopped green chiles, drained
- 2 garlic cloves, minced
- 1 teaspoon ground cumin
- 2 (15-ounce) cans white hominy, drained and rinsed
- ½ teaspoon salt
- ¼ teaspoon pepper
- 1 cup sour cream
- 1 cup shredded cheddar cheese

1. Adjust an oven rack to the middle position and heat the oven to 350 degrees. Grease an 8-inch square baking dish and set aside.

2. Heat the oil in a large skillet over medium heat until shimmering. Add the onion and cook, stirring occasionally, until softened, 5 to 7 minutes. Stir in the chiles, garlic, and cumin and cook until fragrant, about 30 seconds. Add the hominy, salt, and pepper, and cook until the hominy is heated through, 3 to 5 minutes.

3. Off the heat, stir in the sour cream and ¾ cup of the cheese. Transfer the mixture to the prepared baking dish and sprinkle the remaining ¼ cup cheese over the top.

4. Place the baking dish on a foil-lined rimmed baking sheet and bake until the sauce is bubbling and the cheese is melted, about 20 minutes. Cool for 10 minutes before serving.

Notes from the Test Kitchen

With a touch of chile heat, a creamy cheese sauce, and an appealing texture thanks to the hominy, this dish won a lot of fans in the test kitchen, Southerners and Northerners alike. We changed very little from the original recipe, though Tricia's recipe said that topping the casserole with cheese is optional—we thought it was a must.

Baked Eggplant Casserole

M. J. BOJRAB | LAS VEGAS, NEVADA

This family recipe is well loved, and it's easy to understand why. Combining tender rounds of eggplant with ground lamb, cinnamon-accented tomato sauce, and pine nuts, M. J.'s dish is not unlike the classic Greek comfort food, *moussaka*. He tells us he has always served this casserole by request at a dinner party he hosts every February, and each year the roughly sixty guests are sure to polish off every last bite, no matter how much he makes. M. J. recommends serving it over long-grain white rice.

SERVES 4 TO 6

- 2 medium eggplants, sliced into ¼-inch rounds
- 1 teaspoon sugar
  Salt and pepper
- 1 tablespoon olive oil
- 1 onion, minced
- 1 celery rib, chopped fine
- ½ teaspoon ground cinnamon
- 1 pound ground lamb
- 2 (8-ounce) cans tomato sauce
- 3 tablespoons pine nuts, toasted
- ¾ cup grated Parmesan cheese

1. Adjust the oven racks to the upper-middle and lower-middle positions and heat the oven to 450 degrees. Grease an 8-inch square baking dish and set aside. Grease two large rimmed baking sheets.

2. Spread the eggplant out evenly over the prepared baking sheets, overlapping the slices slightly. Sprinkle with the sugar and season with salt and pepper. Roast the eggplant until lightly browned and tender, about 30 minutes, switching and rotating the baking sheets halfway through roasting. Reduce the oven temperature to 350 degrees.

3. Meanwhile, heat the oil in a large skillet over medium heat until shimmering. Add the onion, celery, and ¾ teaspoon salt and cook, stirring occasionally, until softened, 5 to 7 minutes. Stir in the cinnamon and ½ teaspoon pepper and cook until fragrant, about 30 seconds. Add the lamb and cook, breaking up any large clumps with a wooden spoon, until no longer pink, about 5 minutes. Stir in the tomato sauce, bring to a simmer, then set aside off the heat.

4. Arrange one-third of the eggplant in an even layer over the bottom of the prepared baking dish, overlapping the slices slightly. Spoon 1⅓ cups of the meat mixture over the eggplant, then spread it into an even thickness. Sprinkle with 1 tablespoon of the pine nuts and ¼ cup of the cheese. Repeat this layering twice.

5. Place the baking dish on a foil-lined rimmed baking sheet and bake on the upper-middle rack until the sauce is bubbling and the cheese is melted, about 30 minutes. Cool for 10 minutes before serving.

Notes from the Test Kitchen

Moussaka is often laden with a heavy béchamel sauce, so we liked that M. J.'s recipe was cream sauce–free, allowing the eggplant to be the star. To round out the flavors, we added Parmesan cheese to the layers, and after tweaking the seasonings a bit to better complement the lamb, we had a dish that was at once savory and slightly sweet. This casserole is sure to be an appreciated (and beyond-the-ordinary) addition to any potluck table.

Papa's Lasagna

DEBRA CLIFTON | MINCO, OKLAHOMA

"My dad spent three years in concentration camps, and he vowed if he ever got out of there he would never go hungry again, nor would anyone he knew, in or out of his family." This recipe is a direct result of that promise. Of course, it helped that Papa, named Raphaella, was born in Italy and loved cooking. After his first experience as a cook making a meal for the captain of a ship he was working on, he was hooked. He later went on to open two Italian restaurants in the United States, where he became a citizen and lived for 36 years before returning to Italy. "This is one of the dishes that really made him popular. It was passed down to me, his only daughter." This is no ordinary lasagna. With loads of cheese, meat, and sauce, as well as bell pepper and mushrooms, it's beyond hearty—think of it as a super-sized or ultimate lasagna. Debra shares it here in his memory.

SERVES 8 TO 10

SAUCE

- 1 tablespoon olive oil
- 8 ounces white mushrooms, sliced thin
- 2 celery ribs, chopped fine
- 1 onion, minced
- 1 red bell pepper, stemmed, seeded, and chopped fine
  Salt
- 6 garlic cloves, minced
- 2 tablespoons minced fresh oregano
  Pepper
- 1½ pounds 85 percent lean ground beef
- 1 (28-ounce) can tomato puree
- 1 (14.5-ounce) can diced tomatoes, drained

LAYERS

- 12 lasagna noodles
  Salt
- 2 cups whole-milk ricotta cheese
- 1¼ cups grated Parmesan cheese
- ½ cup chopped fresh basil
- 1 large egg
- ½ teaspoon pepper
- 4 cups shredded mozzarella cheese

1. **FOR THE SAUCE:** Heat the oil in a large Dutch oven over medium heat until shimmering. Add the mushrooms, celery, onion, bell pepper, and 1 teaspoon salt and cook, stirring occasionally, until softened, 6 to 8 minutes. Stir in the garlic, oregano, and ½ teaspoon pepper and cook until fragrant, about 30 seconds.

(Continued on page 23)

2. Add the beef, increase the heat to medium-high, and cook, breaking up any large clumps with a wooden spoon, until no longer pink, about 5 minutes. Stir in the tomato puree and diced tomatoes, bring to a simmer, and cook until the flavors are blended, about 3 minutes. Season with salt and pepper to taste, then set aside off the heat. (You should have about 10 cups sauce.)

3. FOR THE LAYERS: Meanwhile, adjust an oven rack to the middle position and heat the oven to 375 degrees. Bring 4 quarts water to a boil in a large pot. Add the noodles and 1 tablespoon salt and cook, stirring often, until al dente. Drain the noodles and rinse them under cold water until cool. Spread the noodles out in a single layer over clean kitchen towels. (Do not use paper towels; they will stick to the pasta.)

4. Mix the ricotta, 1 cup of the Parmesan, the basil, egg, ½ teaspoon salt, and pepper together in a bowl. Spread 1 cup of the meat sauce over the bottom of a 13 by 9-inch baking dish. Place 3 of the noodles in the baking dish to create the first layer. Drop 3 tablespoons of the ricotta mixture on top of each noodle, then spread it into an even thickness. Sprinkle evenly with 1 cup of the mozzarella. Spoon 2½ cups more meat sauce evenly over the cheese. Repeat this layering of noodles, ricotta mixture, mozzarella, and meat sauce twice more.

5. For the final layer, place the remaining 3 noodles on top of the sauce in the baking dish, spoon the remaining 1½ cups sauce evenly over the top, and sprinkle with the remaining 1 cup mozzarella and ¼ cup Parmesan.

6. Place the baking dish on a foil-lined rimmed baking sheet. Lightly coat a large sheet of foil with vegetable oil spray and cover the lasagna. Bake for 15 minutes, then remove the foil and continue to bake until the sauce is bubbling and the cheese is spotty brown, about 35 minutes longer. Let cool for 20 minutes before serving.

Notes from the Test Kitchen

No one will ever go to bed hungry when you serve this super-hearty, meaty lasagna for dinner. Papa's original recipe called for 2 to 3 pounds of meat, 4 eggs, an entire large carton of ricotta, plus feta cheese in addition to the ricotta and mozzarella cheeses. No matter how we tried, we just couldn't fit all that food into a 13 by 9-inch baking dish. We had to scale down and simplify, so we reduced the amounts of the meat, ricotta, and eggs, and for simplicity we left out the small amount of feta in Debra's recipe. Even with these adjustments, our lasagna was still packed full with delicious ingredients.

ASSEMBLING LASAGNA LAYERS

1. After laying down the first layer of sauce and noodles, spoon 3 table-spoons of the ricotta filling onto each noodle and spread it into an even thickness.

2. After sprinkling the mozzarella over the ricotta, spoon 2½ cups more sauce evenly over the mozzarella. Repeat this process two more times before assembling the final layer.

Martini Mac and Cheese

KIM MARTIN | BELLINGHAM, WASHINGTON

When it comes to everybody's preferred comfort foods, few can argue with macaroni and cheese as an all-time favorite. Kim made up this recipe for herself and her husband, since they like stronger flavors. "I call it my 'adult version' of mac and cheese," she says. So how does she do it? First, she makes it incredibly cheesy and rich, calling for a trio of sharp cheddar, Parmesan, and Gorgonzola. Her addition of a few typical martini cocktail garnishes—pearl onions and green olives—adds a salty-briny flavor that perfectly complements the creamy sauce (and, coincidentally, plays off her last name). While this recipe was first made with adults in mind, Kim says she's found that even kids who don't like strong cheeses are likely to enjoy it.

SERVES 8

- 1 pound short shaped or tubular pasta, such as rotellini or orecchiette
  Salt
- 3 tablespoons unsalted butter
- 3 tablespoons all-purpose flour
- 4 cups low-fat milk
- 1 teaspoon ground coriander
- ¼ teaspoon pepper
- 4 cups shredded sharp cheddar cheese
- 1 cup grated Parmesan cheese
- ½ cup crumbled Gorgonzola cheese
- 1 (3.5-ounce) jar cocktail onions, drained, rinsed, and chopped
- 1 cup pimiento-stuffed green olives, chopped

1. Adjust an oven rack to the middle position and heat the oven to 400 degrees. Grease a 13 by 9-inch baking dish and set aside.

2. Bring 4 quarts water to a boil in a large pot. Add the pasta and 1 tablespoon salt and cook, stirring often, until just shy of al dente. Drain the pasta and return it to the pot.

3. Meanwhile, melt the butter in a large saucepan over medium heat. Add the flour and cook for 1 minute. Whisk in the milk, coriander, 1 teaspoon salt, and the pepper, bring to a simmer, and cook until thickened slightly, 5 to 7 minutes.

4. Off the heat, whisk in 3½ cups of the cheddar, ½ cup of the Parmesan, and the Gorgonzola until melted. Stir in the onions and olives.

5. Pour the sauce over the pasta and stir until evenly combined. Transfer the mixture to the prepared baking dish and sprinkle the remaining ½ cup cheddar and ½ cup Parmesan over the top.

6. Place the baking dish on a foil-lined rimmed baking sheet and bake until the sauce is bubbling and the cheese is golden brown, about 20 minutes. Cool for 10 minutes before serving.

Notes from the Test Kitchen

We loved the combination of cheeses in this dish and found the cocktail onions and olives to be a fun, colorful addition that lent a welcome salty flavor to balance the richness. Though the original recipe left the onions and olives whole, we chose to chop them for more even distribution. Kim called for rotellini, but we had a hard time locating it and found that any shaped pasta worked just fine. Feel free to substitute whatever pasta shape you prefer. Make sure to rinse the onions well since they are rather salty straight from the jar.

Mighty Good Shrimp Salad

MARY MRAZ | LA MARQUE, TEXAS

"In the late 1960s I worked at a hospital, and whenever we had a party my coworker Bea brought her famous shrimp salad at the demand of other coworkers. It was always a sensation. It had a different taste and no one could really figure it out. Bea swore that she would never divulge the recipe, not even to her daughter, who worked with us also. When she decided to retire, we all threw a fit because that would be the end of the shrimp salad! So, Bea had a drawing and *everyone* put their name in the hat to get her recipe, and I won! When I read the recipe, it was so simple, I almost died. I've made this recipe for myself and for many different family events, especially summer outings, but one of my nephews requests it each year for Thanksgiving and Christmas as well. I kept Bea's secret until her death in the 1980s, when her daughter asked me for the recipe. She said that Bea's wish was not binding upon her death. So I gave her the recipe, as well as my sisters, brother, and now you."

SERVES 8

- 1 (3-ounce) bag Zatarain's Crawfish, Shrimp, and Crab Boil
- 1 pound large shrimp
  Salt
- 1 pound small pasta shells
- 4 celery ribs, sliced thin
- 1 onion, minced
- 1 cup pimiento-stuffed green olives, chopped fine
- ½ cup drained canned pitted ripe black olives, chopped
- 2 tablespoons sweet pickle relish
- 2 teaspoons garlic powder
- ½ cup mayonnaise
- 2 tablespoons chopped fresh parsley
  Pepper

1. Bring 4 quarts water and the Zatarain's bag to a boil in a large pot. Add the shrimp and 1 tablespoon salt and cook until the shrimp are curled and pink, about 2 minutes. Using a slotted spoon, transfer the shrimp to a bowl and cool to room temperature.

2. While the shrimp cool, return the water to a boil, add the pasta, and cook, stirring often, until al dente. Drain the pasta, discarding the Zatarain's bag, and transfer to a large bowl. Stir in the celery, onion, olives, relish, and garlic powder and cool to room temperature.

3. When the shrimp are cool enough to handle, peel, then cut in half lengthwise. Devein the shrimp and cut in half crosswise into 1-inch pieces.

4. Stir the shrimp pieces, mayonnaise, and parsley into the pasta. Season with salt and pepper to taste. Refrigerate the salad for at least 2 hours, or up to 24 hours, before serving.

Notes from the Test Kitchen

This salad's key ingredient is the Zatarain's spice packet, which works like a seasoning sachet and can be ordered online at the company's website if you can't find it in your area (we tried to come up with a substitute using a combination of pantry spices, but it just wasn't the same). We felt the shrimp-to-pasta ratio was a bit out of balance, more like pasta salad than shrimp salad, so we reduced the amount of pasta and upped the shrimp. Tasters also favored more garnishes and seasoning, so we increased the amounts of celery, olives, and relish.

Corn Pie

SUZANNE OAKLEY | ROCKLAND, MAINE

This old-fashioned pie has roots that run deep into Pennsylvania Dutch country, and while recipes vary on the particulars, in general fresh-cut corn kernels and sliced hard-boiled eggs are cooked with milk and often flour under a flaky pie crust. A corn pie recipe similar to Suzanne's can be found in the *Pennsylvania Trail of History Cookbook* (2004) and is credited to the Cornwall Iron Furnace in Cornwall, Pennsylvania, an iron-making facility that operated from 1742 to 1883 and made pig iron and domestic products, as well as cannon barrels during the Revolution and the Civil War. As in that particular recipe, Suzanne's grandmother made her corn pie in a cast-iron skillet. "It is, for us, the very essence of summer," says Suzanne, "and we usually serve it with fresh, sliced summer tomatoes and homemade mayonnaise. For my family, summer has not arrived (and doesn't dare depart) until we've made this recipe at least once."

SERVES 6 TO 8

CRUST
- 1¼ cups all-purpose flour
- ¼ teaspoon salt
- 3 tablespoons vegetable shortening, cut into ¼-inch pieces and chilled
- 5 tablespoons unsalted butter, cut into ¼-inch pieces and chilled
- 4–6 tablespoons ice water

FILLING
- 4 large eggs
- 12 ears corn, husks and silk removed
- 1 cup heavy cream
- 4 tablespoons (½ stick) unsalted butter
- 1 onion, minced
- 1 celery rib, chopped fine
- 1 teaspoon salt
- 1 garlic clove, minced
- ¼ teaspoon pepper
- ¼ cup chopped fresh parsley

1. FOR THE CRUST: Process the flour and salt together in a food processor until combined. Scatter the shortening over the top and process until the mixture resembles coarse cornmeal, about 10 seconds. Scatter the butter pieces over the top and pulse the mixture until it resembles coarse crumbs, about 10 pulses. Transfer the mixture to a bowl.

2. Sprinkle 4 tablespoons of the ice water over the mixture. Stir and press the dough together, using a stiff rubber spatula, until the dough sticks together. If the dough does not come together, stir in the remaining water, 1 tablespoon at a time, until it does.

3. Turn the dough onto a sheet of plastic wrap and flatten into a 4-inch disk. Wrap the dough tightly in the plastic wrap and refrigerate for at least 1 hour, or up to 2 days. Before rolling out the dough, let it sit on the counter to soften slightly, about 10 minutes.

4. FOR THE FILLING: Adjust an oven rack to the middle position and heat the oven to 375 degrees.

(Continued on page 29)

5. Hard-boil 2 of the eggs by covering them with 1 quart water in a small saucepan and bringing to a boil over high heat. As soon as the water reaches a boil, remove the pan from the heat, cover, and let sit for 10 minutes. Meanwhile, prepare a bowl of ice water. Transfer the eggs to the ice water and cool for 5 minutes. Peel the eggs, cut crosswise into ¼-inch slices, and set aside.

6. Meanwhile, slice the corn kernels from the cobs. Process half of the corn (about 4 cups kernels) in a blender (or food processor) with the cream until smooth, about 30 seconds. Add the remaining 2 eggs and blend until combined, about 5 seconds. Set aside.

7. Melt 2 tablespoons of the butter in a 10-inch cast iron skillet over medium heat. Add the onion, celery, and salt and cook, stirring occasionally, until softened, 5 to 7 minutes. Stir in the garlic and pepper and cook until fragrant, about 30 seconds. Off the heat, stir in the remaining corn kernels, corn-cream mixture, and parsley. Smooth the surface of the filling, then arrange the sliced eggs over the top in an even layer. Using your hands, break up the remaining 2 tablespoons butter into small pieces and scatter evenly over the top.

8. Roll out the dough on a lightly floured counter to a 12-inch circle, about ⅛ inch thick. Cut three oval-shaped vents, each about 1 inch long and ½ inch wide, in the center of the dough. Working quickly, roll the dough loosely over the rolling pin and unroll it evenly over the skillet. Trim the dough, leaving ½ inch hanging over the pan lip. Press the dough firmly to seal it to the lip of the pan. (For a decorative border, press the edges of the pie with the tines of a fork.)

9. Place the skillet on a foil-lined rimmed baking sheet and bake until the filling is bubbling and the crust is golden brown, about 1 hour. Cool for 10 minutes before serving.

Notes from the Test Kitchen

The flavors of the Suzanne's recipe and the history behind it made it a keeper, though we had some trouble getting the filling to hold together like we wanted. Though it's less visually appealing than using only whole kernels, we found that pureeing half of the corn with a couple of eggs helped make the filling more stable. We also opted in favor of using heavy cream versus milk since it created a smoother texture and richer flavor.

ROLLING OUT PIE DOUGH

1. On a lightly floured counter, roll the dough out from its center into a 12-inch circle. Periodically give the dough a quarter turn to keep the circle round.

2. Toss additional flour underneath the dough as needed to keep it from sticking to the counter.

CLASSIC ROAST BEEF AND GRAVY

Sunday Night Suppers

Pan-Fried Chicken with Milk Gravy 32

Chicken Fricassee 34

Oh My God Chicken 36

Chicken 'n' Dumplings 39

Hunter's Chicken 40

Roast Chicken with Orange Cream Gravy 42

Chicken in a Pot 43

Pheasants in Wine Sauce 46

Cornish Game Hens with Rice Stuffing 48

Apple and Sauerkraut Pork Chops 51

Orange Pork Chops 52

Pork Chop Scallop 53

Dr Pepper–Glazed Ham 55

Classic Roast Beef and Gravy 56

Tia's Coffee Pot Roast 57

Horseradish Beef Stew 59

Deviled Beef Tenders 60

Saucy Mustard Beef Steak 61

Grandma Wooly's Beef Barbecue 63

The Meatloaf with the Frosting 64

Sunday Sugo 66

Chili Balls 68

Sunday Tomato Sauce with Meatballs 69

Sweet and Sour Meatballs 70

Loekie's Lamb Shanks 71

Pan-Fried Chicken with Milk Gravy

VICKI WRITER | WAPATO, WASHINGTON

"When I think of Sunday dinners, I think of this recipe. It has been a favorite of mine since I was a little girl. I would often request it for my birthday dinner and I still do! Now, my own family enjoys it as much as I did when I was growing up." Vicki thinks the recipe originated with her grandma or perhaps even her great-grandmother, who came to the States from Denmark. Because the bone-in chicken is pan-fried (or shallow-fried) in less than an inch of oil, the meat is tender inside and crispy outside, similar to what you'd get from deep-frying, but with a lightness that makes it a great match for a creamy milk gravy, a wonderfully old-fashioned addition to this recipe. Such gravies have roots that go back to colonial days, and they have stood the test of time since they are inexpensive and easy to make, keep well, add good flavor, and fill you up. Vicki likes to serve her chicken and gravy with mashed potatoes, corn on the cob, and chocolate cake—classic, down-home comfort food at its finest.

SERVES 4

CHICKEN

- 3 pounds bone-in, skin-on chicken pieces (split breasts cut in half, drumsticks, and/or thighs), trimmed
- 2 cups all-purpose flour
- 1 tablespoon poultry seasoning
  Salt and pepper
- 3 large eggs
- 2½ cups vegetable oil

GRAVY

- 2 tablespoons unsalted butter
- 2 tablespoons all-purpose flour
- 1½ cups whole milk
- ½ cup low-sodium chicken broth
  Pinch cayenne pepper
  Salt and pepper

1. FOR THE CHICKEN: Adjust an oven rack to the middle position and heat the oven to 200 degrees. Set two wire racks inside two large rimmed baking sheets. Line a large plate with paper towels.

2. Pat the chicken dry with paper towels. Whisk the flour, poultry seasoning, 2 teaspoons salt, and 1 teaspoon pepper together in a shallow dish. Whisk the eggs in a bowl.

3. One at a time, dredge the chicken pieces in the flour mixture, dip into the eggs, then dredge in the flour mixture again and coat thoroughly. Place the chicken on one of the prepared wire racks.

4. Heat the oil in a large skillet over medium-high heat to 350 degrees. Add half of the chicken, skin-side down. Cover and cook, flipping every 5 minutes, until the skin is deep golden brown and the chicken is fully cooked and tender, about 20 minutes (160 to

165 degrees on an instant-read thermometer for breasts and 175 degrees on an instant-read thermometer for thighs and drumsticks).

5. Transfer the chicken to the paper towel–lined plate to drain briefly, then lay the chicken on the clean prepared wire rack (do not reuse the one used for the uncooked chicken) and keep warm in the oven. Return the oil to 350 degrees and repeat with the remaining chicken.

6. FOR THE GRAVY: Carefully pour the oil from the skillet. Melt the butter in the skillet over medium-low heat. Add the flour and cook, stirring constantly, until golden brown, about 3 minutes. Slowly whisk in the milk, broth, and cayenne, scraping up any browned bits. Bring to a simmer and cook until thickened, about 5 minutes. Season with salt and pepper to taste. Serve the chicken, passing the gravy separately.

Notes from the Test Kitchen

While Vicki browned her chicken pieces uncovered before covering the dish and cooking them through, we found that covering the skillet the entire time allowed for more even cooking and kept our chicken moist. We also increased the amount of oil from a mere ¼ cup to 2½ cups, enough to give our chicken an even crispier coating but not so much as to turn it into a deep-fry. Since the gravy will continue to thicken after it is removed from the heat, don't over-reduce it; it is best if served immediately. If your gravy does get too thick, whisk in additional water or chicken broth, 2 tablespoons at a time, over the heat until the desired consistency is achieved.

PREPARING CHICKEN FOR PAN-FRYING

1. Pat the chicken dry with paper towels. Working with one piece at a time, dredge the chicken in the seasoned flour, shaking off any excess.

2. Dip the chicken in the beaten eggs, letting the excess drip into the bowl.

3. Return the chicken to the flour mixture to coat thoroughly.

4. Place the chicken on a wire rack set over a rimmed baking sheet.

Chicken Fricassee

WARREN ENG | HARPERS FERRY, WEST VIRGINIA

What better way to end the weekend (or start the week) than with a meal of tender chicken slowly simmered with vegetables and a creamy herb sauce? Fricasseeing chicken is an old-fashioned, simple technique that goes all the way back to medieval times, though the specifics have changed over the ages. In older interpretations (including those found in the French tome *Larousse Gastronomique* and the 1915 edition of *The Fannie Farmer Cookbook*), poultry is stewed in a cream sauce and accented with one or two vegetables. More modern recipes usually define fricassee as chicken poached in stock, which is then made into a sauce that can be a simple reduction or enriched with cream or wine. Warren's mother's recipe builds on the modern fricassee, using broth and enriching it with cream, but then goes on to add some unusual ingredients. Ginger, thyme, and Worcestershire give her sauce a unique depth of flavor you won't find in most fricassees. These days, it seems like fricassee recipes more often than not fall short: gloppy, floury sauces, overcooked meat, and mushy vegetables, not to mention those that take liberties with the help of canned cream-of-something soup. That's why we found this recipe so appealing. There are no shortcuts or canned anything; just perfectly cooked chicken in a creamy, uniquely flavorful (but not too heavy) sauce, accented with tender vegetables. Warren's mother liked to serve it over rice or mashed potatoes.

SERVES 4

- 3 pounds bone-in, skin-on chicken pieces (split breasts cut in half, drumsticks, and/or thighs), trimmed
  Salt and pepper
- 2 tablespoons vegetable oil
- 8 ounces white mushrooms, sliced thin
- 2 leeks, white and light green parts only, halved lengthwise and sliced thin
- 2 teaspoons grated fresh ginger
- 1 teaspoon minced fresh thyme
- 1 tablespoon all-purpose flour
- 2 cups low-sodium chicken broth
- 2 carrots, peeled and cut into 1-inch pieces
- 2 bay leaves
- ½ cup heavy cream
- 1 tablespoon fresh lemon juice
  Dash Worcestershire sauce

1. Pat the chicken dry with paper towels and season with salt and pepper. Heat ½ teaspoons of the oil in a large Dutch oven over medium-high heat until just smoking. Add half of the chicken and cook until golden brown on both sides, about 10 minutes, flipping halfway through. Transfer the chicken to a plate. Return the pot to medium-high heat and repeat with 1½ teaspoons more oil and the remaining chicken.

2. Heat the remaining 1 tablespoon oil in the pot over medium heat until shimmering. Add the mushrooms, leeks, and ¼ teaspoon salt and cook, stirring occasionally, until the leeks are softened and the mushrooms have released their juices and are brown around the edges, 7 to 10 minutes. Stir in the ginger and thyme and cook until fragrant, about 30 seconds. Stir in the flour and cook for 1 minute. Whisk in the broth, scraping up any browned bits.

3. Return the chicken, along with any accumulated juices, to the pot. Add the carrots and bay leaves. Bring to a simmer, cover, and cook until the chicken is fully cooked and tender, about 20 minutes for breasts (160 to 165 degrees on an instant-read thermometer) or 1 hour for thighs and drumsticks (175 degrees on an instant-read thermometer).

(If using both white and dark meat, simmer the thighs and drumsticks for 40 minutes before adding the breasts.)

4. Transfer the chicken to a serving platter and tent loosely with foil. Discard the bay leaves. Skim the fat off the surface of the sauce with a wide spoon. Return the sauce to a simmer and cook until thickened slightly, 4 to 6 minutes. Off the heat, stir in the cream, lemon juice, and Worcestershire sauce, and season with salt and pepper to taste. Pour the sauce over the chicken and serve.

Notes from the Test Kitchen

Warren's version of chicken fricassee impressed us with its incredibly flavorful sauce. But rather than flouring the chicken pieces before browning, we streamlined his technique by browning the chicken plain and adding the flour with the aromatics when building the sauce. This adjustment allowed the chicken to pick up more color during browning and create a flavorful fond for the sauce, and our sauce acquired a smoother texture with the help of the flour. We omitted the water for richer flavor and added a dash of fresh lemon juice before serving to brighten things up.

Oh My God Chicken (Chicken Fricassee with Heads of Garlic)

DAVID LABATE | PARKER, COLORADO

"When my mom passed away, I inherited her little recipe box and found this recipe, which was always one of my favorites. Whenever my mom wanted to get both my sister and me over for a birthday dinner, she knew she only had to tell us she was making this dish. She once gave the recipe to a neighbor, who started calling it 'Oh My God Chicken.' It's that good." Indeed it is. This fricassee starts with the classic components of chicken stewed in a flavorful sauce enriched with wine, but rather than relying on the minor inclusion of a few simple vegetables commonly found in a fricassee (like mushrooms, onions, peas, or carrots), David's mother's recipe turns to a few more unusual choices: olives, a bell pepper, and perhaps most notably, several whole heads of garlic. By the end of the simmer, the garlic is sweet and soft. David suggests eating the cooked garlic as you would an artichoke, using your teeth to squeeze the sweet, nutty paste out of its skin, or removing the cloves from their pods and spreading the soft garlic over the chicken or French bread.

SERVES 4

- 4 slices bacon, chopped
- 4 large garlic heads, rinsed, outer papery skin removed, and top third of heads cut off and discarded
- 3 pounds bone-in, skin-on chicken pieces (split breasts cut in half, drumsticks, and/or thighs), trimmed
  Salt and pepper
- 1 onion, minced
- 1 red bell pepper, stemmed, seeded, and chopped fine
- 4 garlic cloves, minced
- 1 tablespoon all-purpose flour

- 1½ cups low-sodium chicken broth
- ½ cup dry white wine
- 2 bay leaves
- 2 whole cloves
- ½ cup pitted kalamata olives, chopped
- 1 tablespoon fresh lemon juice
- 2 tablespoons chopped fresh parsley

1. Cook the bacon in a large Dutch oven over medium-low heat until crisp, about 10 minutes. Using a slotted spoon, transfer the bacon to a paper towel–lined plate. Place the garlic heads, cut-side down, in the pot and cook over medium-low heat until golden brown, about 3 minutes. Transfer the garlic heads to a plate.

(Continued on page 38)

2. Pat the chicken dry with paper towels and season with salt and pepper. Heat the bacon fat in the pot over medium-high heat until just smoking. Add half of the chicken and cook until golden brown on both sides, about 10 minutes, flipping halfway through. Transfer the chicken to the plate with the garlic heads. Return the pot to medium-high heat and repeat with the remaining chicken.

3. Add the onion and bell pepper to the pot and cook over medium heat, stirring occasionally, until softened, 5 to 7 minutes. Stir in the minced garlic and cook until fragrant, about 30 seconds. Stir in the flour and cook for 1 minute. Whisk in the broth, wine, bay leaves, and cloves, scraping up any browned bits.

4. Return the garlic heads and chicken, along with any accumulated juices, to the pot. Bring to a simmer, cover, and cook until the chicken is fully cooked and tender, about 20 minutes for breasts (160 to 165 degrees on an instant-read thermometer) or 1 hour for thighs and drumsticks (175 degrees on an instant-read thermometer). (If using both white and dark meat, simmer the thighs and drumsticks for 40 minutes before adding the breasts.)

5. Transfer the chicken and garlic to a serving platter and tent loosely with foil. Discard the bay leaves and cloves. Skim the fat off the surface of the sauce with a wide spoon. Add the olives, return the sauce to a simmer, and cook until thickened slightly, 4 to 6 minutes. Off the heat, stir in the lemon juice and season with salt and pepper to taste. Pour the sauce over the chicken and garlic, sprinkle with the reserved bacon and the parsley, and serve.

Notes from the Test Kitchen

Tasters loved both the flavor and the look of this dish; the heads of garlic added a unique savory sweetness, and the rosette pattern of the bulbs made for a very attractive presentation. Instead of using chopped salt pork as the recipe called for, we substituted bacon because we preferred the smoky flavor it added. We cooked the bacon and then reserved the crumbled bits for a garnishing at the end. David halved the garlic heads and used both halves, but we found the top halves tended to fall apart, so we just sliced off the top third and used the root end. Olives and bacon are naturally salty, so be sure to use low-sodium chicken broth and season the chicken lightly in step 2.

BROWNING HEADS OF GARLIC

1. Rinse the garlic heads and remove the outer papery skin. Cut the top third off each head of garlic and discard.

2. Place the garlic heads in the pot with the rendered bacon fat, cut-side down, and cook over medium-low heat until golden brown, about 3 minutes. Transfer to a plate.

Chicken 'n' Dumplings

KATHLEEN JONES | PETALUMA, CALIFORNIA

"My mom cooked frugally but imaginatively, and she involved at least a couple of her five kids in the process. She could do amazing things with one chicken, but my favorite was chicken and dumplings. On cold Minnesota evenings, she would warm the whole house with the inviting fragrance of chicken and vegetables simmering in the Dutch oven." Kathleen's rendition of this classic substitutes chicken thighs for the whole chicken, making the recipe much easier and still amply flavorful. With a rich stew full of vegetables and tender dumplings, it is a guaranteed Sunday supper favorite.

SERVES 4

STEW

- 3 pounds bone-in, skin-on chicken thighs, trimmed
  Salt and pepper
- 1 tablespoon vegetable oil
- 2 celery ribs, chopped fine
- 1 onion, minced
- 2 tablespoons all-purpose flour
- 3 cups low-sodium chicken broth
- 4 carrots, peeled and cut into 1-inch pieces
- 2 bay leaves

DUMPLINGS

- 1½ cups all-purpose flour
- 2 teaspoons baking powder
- ½ teaspoon salt
- ¾ cup whole milk, warmed
- 4 tablespoons (½ stick) unsalted butter, melted and cooled

1. FOR THE STEW: Pat the chicken dry with paper towels and season with salt and pepper. Heat 1½ teaspoons of the oil in a large Dutch oven over medium-high heat until just smoking. Add half of the chicken and cook until golden brown on both sides, about 10 minutes, flipping halfway through. Transfer the chicken to a plate and remove the skin. Return the pot to medium-high heat and repeat with the remaining 1½ teaspoons oil and the remaining chicken.

2. Add the celery, onion, and ¼ teaspoon salt to the pot and cook over medium heat, stirring occasionally, until softened, 5 to 7 minutes. Stir in the flour and cook for 1 minute. Whisk in the broth, scraping up any browned bits. Return the chicken, along with any accumulated juices, to the pot. Add the carrots and bay leaves, bring to a simmer, cover, and cook until the thickest part of the thighs registers 175 degrees on an instant-read thermometer, about 1 hour.

3. Transfer the chicken to a plate. Discard the bay leaves. When the chicken is cool enough to handle, shred the meat into bite-sized pieces and return it to the stew. Season with salt and pepper to taste.

4. FOR THE DUMPLINGS: Whisk the flour, baking powder, and salt together in a bowl. Stir in the milk and butter until incorporated and smooth.

5. Return the stew to a simmer. Using two soup spoons, drop nine golf ball–sized dumplings onto the stew about 1 inch apart. Reduce the heat to low, cover, and cook until the dumplings have doubled in size, 15 to 18 minutes. Serve.

Notes from the Test Kitchen

While Kathleen's dumplings called for cutting in the butter, we found that using melted butter (and warm milk) was key to perfectly tender dumplings. It's important to prepare them just when it's time to cook them; if made too far ahead, the leavening loses its power and the dumplings will be too dense.

Hunter's Chicken

LESLEY PEW | LYNN, MASSACHUSETTS

Lesley tells us this chicken and rice dish is a cross between two classics, hunter's chicken and Mistral's chicken. For a typical hunter's chicken, the meat is slowly cooked in a wine-accented tomato or mushroom sauce, while Mistral's chicken is best known for its 40 cloves of garlic. Lesley incorporates her favorite elements from both: a rich tomato sauce in which the chicken slowly simmers with a hefty amount of garlic. She also adds sweet paprika, a nod to another classic, chicken paprikash. Her twist of cooking rice along with the chicken and sauce creates a flavorful and filling one-pot meal.

SERVES 4

- 4 slices bacon, chopped
- 4 (12-ounce) bone-in, skin-on split chicken breasts, trimmed
  Salt and pepper
- 5 shallots, halved and sliced thin
- 20 garlic cloves, sliced thin
- 1 tablespoon tomato paste
- 1½ cups long-grain white rice
- 3 medium tomatoes, cored and chopped
- 2 tablespoons sweet paprika
- 2½ cups low-sodium chicken broth
- 1 tablespoon fresh lemon juice
- 2 bay leaves
- 2 tablespoons chopped fresh basil

1. Adjust an oven rack to the lower-middle position and heat the oven to 375 degrees.

2. Cook the bacon in a large ovensafe skillet over medium-low heat until crisp, about 10 minutes. Using a slotted spoon, transfer the bacon to a paper towel–lined plate.

3. Pat the chicken dry with paper towels and season with salt and pepper. Heat the bacon fat in the skillet over medium-high until just smoking. Add the chicken and cook until golden brown on both sides, about 10 minutes, flipping halfway through. Transfer the chicken to a plate.

4. Add the shallots, ½ teaspoon salt, and ¼ teaspoon pepper to the skillet and cook over medium heat, stirring occasionally, until softened, about 4 minutes. Add the garlic, reduce the heat to medium-low, and cook, stirring frequently, until the garlic is tender but not browned, about 2 minutes. Stir in the tomato paste and cook until fragrant, about 30 seconds. Stir in the rice, tomatoes, and paprika and cook until the pan is dry, 2 to 4 minutes. Stir in the broth, lemon juice, and bay leaves, scraping up any browned bits.

5. Nestle the chicken, skin-side up, into the rice mixture and bring to a simmer. Transfer the skillet to the oven and cook until the rice is tender and the thickest part of the breasts registers 160 to 165 degrees on an instant-read thermometer, 40 to 45 minutes.

6. Using potholders (the skillet handle will be hot), remove the skillet from the oven and rest for 5 minutes. Discard the bay leaves. Season with salt and pepper to taste, sprinkle with the reserved bacon and the basil, and serve.

Notes from the Test Kitchen

We love garlic, but the 20 minced cloves Lesley used came across as bitter. Slicing rather than mincing them kept the flavor but not the bitterness. We also reserved the bacon as a garnish, since it lost its crispness when cooked with the chicken as Lesley had done. Surprisingly, cooking this dish uncovered didn't dry out the rice, and the chicken's skin got super crispy. Don't use a skillet smaller than 12 inches; it will be quite full before going in the oven in step 5.

Roast Chicken with Orange Cream Gravy

MARCIA HARRINGTON | SYRACUSE, NEW YORK

A golden-skinned roast chicken is quintessential Sunday supper fare; simplify it by using chicken pieces rather than the whole bird and add a fragrant cream sauce like this orange cream gravy flavored with rosemary and thyme, and you've got an old classic taken to the next level. While many of us can recall having a slow-roasted chicken for Saturday or Sunday dinners, for Marcia's family, this recipe is more than just a weekend meal. "This dish is our family's favorite comfort food—it's the birthday dinner of choice, and great for soothing a broken heart. The chicken skin is crisp and the gravy is absolutely luscious and fragrant."

SERVES 4

- 4 (12-ounce) bone-in, skin-on split chicken breasts, trimmed
  Salt and pepper
- 1 tablespoon vegetable oil
- 1 shallot, minced
- 1 teaspoon minced fresh thyme
- 1 teaspoon minced fresh rosemary
- 1 garlic clove, minced
- 1 tablespoon all-purpose flour
- 1¼ cups orange juice
- ¾ cup low-sodium chicken broth
- ½ cup half-and-half
- 2 tablespoons chopped fresh parsley

1. Adjust an oven rack to the lowest position and heat the oven to 450 degrees.

2. Pat the chicken dry with paper towels and season with salt and pepper. Heat 1½ teaspoons of the oil in a large ovensafe skillet over medium-high heat until just smoking. Add the chicken and cook until golden brown on both sides, about 10 minutes, flipping halfway through.

3. Flip the chicken skin-side down and transfer the skillet to the oven. Cook until the thickest part of the breasts registers 160 to 165 degrees on an instant-read thermometer, 15 to 18 minutes.

4. Using potholders (the skillet handle will be hot), remove the skillet from the oven and transfer to the stovetop. Transfer the chicken to a serving platter, tent loosely with foil, and let rest.

5. Add the remaining 1½ teaspoons oil and the shallot to the skillet and cook over medium heat until softened, about 2 minutes. Stir in the thyme, rosemary, and garlic and cook until fragrant, about 30 seconds. Stir in the flour and cook for 1 minute. Whisk in the orange juice and broth, scraping up any browned bits.

6. Bring the sauce to a simmer and cook until reduced to ¾ cup, about 10 minutes. Whisk in the half-and-half, along with any accumulated chicken juices, and cook until heated through, about 1 minute. Season with salt and pepper to taste. Pour the sauce over the chicken, sprinkle with the parsley, and serve.

Notes from the Test Kitchen

Marcia included a homemade chicken stock recipe, and though we generally prefer to use homemade over store-bought, we ultimately decided that for this recipe it just wasn't worth all the trouble. Fortifying the gravy with the drippings from the chicken guaranteed it was still plenty rich and full-bodied. We also found that using orange juice rather than frozen concentrate did a great job of punching up the gravy's orange flavor. While Marcia opted to de-bone the chicken before serving, we left it whole, for both simplicity and presentation.

Chicken in a Pot

THE EDITORS OF COOK'S COUNTRY

Look through nineteenth-century American cookbooks and you'll see that recipes for boiling chicken in a pot abound, promising perfectly velvety meat and a flavorful cooking broth that doubles as a sauce. The skin doesn't bronze like it would on a traditional roast chicken, but rather it protects the meat as it cooks and lends deep, rich flavor to both meat and sauce as it slowly renders. However, none of the old recipes we found agreed on the details—for method *or* ingredients. The bird could be stuffed, bolstered with vegetables, or tarted up with egg sauce or oysters. But all these old recipes did have one thing in common: they were designed for cooking a tough "free-range" bird, since all birds were free-range before World War II. Today's supermarket birds don't have to be boiled to become tender, which explains why few prepare chicken in a pot these days. But with so much potential and appeal as a satisfying and elegant one-dish meal, old-fashioned chicken in a pot, we felt, was primed for a test kitchen makeover. We set out to create a recipe that would be doable by today's home cook. Countless chickens later, we had a recipe that gave us evenly cooked white and dark meat, flavorful vegetables, and an intense, silky broth good enough to sip on its own. Of course, it was even better ladled over our tender, juicy chicken and perfectly cooked vegetables.

SERVES 4

- 1 (4½- to 5-pound) whole chicken, neck and giblets removed
  Salt and pepper
- 2 tablespoons vegetable oil
- 1 pound carrots, peeled and cut into 1-inch pieces
- 1 onion, peeled and halved, root end left intact
- 1 celery rib, halved crosswise
- 6 garlic cloves, minced
- 1 cup dry white wine
- 1 cup low-sodium chicken broth
- 1½ pounds small red potatoes, scrubbed and quartered
- 2 tablespoons unsalted butter
- 1 tablespoon minced fresh chives

1. Adjust an oven rack to the lower-middle position and heat the oven to 350 degrees.

2. Pat the chicken dry with paper towels. Using fingers, loosen the skin from the breasts and legs of the chicken. Rub 1 teaspoon salt and ½ teaspoon pepper all over the chicken and underneath the skin. Tuck the wings behind the back and tie the legs together with kitchen twine.

3. Heat 1 tablespoon of the oil in a large Dutch oven over medium-high heat until just smoking. Add the chicken, breast-side up, and cook until the back is lightly browned, 3 to 4 minutes. Transfer the chicken to a plate.

4. Add the remaining 1 tablespoon oil, the carrots, onion, and celery to the pot and cook,

(Continued on page 45)

stirring occasionally, until beginning to brown, 6 to 8 minutes. Stir in the garlic and cook until fragrant, about 30 seconds. Whisk in the wine and broth, scraping up any browned bits. Place the chicken, breast-side up, on top of the vegetables. Season the potatoes with salt and pepper and arrange around the chicken.

5. Cover the pot, transfer to the oven, and cook until the thickest part of the breast registers 160 to 165 degrees and the thickest part of the thighs registers 175 degrees on an instant-read thermometer, 45 to 60 minutes.

6. Transfer the pot to a wire rack. Remove the lid, tent the pot loosely with foil, and rest for 20 minutes.

7. Transfer the chicken to a carving board. Using a slotted spoon, transfer the vegetables to a serving platter, discarding the onion and celery. Strain the sauce through a fine-mesh strainer into a small saucepan. Skim the fat off the surface of the sauce with a wide spoon. Whisk in the butter and chives and season with salt and pepper to taste. Carve the chicken and serve with the vegetables, passing the sauce separately.

Notes from the Test Kitchen

Traditional chicken in a pot recipes needed a little more definition, as well as some tweaking. First, we ensured that the dark and white meat cooked evenly by cutting the 6 cups of cooking liquid specified by most recipes down to 2 cups, which allowed the legs and thighs to simmer while the breast meat steamed. We also came up with a few good tricks to deepen the flavor, like turning to chicken broth with a slug of white wine for the cooking liquid (rather than using plain old water like old recipes), and browning the vegetables and chicken before adding them to the pot. You will need a Dutch oven with a tight-fitting lid and at least a 6-quart capacity for this recipe.

BUILDING FLAVOR FOR CHICKEN IN A POT

1. After browning the chicken, brown the vegetables in the rendered fat to bring out their sweetness and build flavor for the sauce.

2. Arrange the chicken on top of the aromatics and place the potatoes around the exterior of the pot.

Pheasants in Wine Sauce

MARGARET HOWARD | SAINT LOUIS, MISSOURI

"I'll never forget the aroma of pheasant and mushrooms and wine bubbling away on the stove as I walked through the kitchen door after playing in the sweet fall air. Or the sight of my great-grandpa's hunting boots and coveralls lying over the lawn chair in the carport. Or the sight of the pheasant, blanketed in its beautiful brown mushroom sauce, heaped on the big white platter in the center of the long table. Nothing else could match this day, except maybe Christmas, for pleasing my senses. It was always an extraordinary day when Great-Grandpa Trout came through the door with pheasant for my grandma and my mother to cook. He had to travel a fair distance north from our little southern Illinois town to hunt the birds, and since pheasant was, and is, highly restricted, this meal materialized once a year, tops. I come from a family of fantastic cooks. Still, I do clearly recall the moment when the very idea that we were having pheasant for dinner was suddenly rather remarkable." In Margaret's recipe, the elegant sweet wine–mushroom cream sauce used to dress the prized bird makes it an even more sophisticated meal. Whether you can find a pheasant or choose to substitute chicken, a Sunday dinner featuring this meal will certainly feel like a special and grand event.

SERVES 4 TO 6

- 2 (2½- to 3-pound) whole pheasants, necks and giblets removed, wings discarded, and each bird cut into 6 pieces
  Salt and pepper
- 2 tablespoons vegetable oil
- 2 tablespoons unsalted butter
- 10 ounces wild or cremini mushrooms, quartered
- 1 onion, minced
- 2 tablespoons paprika
- 2 garlic cloves, minced
- 2 teaspoons minced fresh thyme
- 1 tablespoon all-purpose flour
- 1¼ cups Sauternes
- 1 cup low-sodium chicken broth
- 2 bay leaves
- 1 cup heavy cream
- 1 tablespoon fresh lemon juice
- 2 tablespoons chopped fresh parsley

1. Adjust an oven rack to the lower-middle position and heat the oven to 300 degrees.

2. Pat the pheasant dry with paper towels and season with salt and pepper. Heat 1 tablespoon of the oil in a large Dutch oven over medium-high heat until just smoking. Add half of the pheasant and cook until golden brown on both sides, about 10 minutes, flipping halfway through. Transfer the pheasant to a plate. Return the pot to medium-high heat and repeat with the remaining 1 tablespoon oil and the remaining pheasant.

3. Melt the butter in the pot over medium heat. Add the mushrooms, onion, and ¼ teaspoon salt and cook, stirring occasionally, until the onion is softened and the mushrooms have released their juices and are brown around the edges, 7 to 10 minutes. Stir in the paprika, garlic, and thyme and cook until fragrant, about 30 seconds. Stir in the flour and cook for 1 minute. Whisk in 1 cup of the Sauternes, the broth, and bay leaves, scraping up any browned bits.

4. Return the thighs and drumsticks, along with any accumulated juices, to the pot. Bring to a simmer, cover, and transfer the pot to the oven. Cook for 40 minutes, then return the breasts, along with any accumulated juices, to the pot. Cover and continue to cook until the thickest part of the breasts registers 160 to 165 degrees and the thickest part of the thighs and drumsticks registers 175 degrees on an instant-read thermometer, about 20 minutes longer.

5. Transfer the pheasant to a serving platter, tent loosely with foil, and let rest. Discard the bay leaves. Skim the fat off the surface of the sauce with a wide spoon. Return the sauce to a simmer on the stovetop and cook until thickened slightly, 4 to 6 minutes. Off the heat, stir in the remaining ¼ cup Sauternes, the cream, and lemon juice, and season with salt and pepper to taste. Pour the sauce over the pheasant, sprinkle with the parsley, and serve.

Notes from the Test Kitchen

We loved the flavors in this dish and felt the need to make only a few changes. Cooking the pheasant in cream resulted in a flavorful, but curdled, sauce, so we waited until the pheasant was out of the oven and resting to add the cream to the pot, off the heat. Staggering the times when we returned the dark and white meat to the pot to cook through ensured the two were cooked just right. We also stirred in some extra wine and lemon juice to brighten the flavors and balance the cream's richness. Margaret's recipe uses Sauternes, a sweet French white wine usually served with dessert, but you can use another sweet white wine. It's easiest to have your butcher prepare the pheasant for this recipe, as he will break each pheasant down to two breasts, two thighs, and two legs, so you don't have to deal with it at home. You can substitute 3 pounds bone-in, skin-on chicken pieces (split breasts cut in half, drumsticks, and/or thighs), trimmed, for the pheasant, and follow the same procedure.

Cornish Game Hens with Rice Stuffing

MAIRA JARDAK | JAMISON, PENNSYLVANIA

Maira loves this family recipe for its flavorful risotto stuffing, and the irresistible aroma and look of the perfectly bronzed birds. "This recipe has been in my family for many generations. I remember I was 5 years old and my grandmother would be plucking the feathers and trying to gently separate the skin from the breast in preparation for the stuffing." The combination of the cinnamon-spiced stuffing and tender meat with pomegranate molasses glaze gives classic stuffed game hens an appealing, slightly Middle Eastern flavor, with a nice balance between sweet and savory. Maira makes the extra effort to brine the meat (soaking it in a saltwater solution) before cooking it, a step that ensures the meat is extra moist. She likes to make her beautiful Cornish game hens around the holidays.

SERVES 4

GAME HENS

½   **cup salt**
½   **cup sugar**
4   **(1¼- to 1½-pound) Cornish game hens**
    Pepper

STUFFING

2   **tablespoons unsalted butter**
1   **onion, minced**
    Salt
1   **garlic clove, minced**
¼   **teaspoon ground cinnamon**
⅔   **cup Arborio rice**
2   **cups low-sodium chicken broth**
¼   **cup golden raisins**
3   **tablespoons pine nuts, toasted**
2   **tablespoons chopped fresh parsley**
1   **teaspoon fresh lemon juice**
    Pepper

GLAZE

¾   **cup pomegranate molasses**

1. FOR THE GAME HENS: Dissolve the salt and sugar in 2 quarts cold water in a large container. Submerge the hens in the brine, cover, and refrigerate for 30 minutes. Remove the hens from the brine, rinse well, and pat dry with paper towels. Tuck the wings behind the back and season the hens with pepper.

2. Meanwhile, adjust an oven rack to the lower-middle position and heat the oven to 400 degrees. Line a large rimmed baking sheet with foil and set a wire rack inside the baking sheet.

3. FOR THE STUFFING: While the hens brine, melt the butter in a medium saucepan over medium heat. Add the onion and ¼ teaspoon salt and cook, stirring occasionally, until softened, 5 to 7 minutes. Stir in the garlic and cinnamon and cook until fragrant, about 30 seconds. Stir in the rice and cook until the grains are translucent around the edges, about 2 minutes.

4. Stir in the broth and bring to a simmer. Reduce the heat to medium-low, cover, and cook, stirring occasionally, for 10 minutes.

(Continued on page 50)

Uncover, increase the heat to medium, and cook, stirring frequently, until the rice is al dente and the liquid is absorbed, about 5 minutes. Stir in the raisins, pine nuts, parsley, and lemon juice, and season with salt and pepper to taste.

5. Spoon ½ cup packed hot stuffing into the cavity of each hen, then tie each hen's legs together with kitchen twine. Lay the hens, breast-side down, on the prepared wire rack and roast until the backs are golden brown, about 25 minutes.

6. FOR THE GLAZE: Meanwhile, measure out and reserve 2 tablespoons of the pomegranate molasses. After the hens have roasted for 25 minutes, remove them from the oven and brush with some of the remaining molasses. Flip the hens breast-side up and brush again with some of the molasses. Continue to roast until the stuffed cavities register 150 degrees on an instant-read thermometer, 15 to 20 minutes longer.

7. Remove the hens from the oven and increase the oven temperature to 450 degrees.

Brush the hens with the remaining molasses and continue to roast until spotty brown and the stuffed cavities register 160 to 165 degrees on an instant-read thermometer, 5 to 10 minutes longer.

8. Transfer the hens to a serving platter or individual plates, brush with the reserved molasses, and rest for 5 minutes before serving.

Notes from the Test Kitchen

This recipe is ideal for a special occasion or holiday meal. Pomegranate molasses, found in the international food aisle of many supermarkets as well as in Middle Eastern markets, makes a perfect glaze for these game hens: its consistency is just right, it has an appealing sweet-tart taste, and it gives the birds a rich, mahogany-red hue. Preparation of the game hens themselves needed little adjustment, though tasters thought the rice stuffing needed a little extra flavor. Maira suggested garnishing the cooked hens with pine nuts and raisins, so we decided to put them right in the stuffing. That was all it needed.

Apple and Sauerkraut Pork Chops

THERESA CHEVALLIER | EVANS CITY, PENNSYLVANIA

"This dish uses all the best ingredients from the end of the fall harvest. It is really appreciated at the end of a Sunday of yard work, the time of year just before the first crisp snowflake falls." In Theresa's recipe, slow-cooking bone-in pork chops makes the meat so tender it nearly falls off the bone, and their bed of apples and sauerkraut picks up rich, meaty flavor over the long cooking time. A plate of these tender chops served with the apples, cooked down to just shy of applesauce, and tangy, flavorful sauerkraut is a meal sure to warm you through.

SERVES 4

- 1 pound sauerkraut, rinsed and drained
- 1 teaspoon caraway seeds, toasted
- 2 pounds Cortland or Empire apples (about 4 apples), cored
- 4 (10-ounce) bone-in blade-cut pork chops, about 1 inch thick, trimmed and sides slit
   Salt and pepper
- 1 tablespoon vegetable oil
- 2 tablespoons unsalted butter
- 2 teaspoons minced fresh sage
- 2 teaspoons minced fresh thyme
- ⅛ teaspoon ground cinnamon
- ¼ cup apple cider
- 1 tablespoon brown sugar

1. Adjust an oven rack to the lower-middle position and heat the oven to 325 degrees.

2. Spread the sauerkraut evenly across the bottom of a 13 by 9-inch baking dish and sprinkle with ½ teaspoon of the caraway seeds. Peel half of the apples, then cut both the peeled and unpeeled apples into 2-inch-thick wedges.

3. Pat the pork chops dry with paper towels and season with salt and pepper. Heat the oil in a large skillet over medium-high heat until just smoking. Place the pork chops in the skillet in a pinwheel formation with the tips pointing toward the pan edge and cook until golden brown on both sides, about 8 minutes, flipping halfway through. Transfer the pork chops to the baking dish, arranging them in a single layer on top of the sauerkraut.

4. Melt the butter in the skillet over medium heat. Add the remaining ½ teaspoon caraway seeds, the sage, thyme, and cinnamon, and cook until fragrant, about 30 seconds. Stir the cider, sugar, ¼ teaspoon salt, and ⅛ teaspoon pepper into the pot, scraping up any browned bits. Bring the liquid to a simmer and cook until reduced slightly, about 1 minute. Stir the apples into the skillet and cook until just heated through, about 1 minute. Pour the mixture into the baking dish, nestling the apples around the pork chops.

5. Cover the baking dish tightly with foil and bake until the pork chops are tender, 1 to 1½ hours.

6. Remove the foil and continue to cook until the liquid is reduced by half, about 30 minutes longer. Let rest for 5 minutes before serving.

Notes from the Test Kitchen

The flavors in this meal are wonderfully seasonal. We switched from rib chops to blade chops, a better choice for slow-cooking because they become more tender and flavorful. Keeping the apple skins on some of the wedges added color and a nice textural contrast, and cooking the apples in apple cider helped boost the apple flavor even more.

Orange Pork Chops

JOYCE NOWER | LA MESA, CALIFORNIA

Oranges, with their fresh citrus flavor, have always been a great complement to mild pork, whether as a juice-infused glaze, a sauce studded with whole orange segments, or the bittersweet addition of zest. In Joyce's recipe, which her Nana used to make, bone-in chops are braised in orange juice, which is then reduced to create a tangy sauce. It's a homey, comforting dish with an appealingly bright flavor that hits the spot any time of year.

SERVES 4

4	(10-ounce) bone-in blade-cut pork chops, about 1 inch thick, trimmed and sides slit
	Salt and pepper
2	tablespoons vegetable oil
1	onion, minced
3	garlic cloves, minced
2	teaspoons minced fresh oregano
⅛	teaspoon cayenne pepper
2	tablespoons all-purpose flour
3	cups orange juice
1½	cups low-sodium chicken broth
2	bay leaves
1	tablespoon fresh lime juice
2	tablespoons chopped fresh cilantro

1. Pat the pork chops dry with paper towels and season with salt and pepper. Heat 1 tablespoon of the oil in a large Dutch oven over medium-high heat until just smoking. Place the pork chops in the pot in a pinwheel formation with the tips pointing toward the pan edge and cook until golden brown on both sides, about 8 minutes, flipping halfway through. Transfer the pork chops to a plate.

2. Heat the remaining 1 tablespoon oil in the pot over medium heat until shimmering. Add the onion and ¼ teaspoon salt and cook, stirring occasionally, until softened, 5 to 7 minutes. Stir in the garlic, oregano, and cayenne and cook until fragrant, about 30 seconds. Stir in the flour and cook for 1 minute. Whisk in the orange juice, broth, and bay leaves, scraping up any browned bits.

3. Return the pork chops, along with any accumulated juices, to the pot. Bring to a simmer, cover, and cook until the pork chops are tender, about 1½ hours.

4. Transfer the pork chops to a plate and tent loosely with foil. Discard the bay leaves. Skim the fat off the surface of the sauce with a wide spoon. Return the sauce to a simmer and cook until thickened and reduced to 3 cups, about 20 minutes.

5. Stir in the lime juice and season with salt and pepper to taste. Return the pork chops, along with any accumulated juices, to the sauce and heat until the pork chops are warmed through, about 1 minute. Sprinkle with the cilantro and serve.

Notes from the Test Kitchen

We loved the boldness of the orange flavor here, but adding some chicken broth gave the sauce more complexity and cut the juice's sweetness. Garlic, fresh oregano, and a pinch of cayenne added nice depth, and to get a thicker sauce, we added flour and reduced it on the stove for 20 minutes. Lime juice and cilantro gave these chops a fresh finish.

Pork Chop Scallop

JENNIFER KAUFFMAN | ANDERSON, INDIANA

Baking pork chops on a bed of potatoes, carrots, and green beans in a creamy sauce with cheese sounds like food for both the body and the soul. "My mother used to make this for us growing up, and it really is the perfect meal. It has meat, vegetables, and starch all in one dish. As a mother now, I really appreciate all the hard work she put into preparing food for us. She not only worked 40 hours every week, she made sure we sat down to the table together and ate as a family as often as was possible." Without a doubt, Pork Chop Scallop is a meal any family would happily gather around.

SERVES 4

- 4 (8-ounce) boneless center-cut pork chops, about 1 inch thick, trimmed
  Salt and pepper
- 2 tablespoons vegetable oil
- 1 onion, minced
- 2 garlic cloves, minced
- 1 teaspoon dried basil
- ¾ cup heavy cream
- ¾ cup low-sodium chicken broth
- 1 teaspoon Worcestershire sauce
- 2 pounds russet potatoes, peeled and sliced ⅛ inch thick
- 4 ounces green beans, trimmed and cut into 1-inch pieces
- 1 carrot, peeled and sliced ⅛ inch thick
- 1 cup shredded sharp cheddar cheese

1. Adjust an oven rack to the lower-middle position and heat the oven to 425 degrees.

2. Pat the pork chops dry with paper towels and season with salt and pepper. Heat 1 tablespoon of the oil in a Dutch oven over medium-high heat until just smoking. Place the pork chops in the pot and cook until golden brown on both sides, about 6 minutes, flipping halfway through. Transfer the pork chops to a plate.

3. Heat the remaining 1 tablespoon oil in the pot over medium heat until shimmering. Add the onion and 1 teaspoon salt and cook, stirring occasionally, until softened, 5 to 7 minutes. Stir in the garlic, basil, and ¼ teaspoon pepper and cook until fragrant, about 30 seconds. Stir in the cream, broth, and Worcestershire sauce, scraping up any browned bits.

4. Add the potatoes, green beans, and carrot to the pot. Bring to a simmer, cover, and cook over medium-low heat, stirring halfway through, until the potatoes and carrot are almost tender (a paring knife should glide through the potatoes and carrot slices with slight resistance), about 10 minutes.

5. Gently pack the vegetable mixture into an even layer, removing any air pockets, then sprinkle evenly with the cheese. Arrange the pork chops in an even layer on top of the vegetables. Transfer the pot to the oven and bake until the sauce is bubbling and the center of the pork chops registers 140 to 145 degrees on an instant-read thermometer, 15 to 20 minutes. Let rest until the center of the pork chops registers 150 degrees, about 10 minutes. Serve.

Notes from the Test Kitchen

This is one hearty dinner—we found it wouldn't fit in the 13 by 9-inch baking dish called for, so we switched to a Dutch oven and boneless chops. Doing so also allowed us to build flavor all in one pan. Originally the vegetables went into the oven raw and didn't cook evenly, so we parcooked them, and we streamlined by not layering them.

Dr Pepper–Glazed Ham

THE EDITORS OF COOK'S COUNTRY

This recipe, like many of those submitted by our readers, was the creation of a resourceful mother, in this case the mother of one of our editors. "Never one to shy away from the possibility of failure, Mom always experimented with traditional Christmas recipes—even when it came to the ubiquitous spiral-sliced ham. This adventurous (and successful) attempt to dress up the holiday ham with a Dr Pepper glaze may seem strange at first glance, but the combination of flavors from the fruity soda, fresh orange juice, and mustard gives this ham an unbeatable sweet tang that's pure genius. Use of an oven bag gets the ham on the table in record time and ensures that it's moist through and through. This ham is more than enough to serve a crowd and still have some leftovers."

SERVES 20 TO 30

- 1 (7- to 10-pound) spiral-sliced, bone-in half ham, preferably shank end
- 1 plastic oven bag
- ¾ cup packed light brown sugar
- ½ cup Dr Pepper
- 2 tablespoons orange juice
- 2 teaspoons Dijon mustard

1. Remove the ham from the packaging and discard the plastic disk that covers the bone. Place the ham in the plastic oven bag, tie the bag shut, and trim the excess plastic. Set the ham, cut-side down, in a 13 by 9-inch baking dish and cut four slits in the top of the bag. (If you don't have an oven bag, place the ham cut-side down in the baking dish and wrap tightly with foil.) Let sit at room temperature for 1½ hours.

2. Adjust an oven rack to the lowest position and heat the oven to 250 degrees.

3. Bake the ham until the center registers 100 degrees on an instant-read thermometer, 1½ to 2½ hours (about 14 minutes per pound if using a plastic oven bag, about 17 minutes per pound if using foil), depending on the weight of the ham.

4. While the ham bakes, bring the sugar, Dr Pepper, orange juice, and mustard to a simmer in a medium saucepan and cook until syrupy and reduced to ¾ cup, about 8 minutes.

5. Remove the ham from the oven and roll back the sides of the bag to expose the ham. Brush the ham liberally with the glaze and return to the oven until the glaze becomes sticky, about 10 minutes. Brush the entire ham again with the glaze, tent loosely with foil, and rest for 30 to 40 minutes before serving.

Notes From the Test Kitchen

Dr Pepper–glazed ham may sound like a bad idea, but it's definitely a dish that works—and how. The fruity soda has a complexity and real bite you don't find in the typical sweet, one-dimensional glazes usually applied to smoked hams. When we made this dish, we discovered that the key was relying on the orange juice and mustard to cut the sweetness of the Dr Pepper. Also, cooking the ham in an oven bag ensured that it stayed moist, and we only needed to bake it until just warmed through, since the ham was already cooked.

Classic Roast Beef and Gravy

THE EDITORS OF COOK'S COUNTRY

Paired with a rich gravy made from pan drippings, a tender, flavorful beef roast has been a special-occasion meal since our country's youth. Sadly, we've found keeping our roast rosy and juicy means not many drippings get left in the pan—it all stays in the meat. But with a little test kitchen know-how, we found that with the just-rendered fat and fond left from searing the roast, and a few clever ingredients, we could get a flavorful, "beefy" gravy *and* a tender, juicy roast. This recipe turns out picture-perfect every time.

SERVES 6 TO 8

- 1 (4-pound) top sirloin roast, fat trimmed to ¼ inch thick
  Salt and pepper
- 1½ tablespoons vegetable oil
- 8 ounces white mushrooms, chopped
- 2 onions, minced
- 1 carrot, peeled and chopped
- 1 celery rib, chopped
- 4 garlic cloves, minced
- 1 tablespoon tomato paste
- ¼ cup all-purpose flour
- 4 cups low-sodium beef broth
- 1 cup red wine
- 1 teaspoon Worcestershire sauce

1. Pat the beef dry with paper towels. Rub 2 teaspoons salt evenly over the surface of the roast. Cover with plastic wrap and refrigerate for at least 1 hour, or up to 24 hours.

2. Adjust an oven rack to the lower-middle position and heat the oven to 275 degrees. Set a V-rack inside a roasting pan.

3. Pat the beef dry with paper towels and rub 1 teaspoon pepper evenly over the surface of the roast. Heat 1 tablespoon of the oil in a large Dutch oven over medium-high heat until just smoking. Add the roast and cook until well browned on all sides, 8 to 12 minutes, turning as needed. Transfer the roast to the prepared roasting pan and set the Dutch oven aside for the gravy (do not clean). Transfer the roasting pan to the oven and cook until the meat registers 125 degrees (for medium-rare), 1½ to 2 hours.

4. Transfer the roast to a carving board, tent loosely with foil, and let rest for 25 minutes.

5. While the roast rests, heat the remaining 1½ teaspoons oil in the Dutch oven over medium heat until shimmering. Add the mushrooms, onions, carrot, and celery and cook, stirring occasionally, until the vegetables are softened and the mushrooms have released their juices and are brown around the edges, 7 to 10 minutes. Stir in the garlic and tomato paste and cook until fragrant, about 30 seconds. Stir in the flour and cook for 1 minute. Whisk in the broth and wine, scraping up any browned bits.

6. Bring to a simmer and cook until the gravy is thickened, about 10 minutes. Strain the gravy through a fine-mesh strainer into a medium saucepan. Stir in the Worcestershire sauce and season with salt and pepper to taste. Cover to keep warm until ready to serve.

7. Cut the meat crosswise against the grain into ½-inch slices. Serve with the gravy.

Notes from the Test Kitchen

Sautéed mushrooms, tomato paste, beef broth, and Worcestershire sauce combine to mimic the flavor of a drippings-based gravy. For ideal flavor and texture, refrigerate the roast overnight after salting. If you don't have a V-rack, cook the roast on a wire rack set inside a rimmed baking sheet. Look for a roast with at least a ¼-inch fat cap on top; this fat bastes the roast, helping it stay moist.

Tia's Coffee Pot Roast

MARGARET MARTINEZ | TUCSON, ARIZONA

"My Aunt Margaret was not known as the best of the family cooks (of course, we have several great cooks in the family so the competition is fierce), but she had some classic family dinner recipes that held the title of 'Best Of.'" This dish of Margaret's aunt (*tía* means "aunt") is one of those recipes. Braising a roast in coffee is a clever, though not entirely new, idea. It's a thrifty use of the morning's leftover coffee, so it isn't all that surprising that some Amish variations exist, where the use of coffee in such recipes was highlighted as typical of Amish thrift. Coffee also gives the meat a subtle nutty flavor and beautifully deep mahogany color (we found one coffee pot roast recipe titled "Black Pot Roast"). But most importantly, people have found they like to cook roasts in coffee because the acid in the coffee makes the meat unbelievably tender. Make this recipe just once and you might not ever go back to making plain old pot roast again.

SERVES 6 TO 8

1	(3½-pound) boneless beef chuck-eye roast, trimmed
	Salt and pepper
3	tablespoons vegetable oil
1½	pounds small red potatoes, scrubbed and quartered
1½	pounds carrots, peeled and cut into ½-inch pieces
2	teaspoons sugar
1	onion, minced
2	garlic cloves, minced
1	sprig fresh thyme
1	cup low-sodium beef broth
1	tablespoon Worcestershire sauce
2–2½	cups dark coffee
8	ounces white mushrooms, stemmed and halved

1. Adjust an oven rack to the lower-middle position and heat the oven to 300 degrees.

2. Pat the beef dry with paper towels and season with salt and pepper. Heat 2 tablespoons of the oil in a Dutch oven over medium-high heat until just smoking. Add the roast and cook until well browned on all sides, 8 to 10 minutes, turning as needed. Transfer the roast to a plate.

3. Heat the remaining 1 tablespoon oil in the pot over medium heat until shimmering. Add the potatoes, carrots, and sugar and cook, stirring occasionally, until browned, 8 to 10 minutes. Transfer the vegetables to a bowl.

4. Return the pot to medium heat, add the onion and cook, scraping up any browned bits, until softened, 5 to 7 minutes. Stir in the garlic and thyme and cook until fragrant, about 30 seconds.

(Continued on page 58)

5. Return the roast, along with any accumulated juices, to the pot. Add the broth, Worcestershire sauce, and enough coffee to come halfway up the sides of the roast. Bring to a simmer, cover, and transfer the pot to the oven. Cook, turning the roast every 30 minutes, until the roast is almost tender, about 3½ hours. Transfer the roast to a plate.

6. Strain the liquid through a fine-mesh strainer into a large measuring cup. Rinse out the pot. Return the liquid to the pot and let it settle for 5 minutes. Skim the fat off the surface of the sauce with a wide spoon and return the roast to the liquid. Add the potatoes, carrots, and mushrooms, submerging them in the liquid. Bring to a simmer over medium heat, cover, and continue to cook in the oven until the meat is tender, 30 to 40 minutes longer.

7. Transfer the roast to a carving board and tent loosely with foil. Bring the liquid to a simmer over medium-high heat and cook until the vegetables are tender, 10 to 15 minutes.

8. Transfer the vegetables to a serving platter. Cut the meat into ½-inch slices or pull it apart into large pieces. Transfer the meat to the platter with the vegetables. Season the sauce with salt and pepper to taste. Pour about ½ cup of the sauce over the meat and vegetables, and serve, passing the remaining sauce separately.

Notes from the Test Kitchen

We've had our share of pot roasts with tender beef and vegetables in a savory gravy or sauce, but this version made with coffee really impressed us— the robust coffee lent a unique flavor to the beef and a wonderful richness to the sauce. And the meat was amazingly tender. However, Margaret's recipe relied on coffee alone as a braising liquid, and we found it all but dried up by the end of the cooking time. Adding a cup of beef broth solved this issue. To help balance the coffee's bitterness, we caramelized the vegetables in a little sugar before adding them to the pot.

Horseradish Beef Stew

HARRY FEATHERSTONE | WOOSTER, OHIO

Horseradish and beef has long been a favorite pairing, but making them into a stew was new to us. Research turned up wartime recipes for pot roast and horseradish braises (around the time Harry's mother prepared this), but these were thriftier, saucy roasts. Harry's mother likely adapted a standard braise, and later, Harry probably gave it a modern touch or two, like the dill and portobellos. Regardless of how the recipe evolved, one thing is certain: it gives an old comfort food standard a flavorful twist.

SERVES 8

- 4 pounds boneless beef chuck-eye roast, trimmed and cut into 1½-inch cubes
  Salt and pepper
- ¼ cup vegetable oil
- 2 onions, minced
- 3 tablespoons all-purpose flour
- 1½ cups low-sodium chicken broth
- 1½ cups low-sodium beef broth
- 2 (8-ounce) jars prepared horseradish
- 1 teaspoon dill seed
- 1½ pounds red potatoes, scrubbed and cut into 1-inch pieces
- 1 pound carrots, peeled and cut into 1-inch pieces
- 4 large portobello mushroom caps, cut into ½-inch pieces
- 2 tablespoons minced fresh parsley

1. Adjust an oven rack to the lower-middle position and heat the oven to 325 degrees.

2. Pat the beef dry with paper towels and season with salt and pepper. Heat 1 tablespoon of the oil in a large Dutch oven over medium-high heat until just smoking. Add half of the beef and cook until well browned on all sides, about 8 minutes, turning as needed. Transfer the beef to a bowl. Return the pot to medium-high heat and repeat with 1 tablespoon more oil and the remaining beef.

3. Heat 1 tablespoon more oil in the pot over medium heat until shimmering. Add the onions and ¼ teaspoon salt and cook, stirring occasionally, until softened, 5 to 7 minutes. Stir in the flour and cook for 1 minute. Slowly whisk in the broths, scraping up any browned bits. Stir in the horseradish and dill seed.

4. Return the beef, along with any accumulated juices, to the pot. Bring to a simmer, cover, and transfer the pot to the oven. Cook for 50 minutes, then stir in the potatoes and carrots. Cover and continue to cook until the meat is tender, 1 to 1½ hours longer.

5. Meanwhile, heat 1½ teaspoons more oil in a large nonstick skillet over medium-high heat until shimmering. Add half of the mushrooms and cook, stirring occasionally, until they have released their juices and are brown around the edges, 7 to 10 minutes. Season with salt and pepper to taste and transfer the mushrooms to a bowl. Repeat with the remaining 1½ teaspoons oil and the remaining mushrooms.

6. Stir the parsley into the stew and season with salt and pepper to taste. Serve, sprinkling individual portions with the mushrooms.

Notes from the Test Kitchen

Harry's recipe packed the roast in a flour-horseradish-dill paste, which let the roast absorb good flavor but led to scorching when seared. Cubing and searing the meat, and stirring in the horseradish and dill with the broth, kept the flavors fresh. Simmering the mushrooms in the stew gave them an unappealing texture, so we sautéed them and reserved them as a garnish.

Deviled Beef Tenders

SHERRILL DUCHARME | LAWRENCEVILLE, NEW JERSEY

In this recipe, an otherwise simple beef stew becomes "deviled" with the addition of spicy horseradish and Dijon mustard. Served with egg noodles, rice, or potatoes, it is, as Sherrill suggests, perfect comfort food for a fall or winter supper, one that will warm you through on even the chilliest evenings.

SERVES 4 TO 6

- 2 pounds boneless beef chuck-eye roast, trimmed and cut into 1-inch cubes
  Salt and pepper
- 2½ tablespoons vegetable oil
- ½ cup minced onion
- 2 garlic cloves, minced
- 2 tablespoons all-purpose flour
- 1½ cups water
- ½ cup tomato sauce
- 1 tablespoon white wine vinegar
- 1 teaspoon prepared horseradish
- 1 teaspoon Dijon mustard

1. Pat the beef dry with paper towels and season with salt and pepper. Heat 1 tablespoon of the oil in a large skillet over medium-high heat until just smoking. Add half of the beef and cook until well browned on all sides, about 8 minutes, turning as needed. Transfer the beef to a bowl. Return the skillet to medium-high heat and repeat with 1 tablespoon more oil and the remaining beef.

2. Heat the remaining 1½ teaspoons oil in the skillet over medium heat until shimmering. Add the onion and ¼ teaspoon salt and cook, stirring occasionally, until softened, 5 to 7 minutes. Stir in the garlic and ⅛ teaspoon pepper and cook until fragrant, about 30 seconds. Stir in the flour and cook for 1 minute. Whisk in the water, tomato sauce, vinegar, horseradish, and mustard, scraping up any browned bits.

3. Return the beef, along with any accumulated juices, to the skillet. Bring to a simmer, cover, and cook, stirring occasionally, until the sauce is thickened and the meat is tender, 1 to 1½ hours. Season with salt and pepper to taste and serve.

Notes from the Test Kitchen

We prefer chuck-eye roast for this recipe, but any boneless roast from the chuck will work. Sherrill floured the meat before browning, but we opted to add the flour later on, as a way to help thicken the sauce. Cooking the meat unfloured also left a good fond in the pan, which we could use to build an even more flavorful sauce. If the sauce begins to stick to the bottom of the skillet in step 3, add ¼ cup water and continue to simmer.

Saucy Mustard Beef Steak

HEATHER POWELL | YUCAIPA, CALIFORNIA

"The best way to describe our family's recipe is that it is like a beef stroganoff with more flavor." The extra kick in Heather's recipe comes from Dijon mustard, which she adds to sour cream–mushroom sauce. Heather started making this dish for friends when she wanted a meal to deliver to couples who had just had a child. "I had couples claiming they got pregnant specifically to get Saucy Mustard Beef Steak! This recipe is from my now-90-year-old Norwegian grandmother, Marion Matson. My mother started adding mushrooms; I started doubling the sauce ingredients and using stew meat or beef chuck. As with all family recipes, sometimes we go heavy on the meat, sometimes heavy on the mushrooms or mustard—it always comes out fabulous."

SERVES 4 TO 6

- 2 pounds boneless beef chuck-eye roast, trimmed and cut into 1-inch cubes
  Salt and pepper
- 3 tablespoons vegetable oil
- 1 pound white mushrooms, sliced thin
- ½ cup minced onion
- 2 garlic cloves, minced
- 2 tablespoons all-purpose flour
- 1½ cups water
- ½ cup low-sodium beef broth
- ¼ cup Dijon mustard
- 2 tablespoons soy sauce
- 1 cup sour cream
- 1 tablespoon fresh lemon juice
- 2 tablespoons chopped fresh parsley

1. Pat the beef dry with paper towels and season with salt and pepper. Heat 1 tablespoon of the oil in a large Dutch oven over medium-high heat until just smoking. Add half of the beef and cook until well browned on all sides, about 8 minutes, turning as needed. Transfer the beef to a bowl. Return the pot to medium-high heat and repeat with 1 tablespoon more oil and the remaining beef.

2. Heat the remaining 1 tablespoon oil in the pot over medium heat until shimmering. Add the mushrooms, onion, and ¼ teaspoon salt and cook, stirring occasionally, until the mushrooms have released their juices and are brown around the edges, 7 to 10 minutes. Stir in the garlic and ⅛ teaspoon pepper and cook until fragrant, about 30 seconds. Stir in the flour and cook for 1 minute. Whisk in the water, broth, mustard, and soy sauce, scraping up any browned bits.

3. Return the beef, along with any accumulated juices, to the pot. Bring to a simmer, cover, and cook, stirring occasionally, until the sauce is thickened and the meat is tender, 1 to 1½ hours.

4. Stir ½ cup of the warm sauce into the sour cream in a bowl. Off the heat, stir the sour cream mixture and the lemon juice into the pot. Season with salt and pepper to taste. Sprinkle with the parsley and serve.

Notes from the Test Kitchen

Our test kitchen loved this zippy spin on an old classic. We prefer chuck-eye roast for this recipe, but any boneless roast from the chuck will work. If the sauce begins to stick to the bottom of the pot in step 3, add ¼ cup water and continue to simmer. It is important to stir a small amount of the hot sauce into the sour cream before adding it to the pot because it prevents the sour cream from curdling.

Grandma Wooly's Beef Barbecue

CHARLES WOOLEVER | ROCHESTER, NEW YORK

"This recipe comes from my paternal grandmother, Dorothy Woolever, 'Grandma Wooly.' It's remarkable in that the deep flavors of the finished dish belie the simplicity of the ingredients. This recipe is, indeed, way more than the mere sum of its parts!" We found that Grandma's saucy shredded beef barbecue (which is served on buns) has a sweet tang that puts it in a league of its own—most first-timers taking a bite of one of these sandwiches will know there's something different about it but won't be sure exactly what it is. Grandma's secret? A combination of pickling spice, dry mustard, and cider vinegar. It's tangy, sweet, and a perfect complement to the tender meat. "My father and his siblings ate this for dinner during the week when they were growing up. They passed the tradition along to their children, and we all enjoy making it today."

SERVES 8

- 1 tablespoon pickling spice
- 2 pounds boneless beef chuck-eye roast, trimmed and cut into 1½-inch cubes
  Salt and pepper
- 2 tablespoons vegetable oil
- 2½ cups water
- 1½ cups ketchup
- 1 tablespoon cider vinegar
- 1 teaspoon dry mustard
- 8 hamburger buns, toasted

1. Adjust an oven rack to the lower-middle position and heat the oven to 300 degrees. Tie the pickling spice in cheesecloth to make a sachet.

2. Pat the beef dry with paper towels and season with salt and pepper. Heat 1 tablespoon of the oil in a Dutch oven over medium-high heat until just smoking. Add half of the beef and cook until well browned on all sides, about 8 minutes, turning as needed. Transfer the beef to a bowl. Return the pot to medium-high heat and repeat with the remaining 1 tablespoon oil and the remaining beef.

3. Stir the water into the pot, scraping up any browned bits. Return the beef, along with any accumulated juices, to the pot. Bring to a simmer, cover, and transfer the pot to the oven. Cook, stirring occasionally, until the beef is almost tender, about 1 hour.

4. Stir in the ketchup, vinegar, mustard, and spice sack. Continue to cook until the meat is tender, about 1 hour longer.

5. Discard the spice sack and transfer the meat to a plate. When cool enough to handle, pull the meat into thin shreds, discarding the excess fat and gristle. Stir the beef back into the sauce and season with salt and pepper to taste. Serve on the buns.

Notes from the Test Kitchen

We love all the kinds of barbecue our country has to offer, but we'd never had anything like this tangy-sweet-spicy recipe; it immediately earned a high spot on our favorites list. Although Charles slow-cooked the beef on the stovetop, we simplified things by moving it to the oven for more even heat and less need for babysitting. The result was an effortless barbecue packed with all the flavor of Charles's original recipe. Pickling spice can be found in the spice aisle of your supermarket.

The Meatloaf with the Frosting

LAURIE DOWIE | HALIFAX, MASSACHUSETTS

A recipe with a name like this is sure to bring the kids running. The "frosting" is, of course, not a sweet icing, but a blanket of creamy mashed potatoes that surrounds the meatloaf, making this a comforting and filling winter meal. "This meatloaf was a favorite at our house when I was growing up. My mom has made this recipe since I was a child, and her mother before that. I have been making it for my own family for six years. Although I often make more complicated dishes, it still evokes that 'Wow!' look. It's comfort food at its simplest and finest."

SERVES 6 TO 8

MEATLOAF

- 2 slices hearty white sandwich bread, torn into large pieces and pulsed in a food processor to coarse crumbs
- 3 tablespoons vegetable oil
  Salt and pepper
- 1 onion, minced
- ½ cup whole milk
- 2 large eggs
- 1 teaspoon dried thyme
- ½ teaspoon onion powder
- 2 pounds meatloaf mix
- ⅓ cup chopped fresh parsley

FROSTING

- 2 pounds russet potatoes, peeled and sliced ¾ inch thick
- 1 cup heavy cream, warmed
- 2 tablespoons unsalted butter
- ½ teaspoon salt
- ¼ teaspoon pepper
- ¼ cup grated Parmesan cheese

1. **FOR THE MEATLOAF:** Adjust an oven rack to the middle position and heat the oven to 350 degrees. Following the photos on page 75, line a large rimmed baking sheet with foil, set a wire rack over the baking sheet, and place a 9 by 6-inch piece of foil in the center of the rack. Use a skewer to poke holes in the foil at ½-inch intervals.

2. Toss the bread crumbs with 2 tablespoons of the oil, a pinch salt, and a pinch pepper. Toast the bread crumbs in a single layer on a rimmed baking sheet, stirring occasionally, until golden brown and dry, 8 to 10 minutes. Set aside to cool to room temperature.

3. Heat the remaining 1 tablespoon oil in a small skillet over medium heat until shimmering. Add the onion and cook, stirring occasionally, until softened, 5 to 7 minutes. Set aside to cool to room temperature.

4. Whisk the milk, eggs, thyme, onion powder, 1½ teaspoons salt, and ½ teaspoon pepper together in a large bowl. Add the bread crumbs, onion, meatloaf mix, and parsley. Mix with your hands until evenly blended and the meat

mixture does not stick to the bowl.

5. Transfer the meat to the foil rectangle and, using wet hands, pat the mixture into a 9 by 6-inch loaf. Bake until the center of the meatloaf registers 140 degrees on an instant-read thermometer, 45 to 50 minutes. Remove the meatloaf from the oven.

6. FOR THE FROSTING: While the meatloaf bakes, place the potatoes in a colander and rinse under cold running water until the water runs clear. Bring the potatoes and 2 quarts water to a simmer in a medium saucepan and cook until tender, 20 to 25 minutes. Drain the potatoes and return to the saucepan.

7. Stir the potatoes over low heat until thoroughly dried, 1 to 2 minutes. Set a ricer or food mill over a bowl and press or mill the potatoes into the bowl. Gently fold in the cream, butter, salt, and pepper until the cream is absorbed and the potatoes are thick and creamy. Cover and set aside to keep warm until the meatloaf reaches 140 degrees.

8. Once the meatloaf has reached 140 degrees and has been removed from the oven, use a spatula to spread the potatoes over the meatloaf, smoothing the top and the sides. Sprinkle the Parmesan evenly over the potatoes and return to the oven until the center registers 160 degrees on an instant-read thermometer, about 30 minutes.

9. Turn on the broiler and broil the meatloaf until the potatoes are golden brown on top, 3 to 5 minutes. Let rest for 15 minutes before serving.

Notes from the Test Kitchen

We couldn't wait to slice into a finished frosted meatloaf, and we were happily rewarded when the time came. Cooking the loaf on a foil-covered wire rack helped keep the meat from steaming in its own juices and later acted as a pedestal when it came time to frost. We added milk for a moister meatloaf and some seasoning for a boost in flavor. Substituting heavy cream for the chicken broth called for in the original recipe ensured that the frosting was ultra-creamy. If you can't find meatloaf mix, substitute ⅔ pound each of ground pork, ground beef, and ground veal.

FROSTING THE MEATLOAF

1. When the meatloaf reaches 140 degrees, remove it from the oven. With a spatula, spread the potatoes evenly over the meatloaf, then sprinkle on the cheese.

2. After the loaf has baked to 160 degrees, cook the meatloaf under the broiler until the potatoes are golden brown on top, 3 to 5 minutes. Let rest for 15 minutes before serving.

Sunday Sugo

GINA SCHAFER | CHARLOTTE, NORTH CAROLINA

"I stayed overnight with my grandparents many a Saturday night and my grandpa made his Sunday sauce (or *sugo*) every week for family dinner. I would sometimes help him roll meatballs, but sometimes he would just put tons of other meats in it. Either way, it was delicious." With huge chunks of hot and sweet Italian sausage, beef roast, and ground beef, this sugo ladled over pasta guarantees no one will leave supper hungry.

MAKES 15 CUPS, ENOUGH FOR 3 POUNDS OF PASTA

- 3 tablespoons olive oil
- 1 pound hot Italian sausages (4 to 6 links), cut into 1-inch pieces
- 1 pound sweet Italian sausages (4 to 6 links), cut into 1-inch pieces
- 1 pound boneless beef chuck-eye roast, trimmed and cut into 1-inch cubes
  Salt and pepper
- 3 onions, chopped
- 1 red bell pepper, stemmed, seeded, and chopped
- 1 green bell pepper, stemmed, seeded, and chopped
- 1 (6-ounce) can tomato paste
- 8 garlic cloves, minced
- 1 tablespoon minced fresh oregano
- 1–2 teaspoons red pepper flakes
- 1 pound 93 percent lean ground beef
- 3 (28-ounce) cans crushed tomatoes
- 1 (14.5-ounce) can diced tomatoes
- ½ cup grated Parmesan cheese
- 2 tablespoons sugar
- 2 tablespoons plain dried bread crumbs
- ½ cup chopped fresh basil

1. Heat 1 tablespoon of the oil in a large Dutch oven over medium-high heat until just smoking. Add the sausages and cook, stirring occasionally, until well browned, 5 to 7 minutes. Transfer the sausages to a bowl.

2. Pat the beef dry with paper towels and season with salt and pepper. Heat 1 tablespoon more oil in the pot over medium-high heat until just smoking. Add the beef and cook, stirring occasionally, until well browned, about 8 minutes. Transfer the beef to the bowl with the sausages.

3. Heat the remaining 1 tablespoon oil in the pot over medium heat until shimmering. Add the onions, bell peppers, ½ teaspoon salt, and ¼ teaspoon pepper and cook, stirring occasionally, until the vegetables are softened, 8 to 10 minutes. Stir in the tomato paste, garlic, oregano, and pepper flakes and cook until the tomato paste begins to brown, 2 to 4 minutes.

4. Add the ground beef, increase the heat to medium-high, and cook, breaking up any large clumps with a wooden spoon, until no longer pink, about 5 minutes. Stir in the crushed tomatoes, diced tomatoes, cheese, sugar, and bread crumbs. Return the sausages and beef, along with any accumulated juices, to the pot. Bring to a simmer, cover, and cook, stirring occasionally, for 1 hour.

5. Uncover and continue to simmer, stirring occasionally, until the meat is tender and the sauce is dark and thickened slightly, about 1 hour longer.

6. Off the heat, season with salt and pepper to taste and stir in the basil. Serve.

Notes from the Test Kitchen

Tasters raved about the rich flavor of this sauce and the tender meat. We changed little from the original, aside from tweaking a step to cut cooking time, browning the meat in batches, and toning down Gina's 1½ tablespoons of red pepper flakes.

Chili Balls

KATHY K. ANDERSON | EVERETT, WASHINGTON

Both meatballs and chili are quintessential Sunday supper fare, so when you bring the two together by giving meatballs a saucy, chili-spiced kick, it's sure to be a winner. "This is an Anderson family favorite my mother-in-law found, and it is a hit. When my daughter met her future husband, he was in the U.S. Navy. We finally figured out how to pressure-can 6 quarts to send to him. He usually shared his care packages, but when he saw what we had sent, he shouted, 'MINE! Back, all of you, back!'" These chili balls, like the 1940s recipes we found, include rice, a way to stretch meat in wartime. Chili balls were also touted as a great recipe for the working woman. Recipes continued to appear regularly through the 1970s, by then as simply a crowd-pleasing dish. Kathy suggests serving these saucy meatballs over rice; egg noodles would also work well.

SERVES 6 TO 8

- ¼ cup whole milk
- 1 large egg
  Salt
- ¼ cup plus 1½ teaspoons chili powder
- 1 tablespoon ground cumin
- 1 pound 85 percent lean ground beef
- 1 pound ground pork
- ⅔ cup long-grain white rice
- 2 tablespoons olive oil
- 1 onion, minced
- 1 (6-ounce) can tomato paste
- 8 garlic cloves, minced
- ¼ teaspoon pepper
- 2 (28-ounce) cans tomato puree
- 2 cups water

1. Whisk the milk, egg, 1½ teaspoons salt, 1½ teaspoons of the chili powder, and 1 teaspoon of the cumin together in a large bowl. Add the beef, pork, and rice and mix with your hands until well combined. With wet hands, form the mixture into 1¼-inch meatballs (you should have about 40 meatballs).

2. Heat 1 tablespoon of the oil in a Dutch oven over medium-high heat until just smoking. Add half of the meatballs and cook until well browned on all sides, 5 to 7 minutes, turning as needed. Transfer the meatballs to a paper towel–lined plate. Return the pot to medium-high heat and repeat with the remaining 1 tablespoon oil and the remaining meatballs.

3. Add the onion and ½ teaspoon salt to the pot and cook over medium heat, stirring occasionally, until softened, 5 to 7 minutes. Stir in the remaining ¼ cup chili powder, remaining 2 teaspoons cumin, the tomato paste, garlic, and pepper, and cook until the tomato paste begins to brown, 2 to 4 minutes. Stir in the tomato puree and water, scraping up any browned bits.

4. Return the meatballs to the pot, bring to a simmer, cover, and cook until the sauce is thickened slightly and the meatballs are tender, 2 to 2½ hours. Season with salt and pepper to taste and serve.

Notes from the Test Kitchen
We liked the idea behind this dish immediately. To get more chili flavor, we increased the chili powder from 1 teaspoon to more than ¼ cup. We also added tomato paste for depth and increased the cooking time to further thicken the sauce and ensure the rice was tender. It's important to stir the sauce periodically during the last half hour of cooking to avoid scorching.

Sunday Tomato Sauce with Meatballs

LORRAINE STEVENSKI | CLEARWATER, FLORIDA

"About 40 years ago, my Grandpa Cucci grew his own tomatoes that we squeezed by hand and ground through a sieve to extract the seeds, and we made our harvest of tomatoes into large batches of sauce." Lorraine prepares an updated version of her family's recipe, which includes enormous 2½-inch Italian American–style meatballs.

SERVES 6 TO 8

SAUCE

- 3 tablespoons olive oil
- 1 onion, minced
  Salt
- 1 (6-ounce) can tomato paste
- 8 garlic cloves, minced
- 1 teaspoon minced fresh oregano or
  ¼ teaspoon dried
  Pepper
- 3 (28-ounce) cans crushed tomatoes

MEATBALLS

- 4 slices hearty white sandwich bread
- ¾ cup water
- ½ cup chopped fresh basil
- ¼ cup chopped fresh parsley
- 2 large eggs, lightly beaten
- ¼ cup grated Parmesan cheese
- ¼ cup ketchup
- 2 teaspoons salt
- 1 teaspoon pepper
- 2 pounds 80 percent lean ground beef
- 1 pound ground pork
- ¼ cup olive oil

1. **FOR THE SAUCE:** Heat the oil in a large Dutch oven over medium heat until shimmering. Add the onion and ½ teaspoon salt and cook, stirring occasionally, until softened, 5 to 7 minutes. Clear the center of the pot and add the tomato paste, stirring frequently with a wooden spoon, until it begins to brown, 2 to 4 minutes. Stir in the garlic, oregano, and ¼ teaspoon pepper and cook until fragrant, about 30 seconds. Stir in the crushed tomatoes. Bring to a simmer, partially cover, and cook, stirring occasionally, until thickened, about 45 minutes.

2. **FOR THE MEATBALLS:** While the sauce cooks, mash the bread and water together in a large bowl until smooth. Add ¼ cup of the basil, 2 tablespoons of the parsley, the eggs, cheese, ketchup, salt, and pepper, and mash to combine. Add the beef and pork and mix with your hands until well combined. With wet hands, form the mixture into 2½-inch meatballs. (You should have about 16 meatballs.)

3. Heat 2 tablespoons of the oil in a large nonstick skillet over medium-high heat until just smoking. Add half of the meatballs and cook until well browned on two sides, 5 to 7 minutes, flipping halfway through. Transfer the meatballs to a paper towel–lined plate. Return the pot to medium-high heat and repeat with the remaining 2 tablespoons oil and the remaining meatballs.

4. Gently transfer the meatballs to the sauce and continue to cook, partially covered, until the meatballs are tender, 20 to 25 minutes. Off the heat, season with salt and pepper to taste and stir in the remaining ¼ cup basil and the remaining 2 tablespoons parsley. Serve.

Notes from the Test Kitchen

Lorraine's meatballs use an unlikely ingredient—ketchup—to keep them moist. Their flavor was great, but they were too unwieldy to brown all sides. Browning two sides got a good, flavorful crust that held them together, and less exposure to heat ensured they were even more moist.

Sweet and Sour Meatballs

DENISE SIEGAL | DALLAS, TEXAS

Combining tart lime juice and tangy ketchup and tomatoes with sweet brown sugar, these unique meatballs and sauce are truly addictive. Denise learned to make this recipe from her mother-in-law, Mary Siegal, and while it is relatively simple as far as steps and ingredients go, it's also a bit time-consuming—a perfect reason to make it a celebratory Sunday supper, or save it for a special dinner or holiday, as Denise's mother-in-law would do. These meatballs are great served with rice or egg noodles.

SERVES 6 TO 8

- 2 cups water
- 3 large eggs
  Salt and pepper
- 3 pounds 85 percent lean ground beef
- 1 cup matzo meal
- 1 tablespoon unsalted butter
- 1 onion, minced
- 1 (28-ounce) can tomato puree
- 2 cups ketchup
- ½ cup packed brown sugar
- 2 tablespoons fresh lime juice

1. Adjust an oven rack to the middle position and heat the oven to 475 degrees. Set a wire rack over a foil-lined rimmed baking sheet.

2. Whisk 1 cup of the water, the eggs, 1 teaspoon salt, and ½ teaspoon pepper together in a large bowl. Add the beef and matzo meal and mix with your hands until well combined. With wet hands, form the mixture into 1¼-inch meatballs. (You should have about 60 meatballs.) Arrange the meatballs on the prepared wire rack and bake until lightly browned, about 20 minutes.

3. Meanwhile, melt the butter in a large Dutch oven over medium heat. Add the onion and cook, stirring occasionally, until softened, 5 to 7 minutes. Stir in the remaining 1 cup water, the tomato puree, ketchup, sugar, and 1 tablespoon of the lime juice. Transfer the meatballs to the sauce. Bring to a simmer, cover, and cook until the sauce is thickened slightly and the meatballs are tender, about 1 hour.

4. Off the heat, stir in the remaining 1 tablespoon lime juice and season with salt and pepper to taste. Serve.

Notes from the Test Kitchen

Although we found it clever of Denise to drop the raw meatballs right into the sauce to cook them—much like dumplings in a soup—we felt that it caused the sauce to become greasy. Browning 60 meatballs in a skillet would have required three batches, too much work for us, so the easiest way to get around the grease issue was using the oven. We chose to bake them on a wire rack set over a foil-lined rimmed baking sheet in a hot oven before adding them to the sauce. This allowed some of the grease to collect in the baking sheet before we added the meatballs to our sauce.

Loekie's Lamb Shanks

PHYLLIS BLANS | SAN CARLOS, CALIFORNIA

Phyllis's Dutch-born mother, Loekie, prepared these saucy, slow-cooked lamb shanks for Phyllis and her sisters in the winter—even if in California this meant well above freezing. The meat is cooked until it becomes fall-off-the-bone tender, and the liquid in which the shanks simmer is deeply flavorful tomato–white wine sauce that pairs nicely with the gamey meat. With a piece of crusty bread for sopping, this would make a satisfying meal whether it's full-blown winter outside or just hinting of fall.

SERVES 4

4	(12- to 16-ounce) lamb shanks, trimmed
	Salt and pepper
¼	cup vegetable oil
8	ounces cremini mushrooms, quartered
3	onions, halved and sliced ½ inch thick
1	(6-ounce) can tomato paste
1	tablespoon paprika
2	garlic cloves, minced
1	teaspoon minced fresh thyme
1	teaspoon grated fresh ginger
2	cups low-sodium chicken broth
½	cup white wine
2	bay leaves
1	tablespoon fresh lemon juice
2	tablespoons chopped fresh parsley

1. Adjust an oven rack to the lower-middle position and heat the oven to 325 degrees.

2. Pat the lamb dry with paper towels and season with salt and pepper. Heat 1 tablespoon of the oil in a large Dutch oven over medium-high heat until just smoking. Add two of the lamb shanks to the pot and cook until well browned on all sides, about 8 minutes, turning as needed. Transfer the shanks to a plate. Repeat with 1 tablespoon more oil and the remaining lamb shanks.

3. Heat 1 tablespoon more oil in the pot over medium heat until shimmering. Add the mushrooms and ¼ teaspoon salt and cook, stirring occasionally, until the mushrooms have released their juices and are brown around the edges, 7 to 10 minutes. Transfer the mushrooms to a bowl.

4. Heat the remaining 1 tablespoon oil in the pot over medium heat until shimmering. Add the onions and ½ teaspoon salt and cook, stirring occasionally, until softened, 8 to 10 minutes. Clear the center of the pot and add the tomato paste, scraping it along the bottom of the pot with a wooden spoon, until it begins to brown, 2 to 4 minutes. Stir in the paprika, garlic, thyme, and ginger and cook until fragrant, about 30 seconds. Whisk in the broth, wine, and bay leaves, scraping up any browned bits.

5. Return the mushrooms and lamb shanks, along with any accumulated juices, to the pot. Bring to a simmer, cover, and transfer the pot to the oven. Cook until the lamb shanks are browned on all sides and the meat is tender, 2 to 2½ hours, flipping halfway through.

6. Transfer the shanks to a serving platter and tent loosely with foil. Discard the bay leaves. Skim the fat off the surface of the sauce with a wide spoon. Stir in the lemon juice and season with salt and pepper to taste. Pour the sauce over the shanks, sprinkle with the parsley, and serve.

Notes from the Test Kitchen

The long cooking time makes the surprising amount of tomato paste in this recipe deeply flavorful. Phyllis browned the shanks in a skillet and transferred them to a baking dish to braise; we used fewer pots by browning the shanks in a Dutch oven before transferring it to the oven.

MARYLAND CARAMEL TOMATOES

From a Storied Past

Mrs. Rockefeller's Meatloaf **74**

Hamburger Potato Roll **76**

Johnny Marzetti **78**

Mock Chicken Legs **79**

Chicken Vesuvio **82**

Salmon Wiggle **84**

Maryland Caramel Tomatoes **85**

Cheese Frenchees **86**

Mrs. Rockefeller's Meatloaf

MICHELLE RAO | NEW YORK, NEW YORK

We found the original recipe for Mrs. Rockefeller's highly seasoned meatloaf in a book called *Meat* by Leon Lobel (1978). The Lobel brothers run a family meat business in Manhattan, and as Leon noted, this recipe came from the wife of former Arkansas governor Winthrop Rockefeller. We found it to be super-easy to make and very moist thanks to the cottage cheese and sour cream included in the mix of ingredients. Michelle got the recipe from her mother, who claimed she got it from an old cookbook—likely Mr. Lobel's, as many of the unique ingredients (including rye bread, curry powder, and onion soup mix) are found in both versions. Of course, Michelle's mother did lend some touches of her own, adding sage to the mix, while omitting other ingredients, like nutmeg and rosemary. In any event, we can understand why she says, "Everyone who eats it asks for the recipe."

SERVES 6 TO 8

- 1 cup sour cream
- 2 slices rye bread, torn into large pieces and pulsed in a food processor to coarse crumbs
- 1 cup cottage cheese
- 2 large eggs
- 1 envelope onion soup mix
- 2 teaspoons steak sauce
- 2 teaspoons Dijon mustard
- 2 teaspoons chopped fresh sage or ½ teaspoon dried
- 1 teaspoon hot sauce
- ½ teaspoon curry powder
- 1 pound 85 percent lean ground beef
- 1 pound bulk pork sausage
- 8 tablespoons (1 stick) unsalted butter
- 2 onions, minced
- 1½ cups chili sauce

1. Adjust an oven rack to the middle position and heat the oven to 300 degrees. Line a large rimmed baking sheet with foil, set a wire rack over the baking sheet, and place a 9 by 6-inch piece of foil in the center of the rack. Following the photos, use a skewer to poke holes in the foil at ½-inch intervals.

2. Stir the sour cream and bread crumbs together in a bowl. Whisk the cottage cheese, eggs, soup mix, steak sauce, mustard, sage, hot sauce, and curry powder together in a large bowl. Add the sour cream–bread mixture, beef, and sausage to the bowl. Mix with your hands until evenly blended and the meat mixture does not stick to the bowl.

3. Transfer the meat to the foil rectangle and, using wet hands, pat the mixture into a 9 by 6-inch loaf. Bake the meatloaf for 40 minutes.

4. Meanwhile, melt the butter in a large skillet

over medium heat. Add the onions and cook, stirring occasionally, until softened, 5 to 7 minutes. Stir in the chili sauce and cook until the flavors are blended, about 3 minutes.

5. Pour the sauce evenly over the meatloaf and continue to bake until the center registers 160 degrees on an instant-read thermometer, 50 minutes to 1 hour longer. Let rest for 15 minutes before serving.

MAKING MEATLOAF

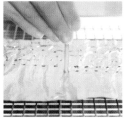 

1. Using a skewer, poke holes about ½ inch apart in the foil placed on the wire rack to allow the fat to drain away.

2. Using wet hands, shape the mixture into a loaf so it covers all the foil.

Notes from the Test Kitchen

We were amazed by the long list of unusual ingredients in this recipe—from onion soup mix to rye bread to curry powder. The recipe Michelle sent in (and the original version of Mrs. Rockefeller's recipe) included two packages of onion soup mix. While we liked the onion flavor, we had a hard time tasting anything else. We used one package of onion soup mix instead, while also reducing the number of other spices in the loaf, which resulted in a cleaner, richer flavor. We did, however, keep the essential ingredients that differentiate this loaf from a typical meatloaf, including curry, mustard, steak sauce, and rye bread. We also made an effort to maintain the low-and-slow cooking method; but at 250 degrees, the original oven temperature was a little too low, so we raised it to 300 degrees. Finally, we cooked the meatloaf on a small piece of foil, arranged on a wire rack set over a foil-lined rimmed baking sheet. This allowed the fat from the meatloaf to drip down into the baking sheet as it cooked, rather than pooling in a baking dish, resulting in a less greasy meatloaf.

Hamburger Potato Roll

BETH VAN KOUTEREN | SANTA FE, NEW MEXICO

According to a 1961 ad for *The New York Times Cook Book*, this was one of the newspaper's most frequently requested recipes in the 1950s—no small feat given a decade of undoubtedly strong competition. Though we felt we needed to make some adjustments to the original recipe, we immediately recognized the appeal of the Hamburger Potato Roll, which is incidentally more of a meatloaf than a hamburger. With mashed potatoes spread over a rectangle of meatloaf that is rolled up jelly-roll style and baked, it's two comfort food classics, all in one package. Beth summed up well why her family loves it: "It's hearty, homey, delicious, and fun."

SERVES 4

POTATOES

- 1 pound Yukon gold potatoes, peeled and sliced ¾ inch thick
- 3 tablespoons heavy cream, warmed
- 2 tablespoons unsalted butter, melted
- ¼ teaspoon salt
- ⅛ teaspoon pepper
- 1 tablespoon chopped fresh parsley

HAMBURGER MEATLOAF

- 3 slices hearty white sandwich bread, torn into large pieces and pulsed in a food processor to coarse crumbs
- 1 tablespoon unsalted butter
- 1 onion, minced
- 2 garlic cloves, minced
- 1 teaspoon minced fresh oregano
- 2 tablespoons whole milk
- 1 large egg
- 2 teaspoons Dijon mustard
- 2 teaspoons Worcestershire sauce
- ¾ teaspoon salt
- ½ teaspoon pepper
- 1 pound 85 percent lean ground beef
- 3 slices bacon

1. FOR THE POTATOES: Place the potatoes in a colander and rinse under cold running water until the water runs clear. Bring the potatoes and 2 quarts water to a simmer in a medium saucepan and cook until tender, 20 to 25 minutes. Drain the potatoes and return to the saucepan.

2. Stir the potatoes over low heat until thoroughly dried, 1 to 2 minutes. Set a ricer or food mill over a bowl and press or mill the potatoes into the bowl. Gently fold in the cream, butter, salt, and pepper until the cream is absorbed and the potatoes are thick and creamy. Stir in the parsley and set aside to cool to room temperature.

3. FOR THE HAMBURGER MEATLOAF: Adjust an oven rack to the middle position and heat the oven to 350 degrees. Measure out ½ cup of the bread crumbs and toast on a rimmed baking sheet until golden brown and dry, 4 to 6 minutes. Cool to room temperature.

4. Melt the butter in a medium skillet over medium heat. Add the onion and cook, stirring occasionally, until softened, 5 to 7 minutes. Stir in the garlic and oregano and cook until fragrant, about 30 seconds. Transfer to a bowl and cool to room temperature.

5. Stir the remaining bread crumbs and the milk together in a bowl. Whisk the egg, mustard, Worcestershire sauce, salt, and pepper together in a large bowl. Add the cooled onion mixture, bread crumb–milk mixture, and beef to the bowl. Mix with your hands until evenly blended and the meat mixture does not stick to the bowl.

6. Following the photos, lay a sheet of foil perpendicularly over another sheet of foil to make a cross. Sprinkle the toasted bread crumbs evenly over the bottom two-thirds of the top piece of foil. Spread the meat mixture over the toasted bread crumbs into a 10 by 7½-inch rectangle. Spread the potatoes evenly over the meat, leaving a ½-inch border around the bottom and sides and a 1-inch border along the top. Using the foil to help, roll the meat and potatoes into a compact log. Lay the bacon strips on top of the loaf and transfer (still in the foil) to an 8½ by 4½-inch loaf pan. Fold back any excess foil.

7. Bake the meatloaf until the bacon is rendered and crisp and the center registers 160 degrees on an instant-read thermometer, 1 hour to 1 hour and 25 minutes. Let rest for 15 minutes. Remove the roll from the pan using the foil sling and serve.

Notes from the Test Kitchen

We loved the idea behind the Hamburger Potato Roll, but the original recipe's flavor needed a boost. Some Dijon mustard, Worcestershire sauce, and fresh oregano did the trick. The original also called for simply "prepared mashed potatoes, warmed." We developed a sturdy mashed potato recipe that worked great, and we found that the potatoes were actually easier to work with when they had cooled. The real challenge was nailing down the rolling method. Making a foil sling and rolling the hamburger and potato on it made for easy rolling and transport to the loaf pan, which we felt was tidier than cooking it free-form, as the original had done.

MAKING A HAMBURGER POTATO ROLL

1. Fold one sheet of foil into an 18 by 7½-inch rectangle, and another into an 18 by 3½-inch rectangle. Lay the wider piece on top to make a cross. Sprinkle the bread crumbs over the bottom two-thirds of the top piece.

2. Spread the meat over the crumbs into a 10 by 7½-inch rectangle, about ¾ inch thick. Spread the mashed potatoes over the meat, leaving a ½-inch border around the bottom and side edges and a 1-inch border at the top.

3. Starting with the shorter side of the rectangle, roll the meat and potatoes into a compact log, using the foil as an aid. Then lay the bacon strips on top of the roll.

4. Using the foil sling, lift the roll and transfer it, in the sling, to an 8½ by 4½-inch loaf pan. Fold back any excess foil so the meatloaf is completely uncovered.

Johnny Marzetti

KATHLEEN COMBS | NORTHBROOK, ILLINOIS

There is no doubt about the inspiration for this comforting, cheesy baked casserole with ground beef, tomatoes, and pasta: it was first served in a restaurant in Columbus, Ohio, founded by an Italian immigrant, Teresa Marzetti, in 1896. Named for her brother-in-law, it soon became popular across Ohio and the Midwest and is now known by many different names—from Yumzetti to Johnny Mazuma to Hamburger Casserole. Says Kathleen, "My mother-in-law made a version of this when my husband was a little boy, and he spoke of it fondly. I did some research and came up with my own recipe a few years ago. It's best made the day before and then baked the day you want to serve it. It's popular with kids and adults alike."

SERVES 6

12	ounces rotini (about 4½ cups)
	Salt
1	tablespoon vegetable oil
2	celery ribs, chopped fine
1	onion, minced
1	green bell pepper, chopped fine
3	garlic cloves, minced
1	tablespoon minced fresh oregano or 1 teaspoon dried
⅛	teaspoon red pepper flakes
	Pepper
1	pound 85 percent lean ground beef
8	ounces sweet Italian sausage, casings removed
1	(15-ounce) can tomato sauce
1	(14.5-ounce) can diced tomatoes
2	tablespoons chopped fresh parsley
2	cups shredded Italian cheese blend

1. Adjust an oven rack to the middle position and heat the oven to 350 degrees. Grease a 13 by 9-inch baking dish and set aside.

2. Bring 4 quarts water to a boil in a large pot. Add the pasta and 1 tablespoon salt and cook, stirring often, until just shy of al dente. Drain the pasta and transfer to the prepared baking dish.

3. Meanwhile, heat the oil in a large skillet over medium heat until shimmering. Add the celery, onion, bell pepper, and 1 teaspoon salt and cook, stirring occasionally, until softened, 5 to 7 minutes. Stir in the garlic, oregano, pepper flakes, and 1 teaspoon pepper and cook until fragrant, about 30 seconds.

4. Add the beef and sausage, increase the heat to medium-high, and cook, breaking up any large clumps with a wooden spoon, until no longer pink, about 5 minutes. Stir in the tomato sauce and diced tomatoes, bring to a simmer, and cook until the flavors are blended, about 3 minutes. Stir in the parsley and season with salt and pepper to taste, then set aside off the heat.

5. Sprinkle 1 cup of the cheese evenly over the pasta, then pour the meat mixture over the top. Sprinkle the remaining 1 cup cheese evenly over the meat mixture.

6. Place the baking dish on a foil-lined rimmed baking sheet, cover with foil, and bake until the sauce is bubbling, about 45 minutes. Remove the foil and continue to bake until the top is spotty brown, about 10 minutes longer. Cool for 10 minutes before serving.

Notes from the Test Kitchen

This baked pasta dish is comfort food at its best. We altered the proportions of a few ingredients to give it a better ratio of pasta to beef and to lighten it up (Kathleen's original had 3½ cups of cheese). We also prefer fresh herbs instead of dried, which help brighten up this appealing casserole.

Mock Chicken Legs

DEBORAH MARCHAND | FRANKLIN, WISCONSIN

These skewers of cubed pork and veal rolled in bread crumbs, deep-fried, then slow-cooked to tenderness raised eyebrows in the test kitchen right off the bat. Considering how readily available and affordable chicken is, why "mock" it in the first place? But a little research turned up the surprising fact that "mock chicken" dishes go back at least as far as the mid-1800s (we found an 1849 recipe for mock chicken pie, made with potatoes and pork). These days it seems odd to "mock" chicken by using more expensive meats like beef or veal, but before the 1940s poultry was actually a luxury, reserved by most families to be eaten only on special occasions and holidays. It wasn't until the advent of large-scale poultry farms that chicken became a competitive option. Mock chicken legs, sometimes called city chicken, usually come in one of two forms: either different types of meat are cubed, then skewered together, breaded, and fried (as in this recipe); or a mixture of ground meat is shaped into the form of a chicken leg, then breaded and fried. In the same family of comfort food as fried chicken, chicken fried steak, and chicken fried chicken, mock chicken legs have a homey appeal that is easy to understand. It's a unique dish that's sure to be a talking point wherever you choose to serve it, whether it's at a special-occasion dinner or the next neighborhood block party.

SERVES 4 TO 6

MEAT
- ½ cup all-purpose flour
- 1 teaspoon dried dill
- Salt and pepper
- ¼ cup Dijon mustard
- 3 large eggs
- 3 slices hearty white sandwich bread, torn into large pieces and pulsed in a food processor to coarse crumbs
- 1½ pounds pork butt, trimmed and cut into 1½-inch chunks
- 1½ pounds veal breast, trimmed and cut into 1½-inch chunks
- 1½–2 cups vegetable oil

SAUCE
- 1 cup sour cream
- 2 tablespoons minced fresh dill
- 1½ teaspoons fresh lemon juice
- 1 garlic clove, minced
- Salt and pepper

1. FOR THE MEAT: Adjust an oven rack to the middle position and heat the oven to 325 degrees. Line a large rimmed baking sheet with foil, set a wire rack over the baking sheet, and coat the rack with vegetable oil spray. Line a second rimmed baking sheet with parchment paper.

(Continued on page 81)

2. Whisk the flour, dried dill, ½ teaspoon salt, and ¼ teaspoon pepper together in a shallow dish. Whisk the mustard and eggs together in a second shallow dish. Toss the bread crumbs with ½ teaspoon salt and ½ teaspoon pepper in a third shallow dish.

3. Thread a 7-inch wooden skewer with 2 pieces of pork and 2 pieces of veal, alternating the two meats. Pat the skewered meat dry with paper towels and season with salt and pepper. Repeat with additional skewers.

4. One at a time, dredge the skewers in the flour, dip into the egg mixture, then coat with the bread crumbs, pressing to adhere. Place on the parchment-lined baking sheet.

5. Pour the oil into a large skillet until it measures ½ inch deep. Heat the oil to 375 degrees over medium-high heat. Lay half of the skewers in the oil and fry until light golden brown on all sides, 2 to 3 minutes, turning as needed. Transfer the skewers to the prepared wire rack over the baking sheet. Repeat with the remaining skewers.

6. Transfer the mock chicken legs to the oven and bake until the meat is tender, about 1 hour. Let rest for 5 minutes.

7. FOR THE SAUCE: While the mock chicken legs bake, combine the sour cream, 1 tablespoon of the fresh dill, the lemon juice, and garlic in a bowl. Season with salt and pepper to taste, cover, and refrigerate until ready to serve.

8. Transfer the mock chicken legs to a platter, sprinkle with the remaining 1 tablespoon fresh dill, and serve, passing the sauce separately.

Notes from the Test Kitchen

Making mock chicken legs was a new adventure for us in the test kitchen. The instructions and quantities in Deborah's original recipe were very loose, so we started by giving it some structure. We saw the appeal in the simple flavors, but adding Dijon lent a very welcome depth. The mustard also helped the bread crumbs stick to the meat. We found that baking our mock chicken legs on a wire rack set over a rimmed baking sheet, uncovered, rather than covered in a roasting pan as the original recipe required, was best for keeping the coating crisp. A simple sour cream dipping sauce made a nice finishing touch. You will need about ten to twelve 7-inch wooden skewers for this recipe.

Chicken Vesuvio

THE EDITORS OF COOK'S COUNTRY

A large contingent of Chicagoans agree the name "Vesuvio" was probably the Chicago touch on a native Italian dish; some believe it stems from a 1930s restaurant of the same name. Despite uncertainty, newspapers, travel books, cookbooks, and magazines all tout the Windy City connection—the earliest we found was in a 1938 Nevada newspaper. The writer mentions a restaurant where the Vesuvio is so good it makes you want to sing. The problem, we found, is that this dish is a labor of love. Bone-in chicken, potato wedges, and a sauce (garlic-lemon, usually with oregano and peas) are each started in the pan in stages, then combined to cook in the oven before the sauce is reduced on the stove. We streamlined this classic to be made entirely in a skillet on the stovetop. And our simple version has all the flavor of the original—now that's something to sing about!

SERVES 4

- 4 (6-ounce) boneless, skinless chicken breasts, trimmed
  Salt and pepper
- 2 tablespoons olive oil
- 1½ pounds baby red potatoes, scrubbed and halved
- 2 garlic cloves, minced
- 1 teaspoon minced fresh rosemary
- ½ teaspoon dried oregano
- 1½ cups low-sodium chicken broth
- ½ cup dry white wine
- 1 cup frozen peas, thawed
- 2 tablespoons unsalted butter
- 2 teaspoons fresh lemon juice

1. Pat the chicken dry with paper towels and season with salt and pepper. Heat 1 tablespoon of the oil in a large nonstick skillet over medium-high heat until just smoking. Cook the chicken until golden brown on both sides, about 5 minutes, flipping halfway through. Transfer the chicken to a plate.

2. Heat the remaining 1 tablespoon oil in the skillet over medium heat until shimmering. Cook the potatoes, cut-side down, until golden brown, about 7 minutes. Stir in the garlic, rosemary, oregano, and ½ teaspoon salt and cook until fragrant, about 30 seconds. Stir in the broth and wine, scraping up any browned bits.

3. Return the chicken, along with any accumulated juices, to the skillet. Bring to a simmer, cover, and cook until the thickest part of the breast registers 160 to 165 degrees on an instant-read thermometer and the potatoes are tender, 10 to 15 minutes. Transfer the chicken and potatoes to a serving platter and tent loosely with foil.

4. Increase the heat to medium-high and cook until the sauce is reduced to 1 cup, about 5 minutes. Stir in the peas and cook until heated through, about 1 minute. Off the heat, whisk in the butter and lemon juice and season with salt and pepper to taste. Pour the sauce over the chicken and potatoes and serve.

Notes from the Test Kitchen

Traditionally prepared Chicken Vesuvio utilizes both the stovetop and oven, and dirties multiple pans. We limited ourselves to the stovetop and a skillet. We switched from bone-in, skin-on chicken parts to boneless, skinless breasts. We found the potatoes in our recipe were better halved than in wedges. Leaving the potatoes in the pan while we built the sauce allowed them to soak up lots of flavor—and cut out a step. Adding rosemary to the usual oregano gave it a more assertive flavor.

Salmon Wiggle

JANE AUGER | ARLINGTON, MASSACHUSETTS

With such a name, we knew this recipe had to have a good story behind it. Turns out there is an old expression, first appearing in print in the late 1890s, "get a wiggle on," which means to hurry or bustle. As the first wiggles relied on only canned ingredients—traditionally, a seasoned milk-based white sauce with canned salmon and peas over crackers or toast—they were certainly quick and simple. Wiggles could also be made with lobster, chicken, or shrimp. A 1911 story from Ohio's *Portsmouth Times* recounts the scandal of Massachusetts college women getting caught for enjoying shrimp wiggle at a chafing dish party, a late-night gathering common at the time, held without permission. To the author, the chance to enjoy a wiggle was worth such a risk. Jane brings new life to her Nana's traditional salmon wiggle with fresh salmon and peas, and fresh-baked rustic Italian bread. Any old wiggle fan would tell you it's even more delicious than before.

SERVES 4

1½ pounds skinless salmon fillet, cut into ½-inch pieces
   Salt and pepper
2 tablespoons unsalted butter
2 leeks, white and light green parts only, halved lengthwise and sliced thin
1 garlic clove, minced
¼ cup all-purpose flour
1 tablespoon Dijon mustard
⅓ cup dry vermouth or white wine
1½ cups whole milk
1 (8-ounce) bottle clam juice
1 cup frozen peas, thawed
2 tablespoons chopped fresh tarragon
1 tablespoon fresh lemon juice
8 slices Italian bread, toasted
   Lemon wedges, for serving

1. Pat the salmon dry with paper towels and season with salt and pepper.

2. Melt the butter in a large saucepan over medium heat. Add the leeks and ½ teaspoon salt and cook, stirring occasionally, until softened, 5 to 7 minutes. Stir in the garlic and cook until fragrant, about 30 seconds. Stir in the flour and mustard and cook for 1 minute.

3. Slowly stir in the vermouth and cook until evaporated, about 30 seconds. Slowly stir in the milk and clam juice and bring to a simmer. Add the salmon and cook until the pieces are just opaque in the center, 2 to 3 minutes. Gently stir in the peas and continue to cook until warmed through, about 1 minute longer.

4. Off the heat, gently stir in the tarragon and lemon juice. Season with salt and pepper to taste. Spoon the salmon wiggle over the toasted bread slices and serve, passing the lemon wedges separately.

Notes from the Test Kitchen

This recipe presents a unique combination: comfort food with a touch of upscale flair. However, we found the original recipe's sauce needed a bit more punch. Including vermouth and clam juice with the milk was a good start. Adding mustard and sautéing some leeks and garlic before adding the flour also deepened the flavor, and fresh tarragon and lemon juice added a bright finish. We used frozen peas rather than shelling fresh; it was less trouble and frozen peas are reliably more fresh-tasting since produce-section peas may in fact be several days old.

Maryland Caramel Tomatoes

ELEANOR BLAKE | WINSTON-SALEM, NORTH CAROLINA

Surprisingly, this dish is tied less to a place and more to a person; President Herbert Hoover's wife, Lou Henry Hoover, in fact. Mary Rattley, the Hoovers' cook in the eight years prior to Mr. Hoover winning the White House, invented these sweet treats. Ripe tomatoes are peeled and cored, sprinkled with brown sugar, dotted with butter, and baked. They become soft and sweet with a concentrated tomato flavor, and the syrup created from the juices cooking down with the sugar is irresistible. Eleanor found the recipe in *The First Ladies Cook Book* (1969), so it seems certain that they were made in the White House even when Mary was no longer their cook. So where does the "Maryland" come from? Its inclusion is simply a tribute to Mary Rattley's native state. These tomatoes are particularly great alongside a nice steak or a simple roast chicken.

SERVES 8

- 8 large ripe but firm tomatoes, cored and peeled
- 1 tablespoon salt
- 1 teaspoon white pepper
- 1 cup packed light brown sugar
- 4 tablespoons (½ stick) unsalted butter, cut into ¼-inch pieces

1. Adjust an oven rack to the upper-middle position and heat the oven to 400 degrees.

2. Arrange the tomatoes in a large ovenproof skillet, cored-side up. Season the tomatoes with the salt and pepper, then sprinkle the brown sugar over the top. Dot the tomatoes evenly with the butter.

3. Bake until the tomatoes are tender and lightly browned, about 1 hour, basting with the juices every 15 minutes.

4. Using potholders (the skillet handle will be hot), remove the skillet from the oven and transfer to the stovetop. Cook the tomatoes over medium-low heat, basting every 5 minutes and adjusting the heat as needed to maintain a rapid simmer, until the sauce is thick and syrupy, 25 to 30 minutes. Serve.

Notes from the Test Kitchen

There's just something so incredibly appealing about a sweet side dish. The original called for a buttered baking dish, but because they aren't always safe to put over direct flame, we switched to an ovensafe skillet. Eleanor's recipe required back and forth between the oven and stovetop, which we streamlined. We also found the original sweetness overwhelming, so we reduced the sugar from 1½ cups to 1 cup. Regularly basting the tomatoes helped them brown and intensified their flavor.

PEELING TOMATOES

1. With a paring knife, score an X at each tomato's base. Simmer the tomatoes in boiling water for 30 to 60 seconds.

2. After cooling the tomatoes in ice water for 1 minute, use the knife to remove strips of loosened peel, starting at the X on each tomato's base.

Cheese Frenchees

PAM PATTERSON | LEON, KANSAS

"Dining out was a rare and special occasion when I was a child during the sixties in Lincoln, Nebraska. A local favorite family restaurant was King's Food Host. The novelty of this restaurant was the telephone at each booth. You placed your order by giving it to the hostess over the phone. In a time when many households had only one phone, having a telephone tableside was very thrilling! The kids' indisputable menu favorite was King's take on grilled cheese, a deep-fried grilled cheese sandwich, served with a side of french fries or onion rings." But a Frenchee has more to it than that. It's a grilled cheese sandwich made with a touch of mayo and cut into triangles, which are battered, rolled in a crunchy coating, and deep fried. Who first came up with the concept is uncertain, but it is clear it won King's restaurants hordes of devoted patrons. (King's Food Host USA, now no longer in business, had at its peak around 160 restaurants in 17 states, mostly in the Midwest.) Adds Pam: "After having children of my own and King's Food Host was a distant memory, I came across a recipe that attempted to replicate this childhood treat. It remains a family favorite to this day."

SERVES 4

- 1½ sleeves Ritz crackers (50 crackers), pulsed in a food processor to coarse crumbs
- ⅔ cup milk
- 2 large eggs
- ½ cup mayonnaise
- 8 slices hearty white sandwich bread
- 6 (¾-ounce) slices American cheese
- 3–4 quarts vegetable oil

1. Line a large rimmed baking sheet with parchment paper. Spread the cracker crumbs in a shallow dish. Whisk the milk and eggs together in a medium bowl.

2. Spread 1 tablespoon of the mayonnaise on one side of each slice of bread. Arrange 1½ slices of the cheese on 4 of the slices of bread and top with the remaining 4 slices bread, with the mayonnaise side facing the cheese. Cut each sandwich diagonally into quarters.

3. One at a time, dip the sandwich quarters into the egg mixture, then coat with the cracker crumbs, pressing to adhere. Place on the prepared baking sheet and refrigerate until set, about 1 hour.

4. Pour the oil into a large Dutch oven until it measures 2 inches deep. Heat the oil to 375 degrees over medium-high heat. Lay half of the chilled sandwich quarters in the oil and fry until golden brown on both sides, 2 to 3 minutes, flipping halfway through. Transfer the sandwich quarters to a large, paper towel–lined plate to drain briefly. Repeat with the remaining sandwich quarters. Serve.

Notes from the Test Kitchen

These fried mini–grilled cheeses were a test kitchen favorite at first bite—not to mention, they just *look* like they're going to be fantastic! Pam's recipe needed only a single minor tweak, just a little extra cheese to cover the bread. The recipe didn't specify a cracker type for the coating, but we favored Ritz. We liked to dip the sandwiches in ketchup (which, we were told by a genuine Frenchee fanatic, is how she ate them growing up in Oklahoma).

BLACK AND WHITE CHICKEN CHILI

Easy Family Favorites

Black and White Chicken Chili **90**

Crunchy Chicken **91**

International Dateline Chicken **92**

Olive Martini Chicken **94**

Lorraine's Pork Chops and Corn **95**

Southern Braised Pork Chops 'n' Gravy **96**

Kids' Favorite Shepherd's Pie **97**

Cornbread Meatloaf **99**

Glop **100**

Green Mountain Surprise **101**

Screaming Noodles **102**

Creamy Potato Puff **104**

"Candied" Apples in Cinnamon Syrup **105**

Black and White Chicken Chili

JENNIFER NYSTROM | MORROW, OHIO

Though chili is an American classic, there really isn't a single classic recipe. It can be made with ground beef or stew meat, venison, pork, or poultry, beans or no beans. Some are tomato-y, thick, and spicy. Others are brothy and light. Says Jennifer of her brothy chicken-based version with black and white beans, corn, and green chiles: "I came up with this recipe after eating something similar at a local restaurant. I wanted a healthy chili that was quick to make and good for us. This is now one of my family's favorite meals and a recipe I go back to all the time. It's great on a cold winter day or for a festive Cinco de Mayo party. I recently won a chili cook-off at my office with this recipe!"

SERVES 4 TO 6

- 1½ **pounds boneless, skinless chicken breasts, trimmed**
  Salt and pepper
- 2 **tablespoons olive oil**
- 1 **onion, minced**
- 4 **garlic cloves, minced**
- 1½ **teaspoons ground cumin**
- 1½ **teaspoons dried oregano**
- 4 **cups low-sodium chicken broth**
- 1 **(15.5-ounce) can cannellini beans, drained and rinsed**
- 1 **(15.5-ounce) can black beans, drained and rinsed**
- 1½ **cups frozen corn, thawed**
- 1 **(8-ounce) can chopped green chiles, drained**
- ¼ **cup chopped fresh cilantro**

1. Pat the chicken dry with paper towels and season with salt and pepper. Heat 1 tablespoon of the oil in a Dutch oven over medium-high heat until just smoking. Cook the chicken until golden brown on both sides, about 5 minutes, flipping halfway through. Transfer the chicken to a plate.

2. Heat the remaining 1 tablespoon oil in the pot over medium heat until shimmering. Add the onion and ½ teaspoon salt and cook, stirring occasionally, until softened, 5 to 7 minutes.

Stir in the garlic, cumin, oregano, and ½ teaspoon pepper and cook until fragrant, about 30 seconds. Stir in the broth, scraping up any browned bits.

3. Return the chicken, along with any accumulated juices, to the pot. Bring to a simmer and cook until the thickest part of the breasts registers 160 to 165 degrees on an instant-read thermometer, 10 to 15 minutes.

4. Transfer the chicken to a plate. When the chicken is cool enough to handle, shred the meat into bite-sized pieces and return it to the chili; add the beans, corn, and chiles. Return to a simmer, cover, and cook, stirring occasionally, until thickened, about 15 minutes.

5. Off the heat, stir in the cilantro and season with salt and pepper to taste. Serve.

Notes from the Test Kitchen

This broth-based, fresh-flavored chili warmed us up like other bowls of the all-American favorite, but without any heaviness. Plus we loved the visual appeal of the black and white beans, yellow corn, and green chiles. To boost the overall flavor, we began by quickly searing the chicken in a Dutch oven and then poached it in the broth with the onions, garlic, and spices, rather than sautéing it until cooked through before adding the broth as Jennifer had done. Adding a little cilantro at the end was just the right touch to further the fresh appeal of this chili.

Crunchy Chicken

GILLIAN JACKSON-CHAMPLAIN | CROTON-ON-HUDSON, NEW YORK

"Crunchy Chicken was served often in our house growing up. It was the requested dish by both of my brothers for their birthday dinners and still is." Gillian's mother relies on cornflakes for her chicken's crispy coating, a technique that has been around longer than you might think. Cornflakes hit the market at the end of the 1800s, and by 1910 recipes calling for cornflake coatings began appearing, offering a novel crunchiness compared to the centuries-old cracker-crumb technique. "Fighting over the 'crunchies' in the bottom of the pan has gotten to a point where my mother now makes more than an army should eat and serves them alongside—it is still never enough. One time my brother's friend met him at one end of a bridge at 11:30 at night just to get a box of the chicken. This is one meal that will guarantee that the entire family will go to great lengths to come together and have a meal, from across the river to across the country."

SERVES 4

- 2 cups buttermilk
- 1½ teaspoons garlic powder
- 1 teaspoon hot sauce
  Salt and pepper
- 3 pounds bone-in, skin-on chicken pieces (split breasts cut in half, drumsticks, and/or thighs), trimmed
- 3½ cups cornflakes, crushed
- 2 slices hearty white sandwich bread, torn into large pieces and pulsed in a food processor to coarse crumbs
- ½ teaspoon paprika
- 3 tablespoons vegetable oil

1. Whisk the buttermilk, 1 teaspoon of the garlic powder, the hot sauce, 2 teaspoons salt, and 1 teaspoon pepper together in a large bowl. Add the chicken to the mixture and turn to coat. Cover and refrigerate for at least 1 hour, or up to 12 hours.

2. Adjust an oven rack to the upper-middle position and heat the oven to 400 degrees. Set a wire rack inside a foil-lined rimmed baking sheet and coat the rack with vegetable oil spray.

3. Combine the cornflakes, bread crumbs, remaining ½ teaspoon garlic powder, the paprika, ¼ teaspoon salt, and ⅛ teaspoon pepper in a shallow dish. Drizzle the oil over the crumbs and toss until well coated.

4. Working with one piece at a time, remove the chicken from the marinade and dredge in the crumb mixture, firmly pressing the crumbs onto all sides of the chicken. Place the chicken on the prepared wire rack, leaving ½ inch between each piece.

5. Bake the chicken until deep golden brown and the thickest part of the breasts registers 160 to 165 degrees and the thickest part of the thighs registers 175 degrees on an instant-read thermometer, 35 to 45 minutes. Serve.

Notes from the Test Kitchen

To ensure Gillian's chicken stayed ultra-crispy, we soaked the chicken pieces in buttermilk to help the crust adhere, and seasoning the buttermilk added good flavor to the meat and kept it juicy. Mixing fresh bread crumbs with the cornflakes and baking the chicken at 400 degrees on a wire rack instead of at 350 degrees in a baking dish gave us even bigger crunch.

International Dateline Chicken

JACKLYNN GROSS | LITTLETON, COLORADO

The colorful, sweet and savory combination of bell pepper, dates, oranges, and curry gives Jacklynn's dish a tropical, South Pacific islands feel, making the name International Dateline Chicken a perfect fit for her creative recipe. "I first tasted this recipe at the home of my then-future in-laws when I was dating my husband in the 1960s. It is very different, and I do not believe I have ever been served this anywhere else. I serve it, as my mother-in-law did, on special occasions."

SERVES 4

- 4 (12-ounce) bone-in, skin-on split chicken breasts, trimmed
  Salt and pepper
- 1 tablespoon vegetable oil
- 1 red bell pepper, stemmed, seeded, and chopped fine
- ½ cup minced onion
- 1 garlic clove, minced
- ½ teaspoon curry powder
- 1 cup low-sodium chicken broth
- 1 cup orange juice
- 1 tablespoon cornstarch
- ¾ cup pitted dates, finely chopped
- 1 (11-ounce) can Mandarin oranges, drained
- 1 tablespoon chopped fresh parsley

1. Pat the chicken dry with paper towels and season with salt and pepper. Heat 1½ teaspoons of the oil in a Dutch oven over medium-high heat until just smoking. Cook the chicken until golden brown on both sides, about 10 minutes, flipping halfway through. Transfer the chicken to a plate and remove the skin.

2. Heat the remaining 1½ teaspoons oil in the pot over medium heat until shimmering. Add the bell pepper, onion, and ½ teaspoon salt and cook, stirring occasionally, until the vegetables are softened, 5 to 7 minutes. Stir in the garlic and curry powder and cook until fragrant, about 30 seconds. Stir in the broth, scraping up any browned bits.

3. Return the chicken breasts, along with any accumulated juices, to the pot. Bring to a simmer, cover, and cook until the thickest part of the breasts registers 160 to 165 degrees on an instant-read thermometer, 20 to 25 minutes. Transfer the chicken to a serving platter and tent loosely with foil.

4. Mix the orange juice and cornstarch together in a bowl. Add the juice mixture and the dates to the pot and cook, stirring constantly, until the sauce is thickened, about 5 minutes. Off the heat, stir in the oranges and parsley and season with salt and pepper to taste. Pour the sauce over the chicken and serve.

Notes from the Test Kitchen

We couldn't get enough of this savory-sweet dish. By trading out green bell pepper for red, we gave Jacklynn's recipe even more color, and we liked that the red pepper's flavor was less bitter. Toasting the curry with the garlic brought out its flavor even more, and while Jacklynn used the syrup from the can of oranges, we found orange juice gave us a more balanced sauce with a purer orange flavor.

Olive Martini Chicken

LINDA FOREMAN | LOCUST GROVE, OKLAHOMA

It may sound like an adults-only entrée, but this is a dish that will appeal to young and old alike. Linda cooks it for everyone from her husband and 92-year-old mother to her daughter, son-in-law, and 9-year-old grandson when they come to visit. "This is easy, it looks great, and no one has to know it was so simple!" Sure, it has all the classic martini ingredients and garnishes—vermouth, gin, onion, and olives—but don't worry, it won't knock you off your feet. As the alcohol simmers with the chicken broth, the flavors combine to become a mellow, well-balanced sauce. It's an easy yet elegant dish that everyone will enjoy.

SERVES 4

- 4 (6-ounce) boneless, skinless chicken breasts, trimmed
  Salt and pepper
- 2 tablespoons olive oil
- ¼ cup minced onion
- 3 garlic cloves, minced
- ½ cup low-sodium chicken broth
- ⅓ cup pimiento-stuffed green olives, sliced thin
- ¼ cup gin
- 1 tablespoon dry vermouth
- 1 teaspoon fresh lemon juice

1. Pat the chicken dry with paper towels and season with salt and pepper. Heat 1 tablespoon of the oil in a large skillet over medium-high heat until just smoking. Cook the chicken until golden brown on both sides, about 5 minutes, flipping halfway through. Transfer the chicken to a plate.

2. Heat the remaining 1 tablespoon oil in the skillet over medium heat until shimmering. Add the onion and cook, stirring occasionally, until softened, 3 to 5 minutes. Stir in the garlic and cook until fragrant, about 30 seconds. Stir in the broth, olives, gin, vermouth, and lemon juice, scraping up any browned bits.

3. Return the chicken breasts, along with any accumulated juices, to the skillet. Bring to a simmer, cover, and cook until the thickest part of the breasts registers 160 to 165 degrees on an instant-read thermometer, 10 to 15 minutes.

4. Transfer the chicken to a serving platter. Season the sauce with pepper to taste, pour the sauce over the chicken, and serve.

Notes from the Test Kitchen

By tapping into the components of a classic cocktail, Linda's recipe gives new life to the humble chicken breast. We didn't need to change much—we found that the meat was flavorful and moist after it poached in the sauce—so the only step we added was browning the onion and garlic before adding the other ingredients to the skillet, a change that gave the aromatics a chance to soften and mellow. Make sure not to over-season the chicken breasts before browning, since the olives will provide the sauce with a fair amount of salt.

Lorraine's Pork Chops and Corn

RON ERICKSON | PORTLAND, OREGON

"My mother made this on special occasions—actually, it was a special occasion when she made it! She and a girlfriend of hers invented this when they were in their late teens, and it became one of our family's favorite meals." It's easy to understand why. This simple dish pairs tender pork chops with creamed corn, a combination that is both comforting and satisfying. You'll find it's a perfect meal for any time of year. "Despite its simplicity, this dish is incredibly good. Once you taste it, you just want more!"

SERVES 4

- 5 ears corn, husks and silk removed
- 4 (10-ounce) bone-in center-cut pork chops, about ¾ inch thick, trimmed and sides slit
  Salt and pepper
- 2 tablespoons vegetable oil
- ½ cup minced onion
- 1 garlic clove, minced
- ½ teaspoon minced fresh thyme
  Pinch cayenne pepper
- 1½ cups heavy cream
- 1 tablespoon chopped fresh parsley

1. Stand the corn upright inside a bowl and carefully cut the kernels from 3 ears of the corn, using a paring knife. Grate the remaining 2 ears corn on the large holes of a box grater set in the bowl with the cut kernels. Before discarding the cobs, scrape any remaining pulp and milk from them using the back of a butter knife.

2. Pat the pork chops dry with paper towels and season with salt and pepper. Heat 1 tablespoon of the oil in a large skillet over medium-high heat until just smoking. Place the pork chops in the skillet in a pinwheel formation with the tips pointing toward the pan edge and cook until golden brown on both sides, about 8 minutes, flipping halfway through. Transfer the pork chops to a plate.

3. Heat the remaining 1 tablespoon oil in the skillet over medium heat until shimmering. Add the onion and ¼ teaspoon salt and cook, stirring occasionally, until softened, 5 to 7 minutes. Stir in the garlic, thyme, cayenne, and ⅛ teaspoon pepper and cook until fragrant, about 30 seconds. Stir in the corn mixture and cream, scraping up any browned bits.

4. Return the pork chops, along with any accumulated juices, to the skillet. Spoon the corn mixture over the pork chops to cover. Bring to a simmer and cook until the center of the pork chops registers 140 to 145 degrees on an instant-read thermometer, about 10 minutes.

5. Transfer the pork chops to a serving platter, tent loosely with foil, and let rest until the center of the pork chops registers 150 degrees, about 10 minutes. Return the corn mixture to a simmer and cook until thickened, 5 to 7 minutes. Off the heat, stir in the parsley and season with salt and pepper to taste. Pour the corn mixture over the pork chops and serve.

Notes from the Test Kitchen

One-pot meals are some of our favorites since they are a great way to enjoy a delicious supper without creating a sink full of dirty dishes. Ron's original recipe called for canned creamed corn, but we opted to make our own creamed corn for a fresher flavor. Ron also breaded his chops, but we found that the coating only became gummy, so we simply browned them. To streamline his recipe, we kept the chops and corn in the skillet and on the stovetop the whole time, rather than transferring it all to a baking dish to go in the oven.

Southern Braised Pork Chops 'n' Gravy

VIDA FONSECA | NEW ORLEANS, LOUISIANA

A little gravy can go a long way in making a simple dinner feel special. And since Southerners have always had a love affair with their gravy, we weren't surprised to see this recipe for simmering bone-in pork chops in an onion-mushroom gravy come from the Deep South. Vida tells us this recipe is a family specialty, one she always requested on her birthday when she was young. These tender, flavorful chops pair perfectly with a side of greens and mashed potatoes. And don't forget the dinner roll or biscuit to sop up all that wonderful gravy.

SERVES 4

- 4 (10-ounce) bone-in center-cut pork chops, about ¾ inch thick, trimmed and sides slit
  Salt and pepper
- 2 tablespoons vegetable oil
- 8 ounces white mushrooms, sliced thin
- 1 onion, halved and sliced thin
- 2 garlic cloves, minced
- ½ teaspoon dried marjoram
- 2 tablespoons all-purpose flour
- 1 cup low-sodium chicken broth
- ¾ cup dry sherry
- 1 tablespoon fresh lemon juice
- 1 tablespoon chopped fresh parsley

1. Pat the pork chops dry with paper towels and season with salt and pepper. Heat 1 tablespoon of the oil in a large skillet over medium-high heat until just smoking. Place the pork chops in the skillet in a pinwheel formation with the tips pointing toward the pan edge and cook until golden brown on both sides, about 8 minutes, flipping halfway through. Transfer the pork chops to a plate.

2. Heat the remaining 1 tablespoon oil in the skillet over medium heat until shimmering. Add the mushrooms, onion, and ½ teaspoon salt and cook, stirring occasionally, until the onion is softened and the mushrooms have released their juices and are brown around the edges,

7 to 10 minutes. Stir in the garlic, marjoram, and ¼ teaspoon pepper and cook until fragrant, about 30 seconds. Stir in the flour and cook for 1 minute. Whisk in the broth and sherry, scraping up any browned bits.

3. Return the pork chops, along with any accumulated juices, to the skillet. Spoon the mushroom mixture over the pork chops to cover. Bring to a simmer, cover, and cook until the meat is tender, about 30 minutes.

4. Transfer the pork chops to a serving platter and tent loosely with foil. Return the mushroom mixture to a simmer and cook, stirring frequently, until thickened, 4 to 6 minutes. Off the heat, stir in the lemon juice and parsley and season with salt and pepper to taste. Pour the sauce over the pork chops and serve.

Notes from the Test Kitchen

Vida's recipe called for two thinner chops per person. So that the chops could stand up to the long braising time, we switched to one thicker chop per person. She also made her sauce from a combination of water, beef bouillon, and a touch of sherry, but for a more balanced flavor, we went with a full ¾ cup of sherry and traded in the water and beef bouillon for chicken broth. Using flour to thicken the sauce instead of cornstarch gave it a silkier texture, and a little lemon juice and parsley added at the end gave it a bright finish.

Kids' Favorite Shepherd's Pie

KATHRYN PELOSI | ENGLEWOOD, FLORIDA

"Because I enjoyed it so much as a kid, I did my best to re-create the shepherd's pie served for lunch at North Yarmouth Elementary School, in North Yarmouth, Maine. This recipe was one of my kids' favorites." Shepherd's pie is a satisfying comfort food, but it started as a thrifty recipe for using leftover meat. Kathryn uses ground beef rather than the old-fashioned choice of lamb, and she adds cheese to the topping—changes sure to make this pie sound great to youngsters (as well as grown-ups).

SERVES 4 TO 6

FILLING

- 1 tablespoon olive oil
- 2 celery ribs, chopped fine
- 1 onion, minced
  Salt
- 2 garlic cloves, minced
- 2 teaspoons minced fresh thyme
  Pepper
- 1½ pounds 85 percent lean ground beef
- 3 tablespoons all-purpose flour
- 2 tablespoons tomato paste
- 1¾ cups low-sodium beef broth
- 2 cups frozen corn, thawed

TOPPING

- 2 pounds russet potatoes, peeled and sliced ¾ inch thick
- 1 cup shredded sharp cheddar cheese
- ¼ cup sour cream
- ½ teaspoon salt
- ¼ teaspoon pepper

1. Adjust an oven rack to the upper-middle position and heat the oven to 375 degrees.

2. FOR THE FILLING: Heat the oil in a large skillet over medium heat until shimmering. Add the celery, onion, and ½ teaspoon salt and cook, stirring occasionally, until softened, 5 to 7 minutes. Stir in the garlic, thyme, and ½ teaspoon pepper and cook until fragrant, about 30 seconds.

3. Add the beef, increase the heat to medium-high, and cook, breaking up any large clumps with a wooden spoon, until no longer pink and beginning to brown, 6 to 8 minutes. Stir in the flour and tomato paste and cook until the tomato paste begins to brown, about 1 minute. Stir in the broth, scraping up any browned bits.

4. Bring to a simmer and cook, stirring frequently, until the mixture is thick but still saucy, 15 to 20 minutes. Off the heat, stir in the corn and season with salt and pepper to taste. Pour the filling into a broiler-safe 2-quart casserole dish.

5. FOR THE TOPPING: While the filling cooks, bring the potatoes and 2 quarts water to a simmer in a medium saucepan and cook until tender, 20 to 25 minutes. Drain the potatoes and return to the saucepan. Stir the potatoes over low heat until thoroughly dried, 1 to 2 minutes. Mash the potatoes until smooth, then gently fold in the cheese, sour cream, salt, and pepper until the potatoes are thick and creamy.

6. Spread the potatoes in an even layer over the filling. Place the casserole dish on a foil-lined rimmed baking sheet and bake until the filling is bubbling, about 15 minutes. Turn on the broiler and broil the shepherd's pie until the potatoes are golden brown on top, 3 to 5 minutes. Cool for 10 minutes before serving.

Notes from the Test Kitchen

Winter comfort food doesn't get much better than this. To deepen the filling's flavor, we cooked tomato paste with the flour. It is important to spread the potatoes to the very edge of the dish to prevent the filling from bubbling out of the pan.

Cornbread Meatloaf

BEVERLY RILEY | EVERETT, WASHINGTON

"This recipe was the result of a compromise made by my mother when I wanted corn in our meatloaf and my siblings didn't. Everyone loved it!" This light, tender meatloaf, with its unusual choice for a binder, makes a loaf that is slightly sweet and nutty, and the tangy molasses-tomato glaze is the perfect complement. Whether you make it for a family dinner or a neighborhood potluck, this is one meatloaf that is sure to disappear quickly.

SERVES 6 TO 8

MEATLOAF

- 1 tablespoon vegetable oil
- 2 celery ribs, chopped fine
- 1 onion, minced
- 1 green bell pepper, stemmed, seeded, and chopped fine
  Salt
- 1/3 cup tomato paste
- 2 large eggs
- 1 tablespoon yellow mustard
- 1/2 teaspoon ground coriander
- 1/2 teaspoon dried basil
- 1/2 teaspoon pepper
- 1 1/2 pounds 85 percent lean ground beef
- 8 ounces bulk pork sausage
- 3 cups cornbread crumbs
- 1/3 cup chopped fresh parsley
- 1/4 cup drained jarred roasted red peppers, chopped

GLAZE

- 1/2 cup tomato juice
- 2 tablespoons molasses

1. FOR THE MEATLOAF: Adjust an oven rack to the middle position and heat the oven to 350 degrees. Line a large rimmed baking sheet with foil, set a wire rack over the baking sheet, and place a 9 by 6-inch piece of foil in the center of the rack. Following the photos on page 75, use a skewer to poke holes in the foil at 1/2-inch intervals.

2. Heat the oil in a large skillet over medium heat until shimmering. Add the celery, onion, bell pepper, and 1/2 teaspoon salt and cook, stirring occasionally, until the vegetables are softened, 5 to 7 minutes. Set aside to cool to room temperature.

3. Whisk the tomato paste, eggs, mustard, coriander, basil, pepper, and 1 1/2 teaspoons salt together in a large bowl. Add the onion mixture, beef, sausage, cornbread, parsley, and roasted red peppers to the bowl. Mix with your hands until evenly blended and the meat mixture does not stick to the bowl.

4. Transfer the meat to the foil rectangle and, using wet hands, pat the mixture into a 9 by 6-inch loaf. Bake the meatloaf until the center registers 160 degrees on an instant-read thermometer, about 1 hour. Remove the meatloaf from the oven and turn on the broiler.

5. FOR THE GLAZE: While the meatloaf bakes, bring the tomato juice and molasses to a simmer in a small saucepan and cook until thickened, 5 to 7 minutes. Spread the glaze evenly over the meatloaf and broil until the glaze begins to bubble, 3 to 5 minutes. Let cool for 15 minutes before serving.

Notes from the Test Kitchen

We were huge fans of Beverly's cornbread binder and the light texture and sweet flavor it lent, but Beverly used roughly 5 cups of cornbread, which we reduced to 3 cups. Use a savory Southern-style cornbread for its balanced sweetness and large crumb. Beverly baked her meatloaf in a casserole dish, but we found it cooked best on a piece of foil with holes in it and placed on a wire rack.

Glop

JENNIFER CHACON | CROWN POINT, INDIANA

"Everyone in my family loves Glop! My mother made Glop from her mother's recipe, and now I make my own version for my family." Glop, believe it or not, is a classic, with recipes first appearing in the 1950s. Usually with hamburger meat as the foundation, it was touted as easy to prepare, as it could change according to what was on hand. With a name that sounds straight from Dr. Seuss, Glop will have kids excited about dinner before they even take a bite. And after one helping of this casserole of ground turkey and macaroni in a chili-spiced tomato sauce with cheese, adults will be lining up with the kids for seconds.

SERVES 6 TO 8

- 2 cups shredded Co-Jack cheese
- 2 cups shredded sharp cheddar cheese
- 1 pound elbow macaroni
   Salt
- 2 tablespoons vegetable oil
- 1 onion, minced
- 1 green bell pepper, stemmed, seeded, and chopped fine
- 2 tablespoons tomato paste
- 3 garlic cloves, minced
- 2 teaspoons dried oregano
- 1 teaspoon chili powder
- 1 teaspoon chipotle chile powder
- 1 pound 93 percent lean ground turkey
- 1 (28-ounce) can tomato puree
- 1 (14.5-ounce) can diced tomatoes
   Pepper

1. Adjust an oven rack to the middle position and heat the oven to 350 degrees. Combine the cheeses in a bowl.

2. Bring 4 quarts water to a boil in a large Dutch oven. Add the macaroni and 1 tablespoon salt and cook, stirring often, until just shy of al dente. Reserve ¾ cup of the pasta cooking water, then drain the macaroni. Toss the macaroni with 1 tablespoon of the oil and set aside.

3. Wipe the pot dry with paper towels. Heat the remaining 1 tablespoon oil in the pot over medium heat until shimmering. Add the onion and bell pepper and cook, stirring occasionally, until softened and beginning to brown, 8 to 10 minutes. Stir in the tomato paste, garlic, oregano, chili powder, and chipotle chile powder and cook until fragrant, about 30 seconds.

4. Add the turkey, increase the heat to medium-high, and cook, breaking up any large clumps with a wooden spoon, until no longer pink, about 5 minutes. Stir in the reserved pasta cooking water, tomato puree, and diced tomatoes, scraping up any browned bits. Bring to a simmer and cook, stirring occasionally, until thickened slightly, about 20 minutes.

5. Off the heat, stir in the macaroni and 2 cups of the cheese mixture. Season with salt and pepper to taste. Pour the mixture into a 13 by 9-inch baking dish and sprinkle with the remaining 2 cups cheese mixture. Place the baking dish on a foil-lined rimmed baking sheet and bake until the sauce is bubbling and the cheese is lightly browned, 15 to 20 minutes. Cool for 10 minutes before serving.

Notes from the Test Kitchen

Jennifer called for Velveeta but we chose to use Co-Jack for its stronger, tangier flavor. If you can't find Co-Jack, substitute equal amounts of Colby and Monterey Jack. Be careful not to overcook the pasta in step 2, since it will continue to cook in the oven.

Green Mountain Surprise

EVELYN CHARTERS | MAPLE, ONTARIO

This recipe has "kids' favorite" written all over it. With a mound of rice covered in a bright green, creamy spinach sauce and a fried egg on the peak, Green Mountain Surprise is one of the most colorful recipes we've seen. Says Evelyn: "My favorite comfort meal as a kid, it's light yet satisfying. Mom was happy because it was very nutritious, with protein, carbs, and vegetable all at once. It's a lovely feast for the senses and an excellent dish for introducing children to the pleasures of delicious and healthy food made from scratch."

SERVES 4

RICE

3¼ cups water
2 cups long-grain white rice, rinsed until water runs clear
1½ teaspoons salt
⅛ teaspoon pepper

SPINACH

2 tablespoons unsalted butter
¼ cup minced onion
Salt
1 garlic clove, minced
Pinch ground nutmeg
¾ cup heavy cream
1 (10-ounce) bag curly-leaf spinach, stemmed
Pepper

EGGS

2 tablespoons olive oil
4 large eggs
Salt and pepper

1. FOR THE RICE: Bring the water, rice, salt, and pepper to a boil in a large saucepan over medium-high heat. Reduce the heat to low, cover, and cook until all the water is absorbed, 16 to 18 minutes. Off the heat, remove the lid and place a clean kitchen towel folded in half over the saucepan. Replace the lid and let sit.

2. FOR THE SPINACH: Melt the butter in a medium saucepan over medium heat. Add the onion and ¼ teaspoon salt and cook, stirring occasionally, until softened, 5 to 7 minutes. Stir in the garlic and nutmeg and cook until fragrant, about 30 seconds. Whisk in the cream, bring to a simmer, and cook until thickened slightly, about 3 minutes. Stir in the spinach, one handful at a time, and cook until wilted, about 1 minute.

3. Transfer the mixture to a blender and process until smooth. Rinse out the saucepan, then return the spinach mixture to the pot. Season with salt and pepper to taste and cover to keep warm.

4. FOR THE EGGS: Heat the oil in a large non-stick skillet over low heat until shimmering. Quickly add the eggs to the skillet and season with salt and pepper. Cover and cook until the whites are set but the yolks are still runny, 2 to 3 minutes. Uncover the eggs and remove the skillet from the heat.

5. Fluff the rice with a fork and divide it onto four serving plates in mounds. Spoon some of the spinach mixture on top of each mound of rice and carefully slide a fried egg on top. Serve.

Notes from the Test Kitchen

This is one of those dishes that turned out to be a really fun, and unexpected, hit. While Evelyn specified brown rice, we actually preferred white (and we have a hunch kids would too). A preheated, nonstick skillet is essential for ensuring the eggs will release easily from the pan. We also streamlined how we cooked the spinach by cooking it right in the sauce rather than steaming it before mixing it in.

Screaming Noodles

ELIZABETH WATSON | CHESTERTOWN, MARYLAND

"This was a family vegetarian favorite (a fast one!) when my two daughters were little. The children named it because one remembers screaming at dinner until she tasted this. It makes a nice party dish or potluck offering because it is so pretty (green, white, gold) and holds up fairly well for reheating or last-minute assembly. I adapted this recipe from a cookbook I no longer remember, back in 1975. Making it over the years, I've adapted it to our own family's preferences and worked out how to assemble it quickly." Elizabeth's inventive and flavorful recipe, made with egg noodles and wilted spinach mixed with a tangy, creamy, and slightly spicy Parmesan–cottage cheese sauce, is an appealing combination of simple flavors. It's sure to be a favorite wherever it's served.

SERVES 4

- 1 **pound wide egg noodles**
  Salt
- 2 **tablespoons olive oil**
- 2 **garlic cloves, minced**
- ½ **teaspoon dried basil**
- ⅛–¼ **teaspoon red pepper flakes**
- 1 **cup cottage cheese**
- ½ **cup grated Parmesan cheese**
- ½ **cup low-sodium chicken broth**
- 2 **(5-ounce) bags baby spinach**
- ½ **cup chopped fresh parsley**
  Pepper

1. Bring 4 quarts water to a boil in a large pot. Add the noodles and 1 tablespoon salt and cook, stirring often, until al dente. Reserve ½ cup of the pasta cooking water, then drain the noodles and return them to the pot.

2. Meanwhile, heat the oil, garlic, basil, red pepper flakes, and ½ teaspoon salt in a medium saucepan over medium heat until sizzling, about 1 minute. Add the cottage cheese, Parmesan, and broth and cook, stirring occasionally, until thickened slightly, 2 to 4 minutes.

3. Stir the sauce into the noodles, adjusting the consistency with the reserved pasta cooking water as needed. Stir in the spinach, one handful at a time, and cook until wilted, about 30 seconds. Add the parsley and season with salt and pepper to taste. Serve.

Notes from the Test Kitchen

Simple to make and appealing to everyone, this dish had many test cooks "screaming" for more. Although Elizabeth's original recipe called for adding either chopped steamed fresh spinach or chopped thawed frozen spinach to the pot before the cheese and broth were added, we preferred to use fresh baby spinach, which gave the dish a fresher color and flavor. We also waited to add our spinach until the last few minutes, as it clumped up too much when added earlier.

Creamy Potato Puff

GAIL LUTZ | QUAKERTOWN, PENNSYLVANIA

Rare is the person who will turn down a heaping spoonful of mashed potatoes, and when you make them into a cheesy, creamy, fluffy casserole as Gail does here, they're nearly impossible to refuse. "I enjoyed this dish at my first holiday meal with my husband's family, and I've been making it ever since. My guests always ask for the recipe, just as I did 24 years ago!" These potatoes are perfect as a quick weeknight side dish or as a potluck contribution that everyone is sure to love.

SERVES 6 TO 8

- 3 pounds russet potatoes, peeled and sliced ¾ inch thick
- 3 tablespoons unsalted butter
- 1 onion, minced
- 1 cup shredded sharp cheddar cheese
- 4 ounces cream cheese, cut into 1-inch chunks
- ½ cup heavy cream
  Salt and pepper
- 1 large egg, lightly beaten
- 1 tablespoon chopped fresh chives

1. Adjust an oven rack to the upper-middle position and heat the oven to 375 degrees. Grease an 8-inch square baking dish and set aside.

2. Bring the potatoes and 3 quarts water to a simmer in a large saucepan and cook until tender, 20 to 25 minutes. Drain the potatoes and transfer to a large bowl.

3. Meanwhile, melt the butter in a small saucepan over medium heat. Add the onion and cook, stirring occasionally, until softened, 5 to 7 minutes. Stir in the cheddar, cream cheese, cream, 1½ teaspoons salt, and ¼ teaspoon pepper and cook until smooth, about 5 minutes. Cover and set aside off the heat to keep warm.

4. With an electric mixer on medium-low speed, beat the potatoes, slowly adding the cheese mixture, until smooth and creamy, about 1 minute. Scrape down the bowl and beat in the egg until incorporated, about 1 minute.

5. Transfer the potato mixture to the prepared baking dish and bake until the potatoes rise slightly and begin to brown, about 40 minutes. Let cool for 10 minutes. Sprinkle with the chives and serve.

Notes from the Test Kitchen

This mashed potato casserole reminded us of twice-baked potatoes, so it was pretty hard for us to find a single fault with the concept. Gail's original recipe called for dried onion, but we felt that this dish benefited from the deeper flavor of fresh onion softened in a little butter. We also substituted half of her cream cheese with cheddar cheese for a more robust flavor. Gail notes that you can use parsley instead of chives if you prefer.

"Candied" Apples in Cinnamon Syrup

SARAH MERCER | WICHITA, KANSAS

"My grandmother was born in 1910 in a small town in southeast Kansas. When she was growing up, there was an abundance of apples to cook with, either from a nearby orchard or from her parents' property. One of the apple recipes she made for her children and grandchildren in later years was this recipe for candied apples." These apples aren't what you are likely thinking of—that state fair staple of an apple on a stick coated with a cinnamon-flavored syrup that's either gooey or crackly-hard. Sarah's apples are not a dessert at all, but a dinnertime side dish. Sliced apples are cooked in a cinnamon candy–syrup and served cold, a great match for meat entrées and particularly pork. This tradition of baking with cinnamon candy appears to have really hit its stride in the early twentieth century, since the classic candy known as Cinnamon Imperials were being made on a large scale as of the mid- to late-1800s and Red Hots hit the market in the 1930s. Whether it's a recipe for whole baked apples with Red Hots, Cinnamon Imperial and apple Jell-O salad, or a side dish of cinnamony apples like Sarah's, cooking with these candies is not only big on flavor but also lots of fun.

SERVES 6

- 2 cups water
- ½ cup sugar
- ½ cup red cinnamon candies
- 2 Granny Smith apples, cored, peeled, and sliced into ¼-inch-thick rings

1. Bring the water, sugar, and cinnamon candies to a simmer in a medium saucepan and cook, stirring frequently, until the sugar and candies are dissolved, about 3 minutes.

2. Add the apples to the liquid and cook, stirring occasionally, until the apples are tender (a paring knife should glide through the apple slices with little resistance), 4 to 6 minutes. Set aside off the heat and cool slightly, then cover and refrigerate until chilled, about 2 hours. Serve.

Notes from the Test Kitchen

Though most of us had never encountered such a side dish before, one of our fellow test cooks knew it well. He told us his family enjoyed nearly identical candied apples alongside pork dishes quite often. It seemed strange to us at first, but once we gave the combination a try, we were completely on board. It was like enjoying applesauce with pork chops, but with a new, and certainly more fun, twist. We agreed with Sarah that Granny Smiths are the perfect choice for this recipe, as their tartness is a nice balance to the candy's sweetness, and they keep their shape during cooking better than other apple varieties. Either Cinnamon Imperials or Red Hot candies will work in this recipe. While Sarah's recipe notes that you can add red food coloring for an even deeper red, we felt the dish had nice color without any additional help.

AUNT FANNY'S PASTA SOUP WITH LITTLE MEATBALLS

Recipes from the Old Country

Traditional Upper Peninsula Pasties **108**

Savory Strudel with Beef, Potatoes, and Onions **111**

Kotlety **113**

Sicilian Meatloaf **115**

Aunt Fanny's Pasta Soup with Little Meatballs **116**

Braciole with Neapolitan Sauce **117**

Nonni's Pasta Mollica (Pasta with Bread Crumbs) **119**

Delicate Manicotti **120**

Shall's Classic Lasagna **122**

Bubie Alte's Lukshen Kugel **126**

Grandma's Borscht **127**

Prune Meat **128**

Outrageous Gulyás **129**

Chicken Paprikash **130**

Italian Pesto Lamb **132**

Traditional Upper Peninsula Pasties

CHRISTI HALL | LEBANON, OHIO

These old-fashioned savory hand-pies have a wonderful workingman's history dating back to the 1800s. As Christi recounts, "Immigrants from Cornwall who flocked to Michigan's Upper Peninsula to work in the copper and iron mines in the nineteenth century brought the pasty, or 'tiddy oggie,' with them from the old country. A pasty is a type of pie, a baked savory pastry case traditionally filled with diced meat, sliced potato, rutabagas, and onion. Carried deep within the mine in the morning, pasties could be eaten like sandwiches and made a convenient and hearty meal." While in Cornwall the pasty could be filled with countless different ingredients, including lamb or fish, rice, eggs, leeks, and even apples, the pasty Christi describes is particular to Michigan, as these pasties vary only within the limits of combining meat with root vegetables. Christi's family recipe is a quintessential U.P. pasty. "My grandparents, Brick and Glen Wuest, were from Michigan. Gramma was born in the Upper Peninsula and then moved to St. Clair where she met Grampa. Gramma's father was originally a traveling preacher to the mining camps of the U.P., which is probably where this recipe comes from. With eighteen people in the immediate family, we get together a lot, and our family gatherings often include this family staple."

SERVES 6

PASTRY

- 3¾ cups all-purpose flour
- 2 teaspoons salt
- 12 tablespoons (1½ sticks) unsalted butter, cut into ½-inch pieces and chilled
- 1–1¼ cups ice water

FILLING

- 2 tablespoons unsalted butter
- 1 onion, minced
- 3 garlic cloves, minced
- 2 teaspoons minced fresh thyme
- 1 pound Yukon gold potatoes, peeled and chopped medium
- 1 small rutabaga, peeled and chopped medium
- ¼ cup heavy cream
- ¼ cup low-sodium chicken broth
- 1 tablespoon Dijon mustard
- 12 ounces blade steak, cut into ½-inch pieces, trimmed
- 1¼ teaspoons salt
- 1 teaspoon pepper
- 1 large egg, lightly beaten

(Continued on page 110)

1. FOR THE PASTRY: Process the flour and salt together in a food processor until combined. Scatter the butter pieces over the top and pulse until the mixture resembles coarse cornmeal, about 16 pulses.

2. Transfer the mixture to a large bowl. Sprinkle the ice water, ¼ cup at a time, over the flour mixture. Stir and press the dough together, using a stiff rubber spatula, until the dough sticks together. (You may not need all of the water.)

3. Divide the dough into six even pieces. Turn each piece of dough onto a sheet of plastic wrap and flatten each into a 5-inch disk. Wrap each disk in the plastic wrap and refrigerate until firm, about 1 hour.

4. FOR THE FILLING: Melt the butter in a large skillet over medium heat. Add the onion and cook, stirring occasionally, until softened, 5 to 7 minutes. Stir in the garlic and thyme and cook until fragrant, about 30 seconds. Stir in the potatoes and rutabaga and cook until the edges of the vegetables have softened slightly, about 5 minutes. Stir in the cream, broth, and mustard and cook until thickened, about 30 seconds. Set aside off the heat to cool to room temperature.

5. Stir the beef, salt, and pepper into the cooled potato mixture.

6. TO ASSEMBLE AND BAKE: Adjust the oven racks to the upper-middle and lower-middle positions and heat the oven to 425 degrees. Line two large rimmed baking sheets with parchment paper and set aside.

7. Working with one disk at a time, roll the dough out on a lightly floured counter to an 8-inch round. Place 1 cup of the filling mixture in the center of each round and gently pack it down. Wet the edges of the dough with water and fold the dough in half over the filling, pressing to seal the edges. Crimp the sealed edge with your thumb and forefinger.

8. Arrange the pies on the prepared baking sheets and brush with the egg. Bake the pies until golden brown, 25 to 30 minutes, switching and rotating the baking sheets halfway through. Cool for 5 minutes before serving.

Notes from the Test Kitchen

We loved the tradition behind this recipe and its simple flavors, so we made an extra effort to preserve these aspects, focusing mostly on the issue of scaling. Christi's original made 15 cups of filling, which we scaled down to 6 cups, just right for filling the six rounds of pastry. We only made a few small ingredient tweaks, making the filling more moist by adding some cream and chicken broth, and using butter instead of lard in the pastry dough since it was easier to find and we preferred the butter's flavor.

MAKING PASTIES

1. After rolling the dough out on a lightly floured counter to an 8-inch round, place 1 cup of the filling mixture in the center of each round and gently pack it down. Wet the edges of the dough with water and fold the dough in half over the filling.

2. Press to seal the edges of the dough, then crimp the sealed edges together with your thumb and forefinger.

Savory Strudel with Beef, Potatoes, and Onions

LINDA ROHR | DARIEN, CONNECTICUT

"As a child, I enjoyed visiting my grandparents' farm. Having emigrated from Europe in the early 1900s, they settled in a town in Pennsylvania aptly named Scenery Hill. Cooking on the farm was always a fun adventure. The first recipe my grandmother taught me was strudel. My grandmother, mother, and I would mix the dough, measuring by the handfuls and adding just enough water until the dough felt right. With my mother being the youngest of fourteen children, food always took center stage at our holiday festivities and Sunday family dinners. When I found my mother's recipe tucked in her 1941 edition of *The Settlement Cookbook*, all the wonderful memories of baking strudel on the farm seemed just like yesterday." Note that you'll need a standing mixer with a dough hook to make this recipe.

SERVES 6 TO 8

FILLING

- 1 slice hearty white sandwich bread, torn into large pieces and pulsed in a food processor to coarse crumbs
- 12 ounces medium red potatoes, scrubbed, halved, and sliced ⅛ inch thick
- 3 tablespoons vegetable oil
- 1 pound white mushrooms, sliced thin
- 1 onion, halved and sliced thin
- 1¼ pounds 90 percent lean ground beef
- 6 ounces cream cheese, cut into ½-inch chunks and softened
- ⅓ cup chopped fresh parsley
- ¼ cup sour cream
  Salt and pepper

DOUGH

- ¾ cup warm water
- 6 tablespoons (¾ stick) unsalted butter, melted and cooled
- 1 large egg
- ¼ teaspoon white vinegar
- 2½ cups all-purpose flour
- ½ teaspoon salt

1. FOR THE FILLING: Adjust the oven racks to the upper-middle and lower-middle positions and heat the oven to 375 degrees. Toast the bread crumbs in a single layer on a rimmed baking sheet, stirring occasionally, until golden brown and dry, 4 to 6 minutes. Set aside to cool to room temperature.

2. Combine the potatoes and 1 tablespoon of the oil in a microwave-safe bowl and cover with plastic wrap. Microwave on high until the edges begin to soften, 2 to 3 minutes, shaking the bowl (without removing the plastic wrap) to redistribute the potatoes halfway through. Set the potatoes aside.

3. Heat the remaining 2 tablespoons oil in a large nonstick skillet over medium heat until shimmering. Add the mushrooms and onion, cover, and cook, stirring occasionally, until the mushrooms have released their juices, 8 to 10 minutes. Remove the cover and continue to cook, stirring occasionally, until the mushrooms are golden brown, 8 to 10 minutes longer.

4. Add the beef, increase the heat to medium-high, and cook, breaking up any large clumps with a wooden spoon, until no longer pink, about 5 minutes. Stir in the cream cheese, parsley, sour cream, 1 teaspoon salt, and

(Continued on page 112)

¼ teaspoon pepper and cook until the cream cheese is melted, about 2 minutes. Set aside off the heat to cool to room temperature.

5. FOR THE DOUGH: Line two baking sheets with parchment paper and set aside. Whisk the water, 1 tablespoon of the melted butter, the egg, and vinegar together in a bowl.

6. Combine the flour and salt in a standing mixer fitted with the dough hook. With the mixer on low speed, add the water mixture and mix until the dough comes together, about 2 minutes. Increase the mixer speed to medium-low and knead until the dough is smooth and elastic, 4 to 6 minutes.

7. Divide the dough in half and turn it out onto a well-floured counter. Gently press each piece of dough into a 6-inch square, cover with a kitchen towel, and let rest for 10 minutes.

8. TO ASSEMBLE AND BAKE: Following the photos, stretch one piece of the dough into an 18-inch square. Brush the dough lightly with some of the melted butter and fold in half so the long side is facing you. Brush the dough again with melted butter and sprinkle with ¼ cup of the bread crumbs, leaving a border on the top, bottom, and sides.

9. Layer half of the potatoes over the bottom half of the bread crumbs, then spread half of the meat mixture over the potatoes. Fold the dough on the sides over the filling, then the dough on the bottom, and continue to roll the dough around the filling to form the strudel. Place the strudel, seam-side down, on one of the prepared baking sheets. Repeat with the remaining dough, some of the remaining melted butter, and the remaining bread crumbs, potatoes, and filling.

10. Brush the strudels with the remaining melted butter and cut four 1-inch slits in the top of each. Bake the strudels until golden brown, 40 to 45 minutes, switching and rotating the baking sheets halfway through. Cool for 15 minutes before serving.

Notes from the Test Kitchen

Its wonderful flavor aside, the size of the strudel in Linda's original recipe made it a challenge to make—she called for pulling the dough to 3 by 3 feet, which took two of us to accomplish, and three to transfer the final strudel to a baking sheet! To make it a one-person job, we simply made two smaller strudels instead of one large one.

ROLLING STRUDEL

1. On a well-floured counter, gently stretch and pull one piece of dough into an 18-inch square with floured hands. Brush the dough lightly with melted butter, fold in half so that the long side is facing you, and brush again with butter.

2. Sprinkle with ¼ cup of the bread crumbs, leaving a 2½-inch border on the top and bottom and a 2-inch border on the sides. Layer half the potatoes over the bottom half of the bread crumbs, then spread half of the meat mixture over the potatoes.

3. Fold the dough on the sides over the filling, then fold the bottom edge over the filling and roll the dough around the filling. Place the strudel, seam-side down, on a prepared baking sheet. Repeat steps to make the second strudel.

4. After brushing the strudels with butter, cut four 1-inch vents across the top of each strudel with a small knife to allow steam to escape.

Kotlety

NINA KIRKLAND | WILLIAMSVILLE, NEW YORK

"These little individual meatloaf-type patties are wonderful served with mashed potatoes or noodles," says Nina, noting they work for a quick dinner or for a buffet. *Kotlety*, a Russian word that translates roughly to "meat cutlets," came to Russia in the mid-eighteenth century from Northern Europe. Simple yet appealing, they are made by rolling chopped meat, bread crumbs, eggs, and seasonings in bread crumbs and frying the patties. They are likely to be served as a second course, modern Russian cooks tell us. Nina's mother made her kotlety simply with ground beef, minced onion, and garlic. She used to shape them into diamonds, but no matter how you shape them, they are sure to be popular with both family and guests.

SERVES 6

- 1 cup plus 2 tablespoons vegetable oil
- 2 onions, minced
- 4 garlic cloves, minced
- 6 slices hearty white sandwich bread, torn into large pieces and pulsed in a food processor to coarse crumbs
- ¼ cup milk
- 2 pounds 90 percent lean ground beef
- 2 large eggs, lightly beaten
- 1 teaspoon salt
- ½ teaspoon pepper

1. Adjust an oven rack to the middle position and preheat the oven to 200 degrees. Set a wire rack over a rimmed baking sheet and set aside.

2. Heat 2 tablespoons of the oil in a large nonstick skillet over medium heat until shimmering. Add the onions and cook, stirring occasionally, until softened, 5 to 7 minutes. Stir in the garlic and cook until fragrant, about 30 seconds. Transfer the onion mixture to a large bowl. Wipe the skillet clean with paper towels.

3. Add 1½ cups of the bread crumbs and the milk to the onion mixture and mash until evenly combined. Add the beef, eggs, salt, and pepper and mix with your hands until evenly blended and the meat mixture does not stick to the bowl. With wet hands, form the mixture into 2¼-inch-wide and about ¾-inch-thick patties (you will have about 18 patties).

4. Spread the remaining 1½ cups bread crumbs in a shallow dish. One at a time, roll each patty in the bread crumbs to coat. Heat the remaining 1 cup oil in the skillet over medium-high heat until just smoking. Add half of the patties to the skillet and cook until golden brown on both sides and the center of the patties registers 160 degrees on an instant-read thermometer, 12 to 14 minutes, flipping halfway through. Transfer the patties to a paper towel–lined plate, then transfer to the prepared wire rack and keep warm in the oven. Repeat with the remaining patties. Serve.

Notes from the Test Kitchen

Cousins to hamburgers and meatballs, kotlety have an approachable comfort-food appeal. We made only a few changes to Nina's recipe: adding more garlic for the flavor and pre-cooking the onion to avoid undercooked onion in our final kotlety. We felt using the traditional choice of milk rather than water improved the flavor. Nina browned her patties on the stove and cooked them through in the oven, but we found cooking them entirely on the stovetop was easy and helped keep the bread-crumb exteriors crisp.

Sicilian Meatloaf

JIM LAIRD | RAYMOND, OHIO

"Back in the 1970s, I was just learning how to cook. Mom's cooking was great—with the exception of her meatloaf. So, I went looking for another way to make a meatloaf and found out how at a friend's grandma's house." The recipe Jim found layers ham and cheese over a meatloaf mixture, which is rolled into a log, jelly-roll style. It's an adaptation of an old Italian recipe, the Sicilian meatloaf *falso magro,* made by taking a thin slice of meat and wrapping it around ground meat and other fillings, like prosciutto, cheese, and even hard-boiled eggs. Jim opts for a meat-cheese filling that gives each slice of this meatloaf great flavor, texture, and visual appeal.

SERVES 4

GLAZE
- 2 large tomatoes, cored and quartered
- ¼ cup packed brown sugar
- ¼ cup lightly packed basil leaves
- 2 tablespoons hot sauce

MEATLOAF
- 12 ounces 85 percent lean ground beef
- 6 ounces sweet Italian sausage, casings removed
- 1 cup tomato juice
- 17 saltine crackers, crushed
- ¼ cup chopped fresh parsley
- 2 tablespoons minced fresh oregano
- 3 garlic cloves, minced
- 1 large egg, lightly beaten
- Salt and pepper
- 4 thin slices ham
- 4 thin slices mozzarella or Swiss cheese

1. FOR THE GLAZE: Process the glaze ingredients together in a food processor until smooth, about 1 minute. Transfer the mixture to a small saucepan and cook over medium-high heat until thickened, about 20 minutes.

2. FOR THE MEATLOAF: Adjust an oven rack to the middle position and heat the oven to 350 degrees.

3. Combine the beef, sausage, tomato juice, crackers, parsley, oregano, garlic, egg, ¾ teaspoon salt, and ½ teaspoon pepper in a bowl and mix with your hands until evenly blended and the meat mixture does not stick to the bowl.

4. Following the photo on page 77, lay a sheet of foil perpendicularly over another sheet of foil to make a cross. Spread the meat mixture over the bottom portion of the top piece of foil to make a 10 by 7½-inch rectangle. Layer the ham and cheese evenly over the meat, leaving a ½-inch border around the bottom and sides and a 1-inch border along the top. Roll the meat and filling into a compact log. Transfer the loaf to an 8½ by 4½-inch loaf pan (still in the foil). Fold back any excess foil.

5. Spread the glaze evenly over the meatloaf and bake until the center registers 160 degrees on an instant-read thermometer, 1 hour to 1 hour 25 minutes. Cool for 15 minutes. Remove the roll from the pan using the foil sling and serve.

Notes from the Test Kitchen

We scaled down the original recipe to make one loaf instead of two—one loaf serves four—but we kept the same amount of glaze and tomato juice, which put the flavors into balance. Jim mixed fresh basil with the ground meat, but basil lost its flavor during cooking, so we swapped it out for a combination of parsley and oregano, which held up better. A foil sling made rolling the meatloaf and transferring it to and from the loaf pan a cinch.

Aunt Fanny's Pasta Soup with Little Meatballs

BARBARA "BEE" ENGELHART | BLOOMFIELD HILLS, MICHIGAN

"My aunt Fanny (Philomena) was the best cook in our excessively large Italian family. She set the standard for preparing feasts for a crowd by using the best ingredients and inventive shortcuts. Her recipes are among my favorite go-to comfort foods. She sometimes made her famous pasta soup, and if she was in the mood, she'd top each bowl with a bruschetta or a bit of shredded mozzarella for a few gooey, stringy bites. You could have her pasta soup pretty much on command if you visited her in later years. She froze the sauce and meatballs in small batches and cooked up the pasta on the spot."

SERVES 6 TO 8

MEATBALLS

- 2 slices hearty white sandwich bread, torn into large pieces
- ½ cup milk
- ½ cup grated Parmesan cheese
- 4 garlic cloves, minced
- 2 teaspoons minced fresh thyme
- 1 large egg, lightly beaten
- ¾ teaspoon salt
- ½ teaspoon pepper
- 1 pound 90 percent lean ground beef

SOUP

- 8 ounces dry elbow macaroni (2 cups)
  Salt
- 2 tablespoons olive oil
- 1 onion, minced
- 2 tablespoons tomato paste
- 4 garlic cloves, minced
- 1 teaspoon minced fresh thyme
- 2 (28-ounce) cans whole tomatoes
- 4 cups low-sodium chicken broth
  Pepper
- ¼ cup grated Parmesan cheese
- ¼ cup chopped fresh basil

1. FOR THE MEATBALLS: Mash the bread and milk together in a large bowl. Stir in the cheese, garlic, thyme, egg, salt, and pepper. Add the meat and mix with your hands until well combined.

With wet hands, form the mixture into 1-inch meatballs (you should have about 30 meatballs).

2. FOR THE SOUP: Meanwhile, bring 4 quarts water to a boil in a Dutch oven. Add the macaroni and 1 tablespoon salt and cook, stirring often, until al dente. Drain the macaroni, rinse under cold water, and set aside. Wipe the pot dry with paper towels.

3. Heat the oil in the pot over medium heat until shimmering. Add the onion and cook, stirring occasionally, until softened, 5 to 7 minutes. Stir in the tomato paste, garlic, and thyme and cook until fragrant, about 30 seconds. Stir in the tomatoes and broth and, using a potato masher, mash the tomatoes until broken into bite-sized pieces. Add the meatballs to the soup (do not stir), bring to a simmer, and cook until the meatballs are tender, 10 to 15 minutes.

4. Stir the pasta into the soup and season with salt and pepper to taste. Sprinkle individual portions with the cheese and basil before serving.

Notes from the Test Kitchen

This dish combines two favorites: hearty pasta with meatballs and a warm bowl of soup. Aunt Fanny's recipe relied on tomato juice and pasta water for its base. Using low-sodium chicken broth instead of pasta water and upping the aromatics created more depth, and using whole tomatoes that we mashed in the pot added good texture. The meatballs were denser than we like, so we added a panade to lighten up this old-world comfort food.

Braciole with Neapolitan Sauce

GILDA LESTER | WILMINGTON, NORTH CAROLINA

"Growing up a latchkey kid was a good thing," recalls Gilda. "I learned to be independent and I learned how to cook. My Italian grandmother lived just a few blocks from our house. On weekends and sometimes after school, I would walk to her house to help out with any chores she needed done. Sometimes the aroma of baking bread filled the neighborhood, so I knew her beehive oven was fired up. On one particular day when I went to visit, my grandfather had just fired up the wood-burning stove, so I knew that spaghetti sauce would be on the menu. Grandmom said that she was going to teach me to make *braciole* for the sauce. I learned the type of meat used, the pounding, the filling, and the rolling. There was no recipe, just a handful of this or a pinch of that. I watched, I listened, and I learned. This recipe for braciole with the Neapolitan sauce is how I remember it and how I cook it to this day." Classic Italian braciole wraps a pounded meat chop or cutlet around a stuffing, then gently braises it in a sauce. It takes time and effort, but the final meal is both attractive and deeply flavorful. Gilda's braciole is filled with seasoned bread crumbs, prosciutto, and cheese (a fairly typical combination), and her tomato-based sauce is seriously hearty, made with a full pound of pork ribs. Using the same pot to first brown the braciole, then build the sauce, and finally cook the braciole, ribs, and sauce together keeps things streamlined. She likes to serve this recipe with fettucine and additional grated cheese on top.

SERVES 4 TO 6

BRACIOLE

- 1 slice hearty white sandwich bread, torn into large pieces and pulsed in a food processor to coarse crumbs
- 5 thin slices prosciutto, chopped fine
- ½ cup grated Pecorino Romano cheese
- ¼ cup chopped fresh parsley
- 3 tablespoons olive oil
- ¼ teaspoon red pepper flakes
- 2 (12-ounce) boneless beef sirloin steaks, trimmed and pounded to a ¼-inch thickness
  Salt and pepper

SAUCE

- 1 pound country-style pork ribs
  Salt and pepper
- 2 tablespoons olive oil
- 1 onion, minced
- 3 tablespoons tomato paste
- 4 garlic cloves, minced
- 1 (28-ounce) can crushed tomatoes
- ½ cup dry red wine
- 1 tablespoon minced fresh oregano
- 1 tablespoon sugar
- 2 tablespoons grated Pecorino Romano cheese
- 2 tablespoons chopped fresh parsley

(Continued on page 118)

1. FOR THE BRACIOLE: Adjust an oven rack to the middle position and heat the oven to 375 degrees. Toast the bread crumbs in a single layer on a rimmed baking sheet, stirring often, until golden brown and dry, 4 to 6 minutes. Set aside to cool to room temperature.

2. Combine the bread crumbs with the prosciutto, cheese, parsley, 2 tablespoons of the oil, and the red pepper flakes in a bowl. Pat the beef dry with paper towels and season with salt and pepper. Sprinkle half of the bread-crumb filling over one of the steaks, leaving a ½-inch border on all sides. Gently press on the filling to pack it together. Following the photos, roll and tie the steak to form a tight roast. Repeat with the remaining steak and filling.

3. Heat the remaining 1 tablespoon oil in a Dutch oven over medium-high heat until just smoking. Add the braciole and cook until well browned on all sides, about 8 minutes, turning as needed. Transfer the braciole to a plate and set aside.

4. FOR THE SAUCE: Pat the ribs dry with paper towels and season with salt and pepper. Heat 1 tablespoon of the oil in the now-empty pot over medium-high heat until just smoking. Add the ribs and cook until well browned on both sides, about 10 minutes, flipping halfway through. Transfer the ribs to a plate.

5. Heat the remaining 1 tablespoon oil in the pot over medium heat until shimmering. Add the onion and cook, stirring occasionally, until softened, 5 to 7 minutes. Stir in the tomato paste and garlic and cook until fragrant, about 30 seconds. Stir in the tomatoes, wine, oregano, sugar, ½ teaspoon salt, and ¼ teaspoon pepper.

6. Return the ribs, along with any accumulated juices, to the pot. Bring to a simmer, partially cover, and cook for 30 minutes. Return the braciole, along with any accumulated juices, to the pot and continue to cook until the meat is tender, 30 minutes to 1 hour longer.

7. Transfer the braciole to a carving board. Remove the twine and slice the braciole into ½-inch-thick slices. Stir the cheese and parsley into the sauce and season with salt and pepper to taste. Serve.

Notes from the Test Kitchen

With its pretty appearance and deep, slow-cooked flavor, this recipe is sure to impress both family and guests. While Gilda cooked her braciole and ribs together in the sauce, we found that the two cooked at different rates, so we waited until the ribs had cooked for 30 minutes before adding the braciole, ensuring both were done at the same time.

ROLLING AND TYING BRACIOLE

1. Sprinkle half of the bread-crumb filling over one steak, leaving a ½-inch border on all sides. Press on the filling to pack it together. Roll the meat into a roast and place it seam-side down on a clean counter.

2. Tie the roast with kitchen twine at 1-inch intervals. Repeat with the remaining steak and filling.

Nonni's Pasta Mollica (Pasta with Bread Crumbs)

ADELE VARENAS | PHILADELPHIA, PENNSYLVANIA

This recipe (we assume it came from Adele's grandmother, though she didn't say directly) is an old-world tradition. *Mollica*, an Italian word that typically refers to the interior crumb of a loaf, alludes to the bread crumbs topping the noodles in this simply flavored dish. About its history, Adele says, "It was traditionally served in the early 1900s in rural Abruzzi and Molise for St. Joseph's Day and distributed to the poor. It could be distributed in napkins, tablecloths, aprons, anything handy that the mother could carry home. It's great freshly made and wonderful the next day." The bread crumbs are not only symbolic of the fertility of spring, which St. Joseph's Day celebrates each March, but they also serve as a thrifty replacement for a more expensive cheese topping. Humble pasta mollica has a texture and flavor that makes it more than the sum of its parts. Adele's inclusion of grated Pecorino, though not traditional, nicely rounds out the appealing meal.

SERVES 4 TO 6

- 4 slices hearty white sandwich bread, torn into large pieces and pulsed in a food processor to coarse crumbs
- ½ cup extra-virgin olive oil
  Salt and pepper
- 6 garlic cloves, minced
- 2 anchovy fillets, rinsed and minced (optional)
- 1 pound linguine
- 1 cup grated Pecorino Romano cheese
- ¼ cup chopped fresh parsley

1. Adjust an oven rack to the middle position, and heat the oven to 375 degrees. Toss the bread crumbs with 2 tablespoons of the oil, ½ teaspoon salt, and ¼ teaspoon pepper. Toast the bread crumbs in a single layer on a rimmed baking sheet, stirring often, until golden brown and dry, 8 to 10 minutes. Set aside to cool to room temperature.

2. Heat the remaining 6 tablespoons oil, the garlic, anchovies (if using), ½ teaspoon salt, and ¼ teaspoon pepper in a medium skillet over medium heat until the garlic is just beginning to turn straw colored, about 2 minutes. Set aside off the heat.

3. Bring 4 quarts water to a boil in a large pot. Add the pasta and 1 tablespoon salt and cook, stirring often, until al dente. Reserve 1 cup of the pasta cooking water, then drain the pasta and return it to the pot.

4. Toss the pasta with the garlic oil, ½ cup of the cheese, and the parsley. Add just enough of the reserved pasta cooking water to keep the pasta strands from sticking together. Toss in 1½ cups of the bread-crumb mixture and season with salt and pepper to taste. Serve, passing the remaining ½ cup cheese and ½ cup bread crumbs separately.

Notes from the Test Kitchen

This dish is comfort food at its simplest and is appealingly light. We did find that the amount of olive oil in the original recipe, 1 full cup, was more than necessary; ½ cup was perfectly sufficient and helped ensure crispier crumbs. We also toasted the crumbs in the oven with only a small amount of the oil, rather than toasting them on the stovetop with most of the oil as Adele had done. Waiting to toss them with the pasta until the very last minute further guaranteed ideally crispy bread crumbs.

Delicate Manicotti

HEIDI FITCH | LAUREL, MONTANA

Though it may feel like an age-old classic, stuffing pasta or *crespelle* (Italian crepes) to make the dish known as manicotti is a relatively modern addition to the Italian culinary tradition. In spite of its late start, when manicotti got big, it got really big. From the 1950s through the 1970s, manicotti grew to become hugely popular, appearing in countless cookbooks, on restaurant menus, and as a frozen packaged food. An old-fashioned, homemade recipe like Heidi's is a welcome addition to any cook's library. Her spinach and cheese version relies on delicate crespelle to hold the filling, making it a much lighter entrée than the pasta-based versions. "The mother of my husband's childhood chum, Vera Gallitano, always made it like this, as did her family before her. We often have this on New Year's Day as a remembrance of her." Topped with a simple tomato sauce, this makes an ideal light yet satisfying supper any time of year.

SERVES 4

SAUCE

- 2 tablespoons extra-virgin olive oil
- 1 onion, minced
- 2 (28-ounce) cans crushed tomatoes
- 3 tablespoons chopped fresh basil
  Salt and pepper

FILLING

- 1 tablespoon olive oil
- 5 ounces curly-leaf spinach (4 cups packed), stemmed
- 2 cups whole-milk ricotta cheese
- 1½ cups shredded mozzarella cheese
- 1 cup grated Parmesan cheese
- 2 large eggs, lightly beaten
- ⅓ cup chopped fresh parsley
- ¾ teaspoon salt
- ¼ teaspoon pepper
  Pinch ground nutmeg

CRESPELLE (CREPES)

- 1½ cups water
- 1 cup all-purpose flour
- 3 large eggs
  Vegetable oil

1. FOR THE SAUCE: Heat the olive oil in a large saucepan over medium heat until shimmering. Add the onion and cook, stirring occasionally, until softened, 5 to 7 minutes. Stir in the tomatoes, bring to a simmer, and cook until thickened slightly, 30 to 35 minutes.

2. Off the heat, stir in the basil and season with salt and pepper to taste. Set aside to cool to room temperature.

3. FOR THE FILLING: Heat the olive oil in a large skillet over medium heat until shimmering. Stir in the spinach, one handful at a time, and cook until wilted, about 4 minutes. Transfer to a colander and gently squeeze any excess liquid from the spinach. Coarsely chop the spinach, then set aside to cool to room temperature.

4. Combine the spinach with the ricotta, ½ cup of the mozzarella, ½ cup of the Parmesan, the eggs, parsley, salt, pepper, and nutmeg in a bowl.

5. Adjust an oven rack to the middle position and heat the oven to 375 degrees.

6. FOR THE CRESPELLE: Whisk the water, flour, and eggs together until just combined. Heat a 10-inch nonstick skillet over medium heat until hot, 3 to 5 minutes. Lightly brush the skillet bottom evenly with vegetable oil to coat. Pour ¼ cup batter into the skillet and rotate the skillet to evenly coat the bottom. Cook until the batter has set on top and the edges are golden, about 1 minute. Transfer the crespella to a plate. Repeat with more oil and the remaining batter. (You should have 12 crespelle.)

7. TO ASSEMBLE AND BAKE: Lay the crespelle out on a counter. Mound ¼ cup of the filling on each crespella 1 inch from the bottom, leaving a 1-inch border on the sides. Following the photos, fold each crespella around the filling and roll into a tidy bundle. Spread half of the sauce over the bottom of a 13 by 9-inch baking dish. Place the manicotti seam-side down in the baking dish. Spoon the remaining sauce evenly over the manicotti. Sprinkle evenly with the remaining 1 cup mozzarella and the remaining ½ cup Parmesan.

8. Place the baking dish on a foil-lined rimmed baking sheet and bake until the sauce is bubbling and the cheese is melted, 30 to 40 minutes. Cool for 10 minutes before serving.

Notes from the Test Kitchen

These were indeed delicate, and judging by how quickly they disappeared, they tasted great too. In her recipe, Heidi simply calls for a good-quality tomato or marinara sauce. We were inspired to add some garlic to our basic sauce recipe, but found even that addition overwhelmed the subtle flavors of the manicotti. So we developed a super simple tomato sauce with only basil, onion, and salt—a perfect complement to the manicotti. We also increased the amount of cheese in the filling and put some on top too. When making the crespelle in step 6, we found it was key to brush the pan with oil after every crespella to guarantee easy release.

MAKING MANICOTTI

1. After mounding ¼ cup filling on each crespella, fold the side closest to you up over the filling.

2. Fold the left and right sides in toward the middle.

3. Continue to roll the manicotti to form a tidy bundle.

4. Arrange the manicotti in the baking dish, seam-side down, in three rows of four.

Shall's Classic Lasagna

HEATHER WARGO | CAMP LEJEUNE, NORTH CAROLINA

"This is a recipe that comes from my deeply rooted Italian family. Dinner was a labor of love in my household growing up and still is today with my own family. Food is tied to love, forgiveness, and a whole gamut of emotions in an Italian household! My (non-Italian) husband absolutely loves lasagna, and my lasagna has spoiled him since the first time I made it for him when we were dating 13 years ago. I have tweaked it and made the family recipe my own over the years. It takes a little time, but is well worth it! I have also made this for many friends, dinner parties, etc., with raves and proposals of marriage ensuing!" Once you've had a bite of this rich, flavorful lasagna, you'll agree such offers wouldn't be all that unexpected. With homemade spinach noodles, a classic creamy béchamel, and a rich, wine-infused meat sauce, this is a lasagna that will win hearts at first bite.

SERVES 6 TO 8

PASTA
- 3 cups all-purpose flour
- ½ teaspoon garlic powder
- Salt
- 4 ounces curly-leaf spinach (3¼ cups packed), stemmed
- 2 large eggs, lightly beaten
- 2 tablespoons olive oil
- 1 teaspoon minced fresh oregano
- Water

MEAT SAUCE
- 3 tablespoons unsalted butter
- 1 onion, minced
- 1 celery rib, chopped fine
- 1 carrot, peeled and chopped fine
- Salt
- 1 (6-ounce) can tomato paste
- 7 garlic cloves, minced
- Pepper
- 1¼ pounds meatloaf mix
- 4 ounces sweet Italian sausage, casings removed
- ⅓ cup red wine
- 2 cups low-sodium chicken broth

BÉCHAMEL
- 3 tablespoons unsalted butter
- ¼ cup all-purpose flour
- 3 cups half-and-half
- Salt and pepper
- Pinch ground nutmeg

- 2½ cups grated Parmesan cheese

(Continued on page 124)

1. **FOR THE PASTA:** Pulse the flour, garlic powder, and ½ teaspoon salt together in a food processor several times to aerate. Add the spinach, eggs, oil, and oregano and process until the dough forms a rough ball, about 30 seconds. If the dough resembles small pebbles, add water, ½ teaspoon at a time, and process until the dough forms a rough ball. Turn the dough out onto a clean counter and knead until smooth, about 2 minutes. Cover with plastic wrap and let rest for at least 30 minutes, or up to 2 hours.

2. Following the photos on page 125, roll out the pasta dough into four 25-inch-long sheets using a manual pasta machine. Trim the ends of the dough, then cut each sheet crosswise into four 6-inch-long noodles (you should have 16 noodles) and transfer to a well-floured baking sheet.

3. Bring 4 quarts water to a boil in a large pot. Add 4 of the noodles and 1 tablespoon salt and cook, stirring often, until the noodles rise to the surface, about 40 seconds. Using tongs, gently transfer the noodles to a colander and rinse under cold water. Spread the cooked noodles out in a single layer over clean kitchen towels. (Do not use paper towels; they will stick to the pasta.) Repeat three more times with the remaining noodles.

4. **FOR THE MEAT SAUCE:** Melt the butter in a Dutch oven over medium heat. Add the onion, celery, carrot, and ½ teaspoon salt and cook, stirring occasionally, until softened, 5 to 7 minutes. Stir in the tomato paste, garlic, and ½ teaspoon pepper and cook until the tomato paste begins to brown, 2 to 4 minutes. Add the meatloaf mix and sausage, increase the heat to medium-high, and cook, breaking up any large clumps with a wooden spoon, until no longer pink, about 5 minutes.

5. Add the wine and cook until almost evaporated, about 1 minute. Stir in the broth, bring to a simmer, and cook until the sauce is thickened, about 30 minutes. Season with salt and pepper to taste. Set aside off the heat.

6. **FOR THE BÉCHAMEL:** Melt 2 tablespoons of the butter in a medium saucepan over medium heat. Stir in the flour and cook until golden, about 1 minute. Whisk in the half-and-half, bring to a simmer, and cook until the sauce is thickened, about 1 minute. Stir in the remaining 1 tablespoon butter, ½ teaspoon salt, ½ teaspoon pepper, and the nutmeg. Season with salt and pepper to taste. Set aside off the heat.

7. **TO ASSEMBLE AND BAKE:** Adjust an oven rack to the middle position and heat the oven to 400 degrees.

8. Spread 1 cup of the meat sauce over the bottom of a 13 by 9-inch baking dish. Place 4 of the noodles in the baking dish to create the first layer. Spoon 1 cup more meat sauce evenly over the noodles. Spoon ¾ cup of the béchamel over the meat sauce. Sprinkle evenly with ½ cup of the cheese. Repeat this layering twice.

9. For the final layer, place the remaining 4 noodles on top of the sauce, spoon the remaining meat sauce and béchamel evenly over the top, and sprinkle with the remaining 1 cup cheese.

10. Place the baking dish on a foil-lined rimmed baking sheet and bake until the sauce is bubbling and the cheese is spotty brown, about 25 minutes. Cool for 20 minutes before serving.

Notes from the Test Kitchen

It's hard not to like good old-fashioned lasagna, especially one that's entirely from scratch, noodles included. The only problem is that it can take a whole day to make. To streamline this recipe but keep its homemade appeal, we used the food processor to help us make the pasta dough, rather than doing it entirely by hand. (You can also make the dough the day before and keep it wrapped in plastic in the refrigerator.) We found both the béchamel and the meat sauce to be a little thick, so we added an extra cup of broth to the meat sauce and loosened up the béchamel by lowering the flour amount. This lasagna can be made with no-boil noodles. Soak the noodles in hot water for 5 minutes, then drain and pat them dry and proceed with the recipe.

MAKING LASAGNA NOODLES

1. Divide the dough into four equal pieces. Pat one piece of the dough into a rough 4-inch square and run the dough through the rollers set to the widest position.

2. Bring the ends of the dough toward the middle and press down to seal. Feed the open side of the pasta through the rollers (the dough should be about 5½ inches wide). Repeat steps 1 and 2 three times.

3. Put the pasta through the machine repeatedly, narrowing the setting each time, until the dough is nickel-thick and about 25 inches long. Lay the pasta on a lightly floured counter and dust with flour. Repeat with the remaining pieces of dough.

4. Trim the ends off each strip of dough to even them, then cut four 6-inch-long noodles out of each strip (you should have 16 noodles). Transfer the noodles to a well-floured baking sheet until ready to cook.

Bubie Alte's Lukshen Kugel

LILY JULOW | GAINESVILLE, FLORIDA

"This is my grandmother's recipe for old-fashioned noodle pudding and can be served as a side dish or dessert, depending on the meal. A kugel can even be used as an entrée in a pinch along with a hearty soup and salad. My Bubie (grandmother) died before I was born, but her recipes lived on through her daughters, one of whom was my mother, Sophie. There are as many versions of *lukshen kugel* as there are Jewish cooks, but this is our family's favorite. Not just because it's so delicious but because our heritage comes alive every time one of us makes it. Alte and all the good things she and my grandfather brought with them when they emigrated in 1913 from Belarus will never be forgotten." Noodle kugels (*lukshen*, often spelled *lokshen*, is Yiddish for "noodle") are a standard of kosher dairy cooking that have a history going back to the sixteenth century. A sweet kugel like Lily's works for any part of the meal. Lily notes that when her mother served this as a side, she paired it with roast chicken or skillet-fried fish.

SERVES 10 TO 12

- 1 (12-ounce) package wide egg noodles
  Salt
- 1¼ cups sugar
- ½ teaspoon ground cinnamon
- 8 ounces cream cheese, cut into 1-inch chunks and softened
- 1 tablespoon unsalted butter, softened
- ½ teaspoon vanilla extract
- 1 cup sour cream
- 6 large eggs, lightly beaten
- ¾ cup golden raisins

1. Adjust an oven rack to the middle position and heat the oven to 350 degrees. Grease a 13 by 9-inch baking dish and set aside.

2. Bring 4 quarts water to a boil in a large pot. Add the noodles and 1 tablespoon salt and cook, stirring often, until al dente. Drain the noodles, rinse under cold water, and set aside.

3. Combine the sugar and cinnamon in a large bowl. With an electric mixer on medium speed, beat in the cream cheese, butter, vanilla, and ¼ teaspoon salt until light and fluffy, 3 to 6 minutes, scraping down the bowl and beaters as needed. Beat in the sour cream until combined, about 1 minute. Add the eggs, one at a time, and beat until incorporated, 2 to 4 minutes. Reduce the mixer speed to low and beat in the raisins.

4. Stir the noodles into the cream cheese mixture until combined. Scrape the noodle mixture into the prepared baking dish and press into an even layer. Bake the kugel until the top is golden brown and the center is set but soft, 35 to 40 minutes. Cool for 10 minutes before serving.

Notes from the Test Kitchen

Lily's recipe called for 1½ sticks of butter, which made the dish nicely rich but too greasy. We reduced the butter to 1 tablespoon and instead turned to cream cheese, a less greasy choice that added richness and tang (and it is found in traditional noodle kugels). Twelve ounces of noodles rather than 1 pound gave us a better custard-to-noodle balance, and incorporating the sour cream into the kugel rather than using it as a garnish also helped. We like our kugel a little bit sweeter than Lily's recipe, so we increased the amount of raisins and sugar, and we added vanilla for depth.

Grandma's Borscht

SHIRLEY HENDEL | THUNDER BAY, ONTARIO

Borscht, the quintessential beet soup of Eastern Europe, has been around since medieval times, if not longer. In addition to the colorful key ingredient, borscht can include other vegetables, meat or meat stock, beans, and almost always sour cream. Though its silky texture, rich flavor, and vibrant color make it feel like a special-occasion meal, borscht actually began as a food prepared by the poor. But from Shirley's family history, it had clearly become food for royalty by the nineteenth century. "My grandmother worked in the kitchen of the German monarch Kaiser Wilhelm back in the late 1800s. She was a wonderful cook, and she made this soup that we could have only in the summertime when the beets were prolific." With beans, cabbage, and pieces of beef roast on the side, Shirley's grandmother's recipe makes for a traditional, hearty meal.

SERVES 10 TO 12

- 1 (1½-pound) boneless beef chuck-eye roast, trimmed
  Salt and pepper
- 1 tablespoon vegetable oil
- 1 onion, minced
- 2½ quarts water
- 1 pound dried navy beans (2 cups), rinsed and picked over
- 5 medium beets, peeled and chopped medium
- ½ medium head green cabbage, cored and cut into 1-inch pieces
- 1½ cups sour cream
- 1 tablespoon all-purpose flour
- 3 tablespoons red wine vinegar

1. Pat the beef dry with paper towels and season with salt and pepper. Heat the oil in a Dutch oven over medium-high heat until just smoking. Cook the roast until well browned on all sides, 8 to 10 minutes, turning as needed. Transfer the roast to a plate.

2. Add the onion and ½ teaspoon salt to the pot and cook over medium heat, stirring occasionally, until softened, 5 to 7 minutes. Stir in the water, beans, and 1 teaspoon salt, scraping up any browned bits.

3. Return the roast, along with any accumulated juices, to the pot. Bring to a simmer, cover, and cook until the roast is tender, 1½ to 2 hours, turning the meat halfway through.

4. Transfer the roast to a carving board and tent loosely with foil. Add the beets and cabbage to the broth, bring to a simmer, and cook until the beets and beans are tender, 50 to 55 minutes.

5. Combine the sour cream and flour in a bowl, then stir in ¼ cup of the warm broth. Stir the sour cream mixture and vinegar into the pot. Season with salt and pepper to taste. Slice the roast into bite-sized pieces and serve with the soup.

Notes from the Test Kitchen

This meal of hearty borscht and roast definitely hits the spot. We did have to scale the original recipe down significantly—it was enough to feed a German army. The original recipe had called for a lot of sour cream, making it far too rich for us, so to solve two issues at once we simply cut down the sour cream to 1½ cups, a change that made the borscht more balanced and ensured it all fit in the pot. Though borscht recipes can be served hot or cold, we think Shirley's is best served hot.

Prune Meat

JUDITH KING | POMPANO BEACH, FLORIDA

Though the idea of this recipe seemed odd to us at first, one bite proved that old-world cooks know how to perfectly balance sweet and savory. Judith's recipe for cooking cubed chuck roast with prunes and prune juice was handed down to her by her mother-in-law, who learned it from her own mother. Their family roots go back to Eastern Europe, where recipes similar to this one first became popular among Ashkenazi (German) Jews in medieval times. As a group, these sweet vegetable or meat dishes were called *tzimmes*, and over the centuries they have evolved to be a typical Sabbath or festival dish. Tzimmes recipes vary greatly—they can be made with or without fresh or dried fruit and they can be highly seasoned with cinnamon and other spices or with nothing more than salt and pepper. Of all the combinations, meat-and-prune dishes are one of the most popular. Though tzimmes recipes typically incorporate one or more root vegetables, Judith instead serves mashed potatoes on the side.

SERVES 8

- 4 pounds boneless beef chuck-eye roast, trimmed and cut into 1½-inch cubes
  Salt and pepper
- 2½ tablespoons vegetable oil
- 1 onion, minced
- 2 garlic cloves, minced
- 2 cups low-sodium chicken broth
- 2 cups prune juice
- 1 pound pitted prunes, halved
- 2 tablespoons fresh lemon juice
- 1 tablespoon chopped fresh tarragon

1. Adjust an oven rack to the lower-middle position and heat the oven to 325 degrees.

2. Pat the beef dry with paper towels and season with salt and pepper. Heat 1 tablespoon of the oil in a Dutch oven over medium-high heat until just smoking. Add half of the beef and cook until well browned on all sides, about 8 minutes, turning as needed. Transfer the beef to a bowl. Return the pot to medium-high heat and repeat with 1 tablespoon more oil and the remaining beef.

3. Heat the remaining 1½ teaspoons oil in the pot over medium heat until shimmering. Add the onion and cook, stirring occasionally, until softened, 5 to 7 minutes. Stir in the garlic and cook until fragrant, about 30 seconds. Stir in the broth, prune juice, and prunes, scraping up any browned bits.

4. Return the beef, along with any accumulated juices, to the pot. Bring to a simmer, cover, and transfer the pot to the oven. Cook until the meat is tender, 2 to 2½ hours.

5. Stir in the lemon juice and tarragon and season the sauce with salt and pepper to taste. Serve.

Notes from the Test Kitchen

This old-world stew proved to be a surprise hit in the test kitchen. To bring the flavors into balance, we left out the 6 tablespoons of sugar called for in the original recipe, and rather than use 2 cups of prune juice alone as the cooking liquid, we stirred 2 cups of chicken broth into the juice to further help balance the sweetness. Doubling the amount of cooking liquid also gave us a better ratio of liquid to meat. For a splash of color and earthy flavor, we stirred in a tablespoon of fresh tarragon just before serving.

Outrageous Gulyás

DEBRA MANSFIELD | HARLEYSVILLE, PENNSYLVANIA

"Blending both sweet and hot Hungarian paprikas gives this hearty beef stew a burst of bright color and taste. My mother, one of nine first-generation Hungarian-American children, taught me how to make it. She never measured anything, but by careful observation and plenty of practice on my own, I have been able to reproduce this fabulous meal. My sister and I could eat this *gulyás* (Hungarian for goulash) every week of our lives and never grow tired of it. I also like it because it's a one-pot dish and easy to prepare. We sometimes make a batch of homemade dumplings or biscuits to go with it. Although this recipe seems like the perfect fall or winter dish, we enjoy it year round with fresh summer produce like corn on the cob, green or yellow wax beans, or cucumber salad as side dishes."

SERVES 4

1½ pounds boneless beef chuck-eye roast, trimmed and cut into 1½-inch cubes
    Salt and pepper
1½ tablespoons vegetable oil
1 onion, minced
1 green bell pepper, stemmed, seeded, and chopped
3 garlic cloves, minced
1 tablespoon sweet paprika
2 teaspoons minced fresh thyme
¼ teaspoon hot paprika
3½ cups low-sodium chicken broth
¼ cup ketchup
¼ cup dry red wine
1½ teaspoons red wine vinegar
1 teaspoon Worcestershire sauce
1 pound Yukon gold potatoes, peeled and cut into 1-inch chunks
3 carrots, peeled and cut into 1-inch pieces

1. Adjust an oven rack to the lower-middle position and heat the oven to 325 degrees.

2. Pat the beef dry with paper towels and season with salt and pepper. Heat 1 tablespoon of the oil in a Dutch oven over medium-high heat until just smoking. Cook the beef until well browned on all sides, about 8 minutes, turning as needed. Transfer the beef to a bowl.

3. Heat the remaining 1½ teaspoons oil in the pot over medium heat until shimmering. Add the onion and bell pepper and cook, stirring occasionally, until the vegetables are softened, 5 to 7 minutes. Stir in the garlic, sweet paprika, thyme, and hot paprika and cook until fragrant, about 30 seconds. Stir in the broth, ketchup, wine, vinegar, and Worcestershire sauce, scraping up any browned bits.

4. Return the beef, along with any accumulated juices, to the pot. Add the potatoes and carrots, bring to a simmer, and transfer the pot to the oven. Cook until the meat and vegetables are tender, 2 to 2½ hours. Season with salt and pepper to taste. Serve.

Notes from the Test Kitchen
Goulash is a hearty stew that always hits the spot on a cold winter evening. We didn't change much in Debra's classic recipe, but we did freshen it up by using low-sodium chicken broth instead of bouillon cubes, and fresh thyme instead of dried.

Chicken Paprikash

JANET HADDER | CROSSVILLE, TENNESSEE

Paprikash is a classic Hungarian stew, similar to paprika-spiced goulash but slightly less soupy and accented with cream. It is a favorite not only in Hungary, but also in the region that was formerly Czechoslovakia (now the Czech Republic and Slovakia), where Janet's mother was from. Janet tells us of her mother's recipe: "My mother, Kristina Buncak, came to the United States in 1938 from Czechoslovakia when she was 16 years old. Her parents, fearing a war was coming, sent her to live with her sister in Chicago. Not speaking a word of English, she secured work as a cook with a Jewish family, and she eventually worked at Campbell Soup Company and met my dad, Jerry Stedronsky, whom she married in 1944. My mom owned a restaurant in Chicago for two years and then we moved to northern Michigan, where she owned a restaurant for 35 years. She loved to cook and we loved to eat. We had this recipe many times." With its rich, classic paprikash flavor and delicious spaetzle-like dumplings, a bowlful of Janet's mother's recipe is perfect for supper on a chilly night.

SERVES 6

STEW

- 3 pounds bone-in, skin-on chicken pieces (split breasts cut in half, drumsticks, and/or thighs), trimmed
  Salt and pepper
- 1 tablespoon vegetable oil
- 1 onion, minced
- 2 tablespoons sweet paprika
- 2 garlic cloves, minced
- 5 cups low-sodium chicken broth
- 2 cups sour cream
- 2 tablespoons all-purpose flour
- 2 tablespoons fresh lemon juice
- 2 tablespoons minced fresh parsley

DUMPLINGS

Salt
- 2 cups all-purpose flour
- 1 cup water
- 2 large eggs

1. FOR THE STEW: Pat the chicken dry with paper towels and season with salt and pepper. Heat 1½ teaspoons of the oil in a Dutch oven over medium-high heat until just smoking. Add half of the chicken and cook until golden brown on both sides, about 10 minutes, flipping halfway through. Transfer the chicken to a plate and remove the skin. Return the pot to medium-high heat and repeat with the remaining 1½ teaspoons oil and the remaining chicken.

2. Add the onion and ½ teaspoon salt to the pot and cook over medium heat, stirring occasionally, until softened, 5 to 7 minutes. Stir in the paprika and garlic and cook until fragrant, about 30 seconds. Stir in the broth, scraping up any browned bits.

3. Return the chicken, along with any accumulated juices, to the pot. Bring to a simmer, cover, and cook until the chicken is fully cooked and tender, about 20 minutes for breasts (160 to 165 degrees on an instant-read thermometer), or 1 hour for thighs and drumsticks (175 degrees on an instant-read thermometer). (If using both white and dark meat, simmer the thighs and drumsticks for 40 minutes before adding the breasts.) Transfer the chicken to a plate.

4. When the chicken is cool enough to handle, shred the meat into bite-sized pieces and return it to the stew. Combine the sour cream and flour in a bowl, then stir in 2 tablespoons of the warm broth. Stir the sour cream mixture, lemon juice, and parsley into the pot. Cover and set aside off the heat to keep warm.

5. FOR THE DUMPLINGS: While the chicken cooks, bring 4 quarts water and 1 tablespoon salt to a boil in a large pot. Whisk the flour, water, eggs, and 1 teaspoon salt together in a bowl until smooth. Set the batter aside to rest for 15 minutes.

6. Following the photos, spread about ⅓ cup of the batter out in a thin, even layer over a small cutting board. Hold the board over the boiling water and, using a bench scraper or chef's knife, scrape the batter into the water to form 2-inch long and 1-inch wide shreds. Cook until the dumplings rise to the surface, about 1 minute. Using a slotted spoon, transfer the dumplings to the stew. Repeat with the remaining batter. Season with salt and pepper to taste and serve.

Notes from the Test Kitchen

We loved the rich flavor of this old-fashioned paprikash, and particularly its traditional spaetzle-like dumplings. The stew made from the original recipe was a bit too rich and thick for us, so we lowered the amount of sour cream and flour and added chicken broth. Onion is a classic paprikash ingredient, and including some along with garlic lent good depth, while a final touch of chopped parsley gave it nice color. When dropping the noodles into the boiling water, just dip the bench scraper or knife into the boiling water if the dough is sticking.

MAKING PAPRIKASH DUMPLINGS

1. Spread about ⅓ cup of the batter out in a thin, even layer about 2 inches wide over a cutting board.

2. Use a bench scraper or chef's knife to scrape 1-inch-wide pieces of the batter into the boiling water. Cook until the dumplings rise to the surface, about 1 minute.

Italian Pesto Lamb

DENNIS VIAU | GOLETA, CALIFORNIA

"There isn't much about my Italian immigrant grandfather I remember, but I do remember his cooking, partly because it was a challenge for him (he had only one arm), and partly because his food was so delicious. There is one recipe that is my favorite. Of all the cooking I do when entertaining friends, this recipe is the most requested."

SERVES 10 TO 14

- **4** cups packed fresh basil leaves
- **1** cup pine nuts or walnuts, toasted
- **1** cup grated Parmesan cheese
- **¾** cup extra-virgin olive oil
- **6** garlic cloves, peeled
  Salt and pepper
- **1** (5- to 7-pound) boneless leg of lamb, trimmed and pounded to a ¾-inch thickness

1. Place the basil leaves in a heavy-duty 1-gallon zipper-lock bag. Pound the bag with the flat side of a meat pounder or rolling pin until the basil is bruised.

2. Process the basil, pine nuts, cheese, oil, and garlic in a food processor until smooth, about 1 minute. Season with salt and pepper to taste. Measure out and reserve ½ cup of the pesto for serving, press a sheet of plastic wrap to the surface, and refrigerate.

3. Pat the lamb dry with paper towels and season with salt and pepper. Using a fork, poke the lamb all over. Transfer the lamb, fat-side down, to a large piece of plastic wrap. Spread ¾ cup of the pesto evenly over the meat. Following the photos, roll and tie the lamb to form a tight roast.

4. Smear the outside of the roast with the remaining pesto. Wrap the roast tightly with the plastic wrap and refrigerate for 24 hours.

5. Adjust an oven rack to the middle position and heat the oven to 350 degrees. Set a wire rack over a large rimmed baking sheet and set aside. Unwrap the lamb, place on the prepared wire rack, and let sit at room temperature for 30 minutes.

6. Cook until the center of the roast registers 120 to 125 degrees (for medium-rare) on an instant-read thermometer, 1 to 1½ hours.

7. Transfer the lamb to a carving board and let rest for 15 minutes. Remove the twine, slice the lamb into ½-inch-thick slices, and serve with the reserved ½ cup pesto.

Notes from the Test Kitchen

Garlicky pesto is perfect paired with bold lamb. To get even more pesto flavor in the meat, we poked the roast all over before coating it. Though Dennis called for a sturdy pesto to cling to the meat, a looser pesto allowed for easier smearing and it still clung well. If you prefer your lamb cooked to medium, the roast should register 130 to 135 degrees, or 140 to 145 degrees for medium-well. Make sure to confirm with your butcher that you are getting a whole leg of lamb and not a half-leg.

ROLLING AND TYING THE LAMB

1. After transferring the lamb to the piece of plastic wrap, spread ¾ cup of the pesto over the meat, then roll it up to form a tight roast.

2. Tie the roast with twine at 1-inch intervals to ensure it holds together and cooks evenly. Smear ½ cup of the pesto over the roast and refrigerate overnight.

SALTINE LASAGNA

Dinner on a Dime

WWII Chicken à la King **136**

Mom's Chicken and Rice Dish **137**

Creamy Chicken and Waffles **138**

Aunt Cho's Chicken with Vinegar and Onions **140**

Saltine Lasagna **141**

Aunt Nina's Breadballs and Sauce **142**

Meat-za Pie **145**

Pot Roast Soup **146**

Salmon Loaf **147**

Tuna-Tater Bake **148**

Snowed-In Potato Hot Dish **149**

Easy Bird's Nest **151**

WWII Chicken à la King

ETHAN ALLEN | TACOMA, WASHINGTON

Title aside, this dish actually got its start long before the war. Allegedly, in the late 1800s the Brighton Beach Hotel's chef tossed poached chicken in a silky cream sauce with mushrooms and bell peppers and, serving it over toast, he presented a luxurious, flavorful, yet inexpensive meal to hotel owners Mr. and Mrs. E. Clark King. It became a symbol of thrifty chafing-dish chic, but during wartime it really hit its stride. "Moms were tasked with coming up with something tasty from limited supplies. Chicken à la King was a perfect example of such a meal, and its popularity carried into the 1950s." But home cooks started taking shortcuts, and its flavor and luxurious feel waned. Ethan's elegant, rich recipe pays tribute to the original from-scratch version.

SERVES 4

- 1½ pounds boneless, skinless chicken breasts, trimmed
  Salt and pepper
- 1 tablespoon vegetable oil
- 2 tablespoons unsalted butter
- 8 ounces white mushrooms, chopped fine
- 1 onion, minced
- 1 carrot, peeled and chopped fine
- 1 red bell pepper, stemmed, seeded, and chopped fine
- 3 tablespoons all-purpose flour
- 2 cups low-sodium chicken broth
- 1 cup heavy cream
- ½ teaspoon dried thyme
- 2 large egg yolks
- ¼ cup drained jarred pimientos, chopped fine
- 1 tablespoon fresh lemon juice
- 1 tablespoon chopped fresh parsley
- 8 slices Italian bread, toasted
  Paprika

1. Pat the chicken dry with paper towels and season with salt and pepper. Heat the oil in a Dutch oven over medium-high heat until just smoking. Cook the chicken until golden brown on both sides, about 5 minutes, flipping halfway through. Transfer the chicken to a plate.

2. Melt the butter in the pot over medium heat.

Add the mushrooms, onion, carrot, bell pepper, and ½ teaspoon salt and cook, stirring occasionally, until the mushrooms have released their juices and are brown around the edges, 10 to 12 minutes. Stir in the flour and cook for 1 minute. Whisk in the broth, cream, thyme, and ¼ teaspoon pepper, scraping up any browned bits.

3. Return the chicken, along with any accumulated juices, to the pot. Bring to a simmer, cover, and cook until the thickest part of the breasts registers 160 to 165 degrees on an instant-read thermometer, 10 to 15 minutes.

4. Transfer the chicken to a plate. When the chicken is cool enough to handle, shred the meat into bite-sized pieces and return it to the sauce. Stir ¼ cup of the warm sauce and the egg yolks together in a bowl. Stir the egg yolk mixture, pimientos, lemon juice, and parsley into the pot and season with salt and pepper to taste. Spoon the chicken mixture over the bread slices, sprinkle with paprika, and serve.

Notes from the Test Kitchen

We gave Ethan's sauce a silkier texture by adding more broth and decreasing the flour, butter, and cream. To boost flavor, we doubled the vegetables and added lemon juice, parsley, and thyme. Cooking the chicken in the sauce rather than cooking chicken and sauce separately helped streamline this flavorful recipe.

Mom's Chicken and Rice Dish

ASHLEY MCNAIR | ARLINGTON, VIRGINIA

With bright vegetables and fresh flavors, Ashley's recipe is able to turn two kitchen staples into a really flavorful dish without breaking the bank. "This is a dish my mom made often when she and my dad lived in Philadelphia in the seventies. My dad was going to law school and my mom was working as a speech therapist. A few years ago, when my husband was going to law school and I was struggling to come up with tasty meals on a student budget, my mom showed me how to make this. It is now a favorite of mine!"

SERVES 4 TO 6

1½ pounds boneless, skinless chicken breasts, trimmed
    Salt and pepper
3   tablespoons vegetable oil
8   ounces white mushrooms, sliced thin
1   onion, minced
1   carrot, peeled and chopped
1   green bell pepper, stemmed, seeded, and chopped
1½ cups long-grain white rice
6   garlic cloves, minced
1   teaspoon dried thyme
2½ cups low-sodium chicken broth
1   (14.5-ounce) can diced tomatoes
½   cup frozen peas, thawed

1. Pat the chicken dry with paper towels and season with salt and pepper. Heat 1 tablespoon of the oil in a Dutch oven over medium-high heat until just smoking. Cook the chicken until golden brown on both sides, about 5 minutes, flipping halfway through. Transfer the chicken to a plate.

2. Heat 1 tablespoon more oil in the pot over medium heat until shimmering. Add the mushrooms, ½ teaspoon salt, and ¼ teaspoon pepper and cook until the mushrooms have released their juices and are brown around the edges, 7 to 10 minutes. Transfer the mushrooms to a bowl.

3. Heat the remaining 1 tablespoon oil in the pot over medium heat until shimmering. Add the onion, carrot, bell pepper, and 1 teaspoon salt and cook, stirring occasionally, until the vegetables are softened, 5 to 7 minutes. Stir in the rice, garlic, and thyme and cook until the grains are translucent around the edges, about 3 minutes. Stir in the broth and tomatoes, scraping up any browned bits.

4. Nestle the chicken into the rice. Bring to a simmer, cover, and cook until the thickest part of the breasts registers 160 to 165 degrees on an instant-read thermometer, 25 to 30 minutes.

5. Transfer the chicken to a plate, brushing any rice that sticks to the chicken back into the pot. Stir the rice, cover, and continue to cook until the rice is tender and the liquid is absorbed, about 15 minutes longer.

6. When the chicken is cool enough to handle, shred the meat into bite-sized pieces and fold it into the rice with the peas and reserved mushrooms. Cover and let sit off the heat until heated through, about 2 minutes. Serve.

Notes from the Test Kitchen

Ashley's recipe leaves other bland chicken and rice recipes far behind. While she cubed her chicken before cooking it, we found cooking it whole, then shredding it, kept the meat more moist. Her recipe called for chopped fresh tomatoes, but fresh tomatoes can be hit or miss, so we used more reliable canned tomatoes and added the juice for more tomatoey punch. Carrots and peas lent fresh color. Work quickly when adding the broth, tomatoes, and chicken, as the rice will cook unevenly if the pot is left uncovered too long.

Creamy Chicken and Waffles

TAMMY WHITEMAN | BERWYN, PENNSYLVANIA

It struck us a strange pairing at first, but with a little research, we discovered the idea of pairing waffles with creamy (or creamed) chicken has been around since the 1890s. The first mention we found was in a *Sunset Magazine* story, where the author called creamed chicken, or chipped beef or ham, and waffles "a grand combination." We quickly discovered this was true! The texture of the waffles with the saucy chicken was a perfect match. Perhaps the idea came from a happy accident when the two were mixed on a plate at a church supper or ladies luncheon, events where both waffles with syrup and creamed chicken (or chicken and gravy) were often on the menu. Not surprisingly, chicken and waffles became popular during World War II, as the dish was a good way to extend protein and make the most of leftovers. As for Tammy's recipe, it's simply an old family favorite. "This recipe comes from my father's nanny and dear friend of the family. My grandmother could not even boil water, so the memories I have of cooking and eating are the wonderful days spent in the kitchen with Ozie, sharing her love of cooking and stories of my dad as a young boy." Note that this recipe calls for making traditional, not Belgian, waffles.

SERVES 4

CHICKEN

- 1½ pounds boneless, skinless chicken breasts, trimmed
- Salt and pepper
- 1 tablespoon vegetable oil
- 2 tablespoons unsalted butter
- 1 onion, minced
- 1 carrot, peeled and chopped fine
- 2 garlic cloves, minced
- 3 tablespoons all-purpose flour
- 1½ cups heavy cream
- 1 cup low-sodium chicken broth
- 1 bay leaf
- ½ teaspoon dried tarragon
- ½ cup frozen peas, thawed
- 1 tablespoon chopped fresh parsley

WAFFLES

- 2 cups all-purpose flour
- 1 tablespoon baking powder
- 1 teaspoon salt
- 1¼ cups whole milk
- 5 tablespoons unsalted butter, melted and cooled
- 3 large eggs, separated
- Pinch cream of tartar

1. FOR THE CHICKEN: Pat the chicken dry with paper towels and season with salt and pepper. Heat the oil in a Dutch oven over medium-high heat until just smoking. Cook the chicken until golden brown on both sides, about 5 minutes, flipping halfway through. Transfer the chicken to a plate.

2. Melt the butter in the pot over medium heat. Add the onion, carrot, and ½ teaspoon salt and cook, stirring occasionally, until softened, 5 to 7 minutes. Stir in the garlic and cook until fragrant, about 30 seconds. Stir in the flour and cook for 1 minute. Whisk in the cream, broth, bay leaf, tarragon, and ¼ teaspoon pepper, scraping up any browned bits.

3. Return the chicken, along with any accumulated juices, to the pot. Bring to a simmer, cover, and cook until the thickest part of the breasts registers 160 to 165 degrees on an instant-read thermometer, 10 to 15 minutes.

4. Transfer the chicken to a plate. Discard the bay leaf. When the chicken is cool enough to handle, shred the meat into bite-sized pieces and return it to the sauce with the peas. Cover and set aside off the heat to keep warm.

5. FOR THE WAFFLES: Adjust an oven rack to the middle position and preheat the oven to 200 degrees. Set a wire rack over a rimmed baking sheet and set aside. Preheat a traditional waffle iron to medium according to the manufacturer's instructions.

6. Whisk the flour, baking powder, and salt together in a large bowl. In a separate bowl, whisk the milk, melted butter, and egg yolks together. In a medium bowl, whip the egg whites and cream of tartar with an electric mixer on medium-low speed until foamy. Increase the speed to medium-high and whip the whites until they form stiff peaks, 1 to 3 minutes.

7. Make a well in the center of the dry ingredients, pour the milk mixture into the well, and whisk very gently until the milk mixture is just incorporated (a few lumps should remain). Gently fold the whipped egg whites into the batter until combined.

8. Following the manufacturer's instructions, spread the appropriate amount of batter onto the preheated waffle iron and cook until golden brown, about 3 minutes. Transfer the waffle to the prepared wire rack, cover with a clean kitchen towel, and keep warm in the oven. Repeat with the remaining batter. (Our waffle iron made six 7-inch waffles, each from ⅔ cup batter.)

9. To serve, return the chicken mixture to a simmer and season with salt and pepper to taste. Off the heat, stir in the parsley and spoon the chicken mixture over the waffles.

Notes from the Test Kitchen

We've seen various recipes for a saucy chicken served over toast or country bread, but we particularly liked this old-fashioned take on the idea. While Tammy cooked the chicken through before combining it with the sauce, we decided that for efficiency and flavor, it was better to poach the browned chicken right in the sauce. We also added onion and garlic, and we used fresh carrots rather than frozen. Switching from milk to cream and adding a touch more flour gave us a richer, silkier sauce. Tammy's waffle recipe made great, light-and-fluffy waffles, and the only change we made was to cut the 2 tablespoons of baking powder in half for a cleaner flavor.

Aunt Cho's Chicken with Vinegar and Onions

DONNA M. PENNATTO | MOUNT VERNON, NEW YORK

This recipe from Donna's aunt transforms a few basic ingredients into a boldly flavored, well-balanced dish. The chicken becomes incredibly tender and infused with flavor from braising in the cooking liquid, which in turn becomes a flavorful sauce. The onions lend a hint of sweetness that perfectly balances the sauce's bite. Braising chicken in vinegar is an old technique, and though it may be one of the thriftiest, simplest methods around, when you take one bite you'll discover it certainly isn't short on flavor.

SERVES 4 TO 6

- 3 pounds bone-in, skin-on chicken pieces (split breasts cut in half, drumsticks, and/or thighs), trimmed
  Salt and pepper
- 1 tablespoon vegetable oil
- 1 onion, minced
- 2 garlic cloves, minced
- 1 teaspoon dried thyme
- 1 tablespoon all-purpose flour
- 1¾ cups low-sodium chicken broth
- ¼ cup red wine vinegar
- 2 tablespoons unsalted butter, cut into ½-inch pieces

1. Pat the chicken dry with paper towels and season with salt and pepper. Heat 1½ teaspoons of the oil in a large Dutch oven over medium-high heat until just smoking. Add half of the chicken and cook until golden brown on both sides, about 10 minutes, flipping halfway through. Transfer the chicken to a plate. Return the pot to medium-high heat and repeat with the remaining 1½ teaspoons oil and the remaining chicken.

2. Add the onion to the pot and cook, stirring occasionally, until softened, 5 to 7 minutes. Stir in the garlic and thyme and cook until fragrant, about 30 seconds. Stir in the flour and cook for 1 minute. Whisk in the broth and vinegar, scraping up any browned bits.

3. Return the chicken, along with any accumulated juices, to the pot. Bring to a simmer, cover, and cook until the chicken is fully cooked and tender, about 20 minutes for breasts (160 to 165 degrees on an instant-read thermometer) or 1 hour for thighs and drumsticks (175 degrees on an instant-read thermometer). (If using both white and dark meat, simmer the thighs and drumsticks for 40 minutes before adding the breasts.)

4. Transfer the chicken to a serving platter and tent loosely with foil. Skim the fat off the surface of the sauce with a wide spoon. Return the sauce to a simmer and cook until thickened slightly, 4 to 6 minutes. Off the heat, stir in the butter and season with salt and pepper to taste. Pour the sauce over the chicken and serve.

Notes from the Test Kitchen

We loved the combination of the tart, vinegary sauce with the tender braised chicken. Donna cooked her chicken in 4 cups of water combined with 2 cups of vinegar, but we wanted more of a sauce than a cooking liquid, so we reduced the liquid ingredients to 2 cups total, which was still plenty to braise the meat. We swapped flavorful chicken broth for the water and used just 1¾ cups, along with ¼ cup of vinegar. If using both white and dark meat chicken, we recommend cutting the breast pieces in half so that each serving can include some white meat and some dark. We liked this dish best served with rice as Donna suggests, but mashed potatoes or buttered egg noodles would also work well.

Saltine Lasagna

JANICE ELDER | CHARLOTTE, NORTH CAROLINA

In this one-of-a-kind recipe, bell peppers, zucchini, onion, and cheese are layered with, yes, saltine crackers rather than noodles, then a custard is poured over before it's baked. This "lasagna"—more like a colorful fresh-vegetable strata—is served with tomato sauce on the side. Says Janice, "I'm not sure of the genesis of this recipe. I suspect someone was out of lasagna noodles and had a box of saltines and decided to make a brave substitution. It has been out of my rotation for years, but I prepared it again and was immediately taken back to the era when we enjoyed this dish." After topping the lasagna with your favorite homemade or store-bought tomato sauce, Janice recommends sprinkling it with Parmesan and basil.

SERVES 4

- 4 teaspoons vegetable oil
- 1 small zucchini, cut into ½-inch chunks
  Salt
- 1 onion, minced
- 1 red bell pepper, stemmed, seeded, and chopped
- 3 garlic cloves, minced
- 1 teaspoon dried Italian seasoning
- 36 saltine crackers
- 2 cups shredded mozzarella cheese
- 2 cups whole milk
- 4 large eggs
- ¼ teaspoon pepper
- ⅛ teaspoon red pepper flakes
- ⅛ teaspoon ground nutmeg
- 2 cups jarred or homemade tomato sauce, warmed

1. Adjust an oven rack to the middle position and heat the oven to 350 degrees. Grease an 8-inch square baking dish and set aside.

2. Heat 2 teaspoons of the oil in a large skillet over medium heat until shimmering. Add the zucchini and ⅛ teaspoon salt and cook, stirring occasionally, until tender and lightly browned, 4 to 6 minutes. Transfer the zucchini to a bowl.

3. Heat the remaining 2 teaspoons oil in the skillet over medium heat until shimmering. Add the onion, bell pepper, and ⅛ teaspoon salt and cook, stirring occasionally, until the vegetables are softened, 5 to 7 minutes. Stir in the garlic and Italian seasoning and cook until fragrant, 30 seconds. Off the heat, stir in the zucchini.

4. Layer half of the crackers in the prepared baking dish, overlapping slightly as necessary to form a single layer. Spoon half of the vegetables over the crackers and smooth into an even layer. Sprinkle evenly with 1 cup of the mozzarella. Repeat with the remaining crackers, vegetables, and cheese for a second layer.

5. Whisk the milk, eggs, pepper, red pepper flakes, nutmeg, and ¼ teaspoon salt together in a bowl. Slowly pour the egg mixture into the baking dish. Place the baking dish on a foil-lined rimmed baking sheet and bake until the eggs are set and the top is beginning to brown, 25 to 30 minutes. Cool for 10 minutes, then serve with the tomato sauce.

Notes from the Test Kitchen

Gooey cheese, fresh vegetables, and a few saltines peeking out meant love at first bite for us. Janice's 2 teaspoons of Italian seasoning and ½ teaspoon of red pepper were too much for us, so we cut the Italian seasoning in half and used ⅛ teaspoon red pepper. A little garlic added depth.

Aunt Nina's Breadballs and Sauce

DONNA BARDOCZ | HOWELL, MICHIGAN

Donna's Aunt Nina learned how to make this simple, satisfying comfort food from her own mother and later shared it at a family reunion. This recipe is for "meatless meatballs," which are prepared in much the same way as meatballs, just with different ingredients. Bread crumbs, eggs, cheese, and herbs are combined and rolled into balls, which are then browned and simmered in a tomato sauce. The idea for breadballs can be traced, not that surprisingly, to Italy, where similar recipes are made as appetizers. Here, Donna turns them into a filling dinner by serving them with sausage and a salad. Among the Italian recipes we found, one compares such breadballs to a light gnocchi, a comment that made us realize this recipe would work just as well as a great vegetarian entrée.

SERVES 6 TO 8

BREADBALLS

- 1 cup water
- 1 large egg
- 3 garlic cloves, minced
- 1 tablespoon chopped fresh parsley or ¾ teaspoon dried
- 1 tablespoon chopped fresh basil or ¾ teaspoon dried
- ¼ teaspoon pepper
- 1 (16-ounce) loaf Italian bread, torn into small pieces
- 1½ cups grated Parmesan cheese
- 6 tablespoons olive oil

SAUCE

- 1 onion, minced
  Salt
- 2 (6-ounce) cans tomato paste
- 1 tablespoon sugar
- 3 garlic cloves, minced
- 2 teaspoons dried oregano
- ⅛ teaspoon red pepper flakes
  Pepper
- 2 cups water
- 1 (28-ounce) can diced tomatoes
- 1 (15-ounce) can tomato sauce
- 1 tablespoon chopped fresh parsley
- ½ cup grated Parmesan cheese
- 1 tablespoon chopped fresh basil

(Continued on page 144)

1. **FOR THE BREADBALLS:** Whisk the water, egg, garlic, parsley, basil, and pepper together in a large bowl. Add the bread and cheese and mix with your hands until well combined. With wet hands, form the mixture into 1½-inch bread-balls (you should have about 30 breadballs).

2. Heat ¼ cup of the oil in a Dutch oven over medium-high heat until shimmering. Add half of the breadballs and cook until well browned on the first side, 2 to 4 minutes. (Do not move the bread-balls until they are well browned on the first side.) Continue to cook until they are well browned on all sides, about 5 minutes longer, turning as needed. Transfer the breadballs to a bowl. Add the remaining 2 tablespoons oil to the pot and return it to medium heat until the oil is shimmering. Repeat with the remaining breadballs.

3. **FOR THE SAUCE:** Pour off all but 1 tablespoon of the oil from the pot and return to medium heat until shimmering. Add the onion and ½ teaspoon salt and cook, stirring occasion-ally, until softened, 5 to 7 minutes. Stir in the tomato paste, sugar, garlic, oregano, red pepper flakes, and ¼ teaspoon pepper and cook until the tomato paste begins to brown, 2 to 4 min-utes. Add the water, tomatoes, and tomato sauce. Bring to a simmer, cover, and cook, stirring occasionally, for 1 hour.

4. Return the breadballs to the pot, cover, and continue to simmer until the sauce is thickened slightly and the breadballs are tender, about 30 minutes longer. Off the heat, stir in the parsley and season with salt and pepper to taste. Serve, sprinkling each portion with Parmesan and basil.

Notes from the Test Kitchen

Simmering balls of bread in tomato sauce sounded like a kitchen disaster waiting to happen. To our surprise they not only held together really well, but one taste and we were sold—they're a satisfying comfort food we'd somehow not discovered until now. We found the key to success was making sure the breadballs formed a good crust during frying so that they did not fall apart when simmered. To give them a bit more flavor, we increased the minced garlic cloves from 2 to 3, and we increased both herbs from 1 teaspoon to 1 tablespoon (we also increased the herbs in the sauce). However, we omitted the onion from the breadballs and just left them in the sauce, since we didn't like the texture it gave the breadballs. Donna's simple tomato sauce was great, though we prefer ours a bit less sweet, so we reduced the sugar from 6 tablespoons to just 1 tablespoon. To ensure the balls do not stick to the pan while frying, avoid moving them for the first 2 to 3 minutes of browning.

Meat-za Pie

ELLEN SCHWARTZ | HOUSTON, TEXAS

A recipe with a name like this is sure to draw a crowd (think teenage boys). Somewhere between pizza and meatloaf, Meat-za Pie features a hearty layer of a meatloaf-like mixture topped with a flavorful tomato sauce, mushrooms, and gooey cheese.

SERVES 6

2	slices hearty white sandwich bread, torn into large pieces and pulsed in a food processor to coarse crumbs
¼	cup olive oil
	Salt and pepper
3	garlic cloves, minced
½	teaspoon dried oregano
½	teaspoon dried basil
1	(6-ounce) can tomato paste
1	cup water
8	ounces white mushrooms, sliced thin
1	onion, minced
¼	teaspoon dried thyme
1	(5-ounce) can evaporated milk
¼	cup grated Parmesan cheese
1	large egg
1½	pounds 85 percent lean ground beef
1½	cups shredded sharp cheddar cheese

1. Adjust an oven rack to the middle position and heat the oven to 350 degrees. Following the photos on page 75, line a large rimmed baking sheet with foil, set a wire rack over the baking sheet, and place a 12 by 12-inch piece of foil in the center of the rack. Use a skewer to poke holes in the foil at ½-inch intervals.

2. Toss the bread crumbs with 2 tablespoons of the oil, a pinch salt, and a pinch pepper in a bowl. Toast the bread crumbs in a single layer on a rimmed baking sheet, stirring occasionally, until golden brown and dry, 8 to 10 minutes. Set aside and cool to room temperature.

3. Heat 1 tablespoon more oil, the garlic, oregano, and basil in a medium saucepan over medium heat until sizzling, about 1 minute. Stir in the tomato paste and cook until beginning to brown, 2 to 4 minutes. Stir in the water, bring to a simmer, and cook until thickened slightly, about 2 minutes. Season with salt and pepper to taste. Set aside.

4. Heat the remaining 1 tablespoon oil in a large skillet over medium heat until shimmering. Add the mushrooms, onion, thyme, and ¼ teaspoon salt and cook until the mushrooms have released their juices and are brown around the edges, 7 to 10 minutes. Set aside to cool to room temperature.

5. Whisk the milk, Parmesan, egg, ½ teaspoon salt, and ½ teaspoon pepper together in a large bowl. Add the bread crumbs and meat and mix with your hands until evenly blended and the mixture does not stick to the bowl.

6. Transfer the meat to the foil square and, using wet hands, pat the mixture into an 11-inch circle. Press all but the outside 1 inch of the meat down with your fingertips to create a slight depression in the center. Spread the tomato sauce over the indented portion of meat. Spoon the cooked mushroom mixture over the sauce, then sprinkle evenly with the cheddar.

7. Bake until the cheese is spotty brown and the center of the meatloaf registers 160 degrees on an instant-read thermometer, about 45 minutes. Cool for 15 minutes before serving.

Notes from the Test Kitchen

Ellen used a 9-inch pie plate, which caused the pie to retain liquid. Using a wire rack topped with foil allowed excess moisture to drain. Fresh garlic instead of garlic powder, and fresh bread crumbs and basil boosted flavor. We also made our own spaghetti sauce instead of using a dry mix.

Pot Roast Soup

CHRISTINE LIBERT | RENO, NEVADA

When you turn old-fashioned, affordable pot roast and vegetables into a hearty noodle soup, you have a whole new dish, one that will fill you up and warm you through. "This soup is a favorite with anyone I serve it to. My friends have asked for the recipe and now make it for their own families. The first time I had this was after flying with my kids and husband to his mom and dad's in Chicago. We got in late, hungry and exhausted from traveling. My mother-in-law, Joyce, sat us down with this piping hot soup and some crackers and we were in heaven. I have since tweaked it to make it more my own, but I will always be grateful to her for the original recipe."

SERVES 6 TO 8

- 1 (3-pound) boneless beef chuck-eye roast, trimmed
  Salt and pepper
- 2 tablespoons vegetable oil
- 1 onion, minced
- 1 tablespoon tomato paste
- ½ teaspoon dried thyme
- 4 cups low-sodium chicken broth
- 4 cups low-sodium beef broth
- 2 cups water
- 2 bay leaves
- 4 carrots, peeled, halved lengthwise, and sliced ¼ inch thick
- 4 celery ribs, chopped
- 1 (14.5-ounce) can diced tomatoes, drained
- 6 ounces wide egg noodles (2¼ cups)

1. Pat the roast dry with paper towels and season with salt and pepper. Heat the oil in a Dutch oven over medium-high heat until just smoking. Cook the roast until well browned on all sides, 8 to 12 minutes, turning as needed. Transfer the roast to a plate.

2. Pour off all but 1 tablespoon of the fat from the pot and return to medium heat until shimmering. Add the onion and cook, stirring occasionally, until softened, 5 to 7 minutes. Stir in the tomato paste and thyme and cook until the tomato paste begins to brown, about 1 minute. Stir in the broths, water, and bay leaves, scraping up any browned bits.

3. Return the roast, along with any accumulated juices, to the pot. Bring to a simmer, cover, and cook until the meat is tender, 2 to 2½ hours, flipping the roast halfway through.

4. Transfer the roast to a plate. Strain the liquid through a fine-mesh strainer into a large measuring cup, discarding the solids. Rinse out the pot. Return the liquid to the pot and let it settle for 5 minutes. Skim the fat off the surface of the broth with a wide spoon.

5. When the roast is cool enough to handle, shred the meat into bite-sized pieces and return it to the broth with the carrots, celery, and tomatoes. Bring to a simmer, cover, and cook until the vegetables are almost tender, 15 to 20 minutes. Add the noodles and cook, stirring often, until al dente, 6 to 7 minutes. Season with salt and pepper to taste. Serve.

Notes from the Test Kitchen

While Christine utilized beef bones to help enrich the flavor of the soup, we thought that was too much trouble. To get rich, meaty flavor without the hassle, we relied on store-bought chicken and beef broths. Browning the onions and adding some tomato paste also helped deepen flavor. Though Christine used fresh linguine noodles, we found they easily overcooked. Egg noodles proved to be an easier option, and they held up much better.

Salmon Loaf

MARILEE KINSELLA | CHICAGO, ILLINOIS

"As a child, the only fish I would eat was in the form of a fried or baked stick, until my mother developed this recipe. My mother used a tall can of salmon. However, I've adapted the recipe so that fresh, cooked salmon is used. I also added fresh dill." Marilee's recipe, which bakes a mixture of fresh salmon, bread crumbs, eggs, milk, and seasoning into a light, savory loaf, is very similar to salmon loaves from the early 1900s, which were in turn based on steamed fish "puddings." Though recipes past and present rely about equally on fresh or canned salmon, loaves with canned salmon endured as an economical choice, particularly during wartime. Marilee takes the recipe into the twenty-first century with fresh ingredients, perfect for a summer lunch or light dinner.

SERVES 4

- 2 slices hearty white sandwich bread, torn into large pieces and pulsed in a food processor to coarse crumbs
- 4 (6-ounce) skinless salmon fillets
  Salt and pepper
- 1 tablespoon vegetable oil
- ¾ cup whole milk
- 3 tablespoons unsalted butter, melted and cooled
- 3 large eggs, separated
- 4 teaspoons Dijon mustard
- 4 teaspoons minced fresh dill or 1 teaspoon dried
- 1 lemon, cut into wedges

1. Adjust an oven rack to the middle position and heat the oven to 325 degrees. Grease an 8½ by 4½-inch nonstick loaf pan well and set aside.

2. Toast the bread crumbs in a single layer on a rimmed baking sheet, stirring occasionally, until golden brown and dry, 8 to 10 minutes. Set aside to cool to room temperature.

3. Pat the salmon dry with paper towels and season with salt and pepper. Heat the oil in a large nonstick skillet over medium-high heat until just smoking. Cook the salmon until golden brown on both sides and just opaque in the center, about 8 minutes, flipping halfway through. Transfer the salmon to a plate and set aside to cool to room temperature.

4. Flake the salmon into bite-sized pieces. Whisk the milk, melted butter, egg yolks, and mustard together in a bowl. Add the bread crumbs, dill, ¾ teaspoon salt, and ¼ teaspoon pepper and mix until evenly incorporated. Gently stir in the salmon until combined.

5. In a medium bowl, whip the egg whites with an electric mixer on medium-low speed until foamy. Increase the speed to medium-high and whip the whites until they form soft peaks, 1 to 2 minutes. Gently fold the whipped egg whites into the salmon mixture until combined.

6. Pour the mixture into the prepared loaf pan, smooth the top with a rubber spatula, and bake until the center registers 180 degrees on an instant-read thermometer and the loaf is lightly browned on the top, 45 to 55 minutes. Let rest for 15 minutes. Run a small knife around the edge of the loaf, then remove the loaf from the pan and serve with the lemon wedges.

Notes from the Test Kitchen

This light meal is a great change of pace. To bring the flavors into balance, we reduced the dill from 2 tablespoons to 4 teaspoons and added Dijon for zing. For better texture, we increased the salmon from 14 ounces to 24 ounces and doubled the bread crumbs. Marilee's recipe called for poached, broiled, or baked salmon; we found pan-searing contributed the most flavor.

Tuna-Tater Bake

JAMES PALM | PENSACOLA, FLORIDA

Tuna noodle casserole has long served as an easy, affordable family dinner option, but we can probably all agree, it gets old after awhile. But combine tuna with fluffy mashed potatoes and a little mustard and seasoning, and top it with crumbled potato chips, and you've got a whole new dish that will have your family asking for seconds. By folding egg whites into the mashed potatoes, James creates a uniquely satisfying casserole that also has a welcome touch of lightness. Paired with green beans or a fresh salad, Tuna-Tater Bake is an ideal easy weeknight dinner.

SERVES 4

- 1 pound russet potatoes, peeled and cut into 1-inch chunks
- ½ cup heavy cream, warmed
- 4 tablespoons (½ stick) unsalted butter, melted
- 2 large eggs, separated
- 2 teaspoons Dijon mustard
- ¾ teaspoon salt
- ¼ teaspoon pepper
- 2 (5-ounce) cans solid white tuna in water, drained
- 1 cup shredded cheddar cheese
  Pinch cream of tartar
- ½ cup potato chips, crushed fine

1. Adjust an oven rack to the middle position and heat the oven to 350 degrees. Grease an 8-inch square baking dish and set aside.

2. Bring the potatoes and 2 quarts water to a simmer in a medium saucepan and cook until tender, 20 to 25 minutes. Drain the potatoes and transfer to a bowl.

3. Mash the potatoes until smooth, then gently fold in the cream, melted butter, egg yolks, mustard, salt, and pepper until thick and creamy. Add the tuna, breaking up any large chunks, and ½ cup of the cheese and mix to combine.

4. In a medium bowl, whip the egg whites and cream of tartar with an electric mixer on medium-low speed until foamy. Increase the speed to medium-high and whip the whites until they form stiff peaks, 1 to 3 minutes.

5. Gently fold the whipped egg whites into the potato mixture until combined. Pour the mixture into the prepared baking dish and smooth the top. Sprinkle evenly with the remaining ½ cup cheese and the potato chips. Place the baking dish on a foil-lined rimmed baking sheet and bake until the cheese is melted and the edges are starting to brown, 25 to 30 minutes. Cool for 10 minutes before serving.

Notes from the Test Kitchen

A good mashed potato casserole is always a welcome side dish, so turning it into an entrée by adding tuna had a lot of appeal right off the bat. Though James simply called for mashed potatoes, we felt we needed to include a mashed potato recipe since it's a core component of the dish. We settled on mashing the potatoes with cream and butter, not only because we liked the rich flavor but also because it gave us potatoes that were ultralight and fluffy, even better when coupled with the whipped egg whites. James cooked his casserole for 45 minutes at 375 degrees, but we reduced both the time and the temperature (to 25 to 30 minutes and 350 degrees, respectively) to ensure that this crowd-pleasing casserole remained moist.

Snowed-In Potato Hot Dish

ARDELLA VON OHLEN | CLARKSTON, WASHINGTON

Whether you're housebound or just want a satisfying dinner on a cold evening, this casserole of rich scalloped potatoes layered with cheese, seasoned with sage, and topped with bacon is sure to hit the spot. As a bonus, it's super simple to prepare and requires only a handful of ingredients. "This recipe was in a farm magazine one winter in the 1950s when we had a lot of snow. The ingredients were something most everyone had in the cupboard even if snowed in for a week. It's easy to fix and tastes really good." If we were snowed in, this meal would surely be at the top of our list as a satisfying meal to warm us through.

SERVES 8 TO 10

- 6 slices bacon
- 3 cups heavy cream
- 1 teaspoon dried sage
- 1 teaspoon salt
- 1/8 teaspoon pepper
- 2½ pounds russet potatoes, peeled and sliced 1/8 inch thick
- 1 onion, halved and sliced thin
- 1½ cups shredded sharp cheddar cheese

1. Adjust an oven rack to the middle position and heat the oven to 350 degrees.

2. Lay the bacon slices evenly on a large plate. Weigh the bacon down with a second plate and microwave on high until the fat is rendered and the bacon is slightly shriveled but still pliable, 1 to 3 minutes. Set aside.

3. Bring the cream, sage, salt, and pepper to a simmer in a Dutch oven and cook until the liquid is reduced to 2½ cups, about 5 minutes. Off the heat, gently stir in the potatoes and onion.

4. Spoon half of the potato mixture into a 13 by 9-inch baking dish and sprinkle with ¾ cup of the cheese. Spoon the remaining potato mixture over the cheese. Gently pack the potatoes into an even layer, removing any air pockets, then sprinkle with the remaining ¾ cup cheese. Lay the bacon strips evenly over the top of the baking dish.

5. Place the baking dish on a foil-lined rimmed baking sheet and bake until the potatoes are tender (a paring knife should glide through the potatoes with little resistance) and the bacon is crisp, 1 to 1½ hours. Cool for 20 minutes before serving.

Notes from the Test Kitchen

We loved the simplicity of this dish, but we did make a few changes to boost the flavor and consistency. We swapped milk for richer cream, which we reduced on the stovetop to get a thicker consistency that allowed us to skip using flour as a thickener, as Ardella had done. To get more sage flavor, we infused the cream with the herb on the stovetop rather than sprinkling it over the potatoes before baking. While Ardella used ground sage, we had problems with it clumping so we switched to dried, which was easier to keep evenly distributed. Make sure to cut the potatoes 1/8 inch thick so they will hold their shape but still be flexible enough to lie together compactly.

Easy Bird's Nest

EMILY KOCH | NISKAYUNA, NEW YORK

"I grew up during World War II, so my mom tried to make meatless meals from ingredients that were easily available. Naturally, we had a Victory Garden with a variety of vegetables. Eggs were rather scarce, but we were sometimes able to buy them from a local farmer. Of course butter was rationed, but we used margarine. (Since we could only buy white margarine, we buckled down and colored it ourselves.) By combining egg noodles, margarine, eggs, and green beans fresh from the garden, we could have a complete, delicious supper." These days, Emily tops this appealing meal with almonds, which add just the right finishing crunch.

SERVES 4

- 1 pound green beans, trimmed and cut into 1-inch pieces
  Salt
- 1 (12-ounce) package egg noodles
- 8 tablespoons (1 stick) unsalted butter, cut into 8 pieces
  Pepper
- 4 large eggs
- ¼ cup sliced almonds, toasted

1. Bring 4 quarts water to a boil in a large pot. Add the beans and 1 tablespoon salt and cook until crisp-tender, about 5 minutes. Using a slotted spoon, transfer the beans to a bowl and cover with foil to keep warm.

2. Return the water to a boil. Add the noodles and cook, stirring often, until al dente. Drain the noodles and return them to the pot. Stir the beans and 7 tablespoons of the butter into the noodles. Season with salt and pepper to taste. Cover to keep warm until ready to serve.

3. Meanwhile, melt the remaining 1 tablespoon butter in a large nonstick skillet over low heat. Quickly add the eggs to the skillet and season with salt and pepper. Cover and cook until the whites are set but the yolks are still runny, 2 to 3 minutes. Uncover the eggs and remove the skillet from the heat.

4. Divide the pasta evenly onto four serving plates and carefully slide a fried egg over the top. Sprinkle 1 tablespoon of the almonds over each egg and serve.

Notes from the Test Kitchen

We loved the bright colors of the egg and green beans in this light yet satisfying summery dish. Though Emily's recipe included slivered almonds as optional, we felt that the nuts added essential texture and were a required ingredient. Instead of slivered almonds, our tasters preferred sliced, which we toasted to deepen the flavor. We cut back the 1 pound of pasta called for in the original to an easier-to-find 12-ounce bag, and with the smaller amount of noodles, we decided to reduce the number of eggs from six to four (though you can certainly fry more or less eggs as desired). Though perhaps not quite as thrifty as the original recipe, we also increased the amount of butter from 2 tablespoons to 8 tablespoons, which we felt gave it great flavor and better coated the pasta and beans.

CHESAPEAKE PARTAN BREE

American Regional Specialties

Quilt-Top Country Ham 154

Crispy Iowa Skinnies 156

Yankee Pot Roast Supper 157

New England Boiled Dinner 158

Pennsylvania Dutch Slippery Chicken Bott Bie 160

Coke Oven Fried Chicken 162

Louisiana Smothered Rabbit 164

Duck Gumbo 165

Blue Ridge Baked Bean Burgoo 167

Cincinnati Chili 169

Pivoto-Robinson Shrimp Creole 170

Chesapeake Partan Bree 172

Char's Maine Fish Chowder 174

Long Island Clam Pie 175

Grandma Taylor's Crab Cakes 177

Great-Grandma's Corn Fritters 179

Baked Boston Brown Bread 180

Quilt-Top Country Ham

KATHLEEN ELLIS | PARIS, TENNESSEE

"My husband's grandparents lived on a farm in Robertson County, Tennessee, where they raised hogs they butchered each fall. After preparing the meat, the hams and shoulders were smoked in the old smokehouse near the barn. Mama Nichols, the beloved matriarch of the family and mother to fifteen children, cooked a ham for holidays and celebrations. This is her method of cooking country ham, which allows the ham to finish cooking wrapped up snugly in a quilt. We continue to prepare it each year as she did to honor her memory." Unlike their wet-cured supermarket cousins (or "city hams") that are either injected with or soaked in a brine, a country ham, a whole bone-in leg, is rubbed with salt (and sometimes also with sugar and other seasonings) and dry-cured, then the salt is washed off, the ham is smoked, and finally it's aged for several months. Aside from being drier and firmer than its city kin, country hams have a salty, meaty, smoky flavor and intensity that the other just can't achieve. These days you can get fully cooked country hams, but most are still sold uncooked. We recommend going the uncooked route so you can enjoy preparing your own old-fashioned ham, just like Kathleen. You will need a very large 30-quart stockpot to make this recipe.

SERVES 15 TO 20

- 1 (11- to 14-pound) bone-in, short-shank, uncooked country ham
- 1 cup Dijon mustard
- 1 cup packed brown sugar
- 2 teaspoons pepper

1. Using a clean, stiff brush, scrub the ham under cold running water to remove the pepper and any traces of mold. Place the ham in a 30-quart stockpot and cover completely with cold water. Cover the pot and soak at room temperature for 48 hours, changing the water six times each day to rid the ham of excess salt.

2. Pour off the soaking liquid, add enough cold water to cover the ham by 2 inches, and bring to a boil over high heat. Reduce the heat to low, partially cover, and simmer the ham for 30 minutes. Turn off the heat, cover tightly, and secure the lid with duct tape so that no steam can escape.

3. Meanwhile, following the photos, line a large metal tub with a capacity of at least 18 gallons with a thick layer of crumpled newspapers and set it on a heat-safe surface. Fold a twin-size quilt or comforter in half twice to form a four-layer square. Carefully remove the sealed pot from the stovetop and place on top of the newspapers in the tub. Surround and cover the pot

with more crumpled newspapers, then place the folded quilt on top. Tuck the edges of the quilt between the newspapers and the inside of the tub to fully insulate the stockpot. The sides of the tub should feel cool to the touch throughout the 24-hour cooking period, indicating that the heat is contained inside the pot.

4. After 24 hours, remove the quilt, newspapers, and duct tape seal and carefully transfer the ham to a large roasting pan. Let the ham cool for 20 minutes before removing and discarding the skin, fat, and loose bone. Brush the ham with the mustard, pat evenly with the brown sugar, and sprinkle with the pepper. Tent the ham loosely with foil and cool to room temperature. Transfer the ham to a carving board and cut against the grain into paper-thin slices. Serve.

Notes from the Test Kitchen

While we love Kathleen's energy-efficient, old school quilt-top method for cooking a country ham, we realize that many home cooks don't keep spare 18-gallon metal tubs or quilts handy for kitchen work. For this reason, we tested a more conventional cooking method that still produces delicious results. Starting with step 2, continue to simmer the ham until the bone becomes loose, 4½ to 6 hours or about 25 minutes per pound, adding water as needed to keep the ham covered. Remove the pot from the heat and cool for 2 hours. Transfer the ham to a large roasting pan and follow the remainder of step 4 to remove the skin, fat, and bone, make the glaze, and carve.

MAKING QUILT-TOP COUNTRY HAM

1. Line an 18-gallon metal tub (24 inches wide and 11 inches deep) with a thick layer of crumpled newspapers and set it on a heat-safe surface, such as a large wooden cutting board or concrete floor. Carefully remove the sealed pot from the stovetop and place on top of the newspapers in the tub.

2. Fold a twin-size quilt or comforter in half horizontally and then vertically to form a four-layer square. After covering the pot on all sides and the top with more crumpled newspapers, place the folded quilt on top. Tuck the edges of the quilt between the newspapers and the inside of the tub to fully insulate the stockpot.

Crispy Iowa Skinnies

THE EDITORS OF COOK'S COUNTRY

In the Midwest, pork is king. That's because the heartland of America (sometimes called the Hog Belt) produces most of our country's pork, and Iowa stands out not only for its pork production, but also for its preparation, including a fried pork sandwich known as the "skinny." A chunk of pork tenderloin is pounded to platter size, lightly breaded and fried, and served on a soft bun with lettuce, tomato, and a slathering of mayo. With its crunchy golden brown coating, the hefty skinny is about as good, and simple, as it gets.

SERVES 4

- ½ cup all-purpose flour
- 2   large eggs
- ¼ cup mayonnaise, plus extra for serving
- 3   slices hearty white sandwich bread, torn into large pieces
- 16 saltine crackers
- 1   (1-pound) pork tenderloin, cut into 4 pieces and pounded to ¼-inch thickness
       Salt and pepper
- 1   cup vegetable oil
- 4   soft hamburger buns
- 1½ cups shredded iceberg lettuce
- 1   medium tomato, sliced

1. Adjust an oven rack to the middle position and heat the oven to 200 degrees. Set a wire rack over a baking sheet and set aside.

2. Place the flour in a shallow dish. Whisk the eggs and the mayonnaise together in a second shallow dish. Process the bread and saltines together in a food processor to fine crumbs and transfer to a third shallow dish.

3. Pat the pork cutlets dry with paper towels and season with salt and pepper. One at a time, dredge the cutlets in the flour, dip into the egg mixture, then coat with the crumbs, pressing to adhere. Place on the prepared wire rack and let dry for 5 minutes, or refrigerate for up to 1 hour.

4. Heat ½ cup of the oil in a large nonstick skillet over medium heat until shimmering. Lay

2 of the cutlets in the skillet and cook until crisp and deep golden brown on both sides, about 2 minutes, flipping halfway through. Transfer the pork cutlets to a paper towel–lined plate and keep warm in the oven. Discard the oil and wipe out the skillet. Return the skillet to medium heat and repeat with the remaining ½ cup oil and the remaining pork cutlets.

5. Place 1 pork cutlet on each bun and top with mayonnaise, lettuce, and tomato. Serve.

Notes from the Test Kitchen

Most recipes agree on the meat type and method, but there's little consensus on the coating for Iowa Skinnies. Saltines added to a bread-crumb mixture created the right saltiness and an extra-crispy coating, and adding mayo to the egg coating allowed for a nice richness and tang.

MAKING PORK CUTLETS

1. After removing any silver skin or extraneous fat from the tenderloin, cut it into 4 equal pieces.

2. Arrange the tenderloin pieces cut-side up on a cutting board. Cover with plastic wrap and pound into ¼-inch-thick cutlets.

Yankee Pot Roast Supper

TRISHA KRUSE | EAGLE, IDAHO

"This recipe was passed down to my mother from my Grandma Ellis. My mom was not a very good cook, but this dish always turned out perfect: tender meat, flavorful gravy, and a tangy sweetness from the apricots." An all-in-one pot roast supper is typical of sensible New England cookery. Trisha's recipe includes traditional vegetables along with one unusual addition: dried apricots. Their sweetness perfectly complements the savory flavors. "We were very thankful to Grandma for handing this down to my mom—a huge improvement over her hockey puck burgers and roof shingle baked chicken breasts!"

SERVES 6 TO 8

1	(3½-pound) boneless beef chuck-eye roast
	Salt and pepper
2	tablespoons vegetable oil
1	onion, halved and sliced thin
1	teaspoon minced fresh thyme
1	teaspoon minced fresh rosemary
1	tablespoon all-purpose flour
3–3½	cups low-sodium beef broth
1½	pounds small red potatoes, scrubbed and quartered
1½	pounds carrots, peeled and cut into ½-inch pieces
⅔	cup dried apricots

1. Adjust an oven rack to the lower-middle position and heat the oven to 300 degrees.

2. Pat the beef dry with paper towels and season with salt and pepper. Heat the oil in a Dutch oven over medium-high heat until just smoking. Cook the roast until well browned on all sides, 8 to 10 minutes, turning as needed. Transfer the roast to a plate.

3. Pour off all but 1 tablespoon of the fat and return the pot to medium heat until shimmering. Add the onion and cook, stirring occasionally, until softened and beginning to brown, 6 to 8 minutes. Stir in the thyme and rosemary and cook until fragrant, about 30 seconds. Stir in the flour and cook for 1 minute.

4. Return the roast, along with any accumulated juices, to the pot. Add enough broth to come halfway up the sides of the roast. Bring to a simmer, cover, and transfer to the oven. Cook until the roast is almost tender, about 3 hours.

5. Remove the pot from the oven. Stir in the potatoes, carrots, and apricots. Bring to a simmer over medium heat, cover, and cook until the meat and vegetables are tender, about 30 minutes.

6. Transfer the roast to a carving board and tent loosely with foil. Transfer the vegetables to a serving platter and tent loosely with foil. Let the liquid in the pot settle for 5 minutes. Skim the fat off the surface of the sauce with a wide spoon. Bring the liquid to a simmer over medium-high heat and cook until thickened slightly and reduced to 1½ cups, 8 to 10 minutes. Season the sauce with salt and pepper to taste.

7. Cut the meat into ½-inch slices or pull it apart into large pieces. Transfer the meat to the platter with the vegetables. Pour ½ cup of the sauce over the meat and vegetables and serve, passing the remaining sauce separately.

Notes from the Test Kitchen
We loved the apricots, and adding them with the potatoes and carrots during the last 30 minutes, rather than the last hour, preserved their texture but still gave them time to infuse flavor. Trisha used savory, but we left it out since it is hard to find. We also found 3½ hours, rather than 2 hours, of cooking was needed for a fall-apart-tender roast.

New England Boiled Dinner

RUTH FISHER | BROWNS MILLS, NEW JERSEY

"I grew up in Maine and when I need comfort food, this is what I cook. I remember well all of the traditional New England foods we ate. This recipe is the way my mother and grandmother made this dish." New England boiled dinner, like a pot roast supper, is emblematic of the region's practicality and frugality. Customarily, the cooking would begin shortly after breakfast, when corned beef was covered with water and set over a fire. After a few hours, vegetables would be added, and by noon a hearty meal was ready. Says Ruth of this nostalgic recipe, "When I eat this, it is like my grandparents and parents are at the table with me."

SERVES 8

- 3 bay leaves
- 1 tablespoon dried thyme
- 2 teaspoons whole black peppercorns
- 2 teaspoons whole allspice
- 1 (3- to 4-pound) corned beef, trimmed
- 1½ teaspoons salt
- 1½ teaspoons paprika
- 1 pound small beets, trimmed and scrubbed
- 1½ pounds small red potatoes, scrubbed
- 1½ pounds carrots, peeled and cut into 2-inch pieces
- 1 pound frozen pearl onions
- 1 medium head green cabbage, cut into 8 wedges (core left intact)

1. Tie the bay leaves, thyme, peppercorns, and allspice together in cheesecloth to make a sachet.

2. Place the corned beef and cheesecloth pouch in a large stockpot. Cover with cold water by 1 inch and bring to a simmer over medium-high heat, skimming any foam from the surface. Add the salt and paprika, cover, and cook until the meat is tender, 2½ to 3 hours.

3. Adjust an oven rack to the middle position and heat the oven to 200 degrees. Transfer the meat to a large baking dish and ladle 1 cup of the cooking liquid over the top. Cover with foil and keep warm in the oven.

4. Add the beets to the pot, return to a simmer, cover, and cook for 20 minutes. Add the potatoes, carrots, and onions, cover, and simmer until the vegetables are almost tender, about 10 minutes. Add the cabbage and continue to simmer until the vegetables are tender, 10 to 20 minutes longer.

5. Transfer the beets to a carving board and, using paper towels, gently peel off and discard the outer skin. Transfer the beets to a serving platter, along with the remaining vegetables. Discard the cheesecloth pouch.

6. Transfer the meat to the carving board, cut against the grain into ¼-inch slices, and transfer to the platter with the vegetables. Drizzle 1 cup of the cooking liquid over the top of the meat and vegetables and serve, passing the remaining cooking liquid separately.

Notes from the Test Kitchen

This otherwise traditional boiled dinner relies on the spice packet sometimes included with prepared corned beef for flavor. We found making our own spice blend lent cleaner flavor and made shopping easier since sometimes we couldn't find corned beef with this packet. Ruth's recipe adds the vegetables to the pot with the meat in stages (which is also the traditional way of doing it), but we found it all cooked more evenly if we waited until the meat was done, removed it from the pot, and then cooked the vegetables.

Pennsylvania Dutch Slippery Chicken Bott Bie

LAURA HOOVER | MIDDLETON, WISCONSIN

This Hoover family recipe isn't a crust-encased pot pie like you might think from the sound of its name. Laura's dish is rooted in the Pennsylvania Dutch tradition of the *botboi*, which does mean "pot pie," but these pot pies were actually stews with large, flat noodles—no crust at all. Laura's recipe takes this regional stew-based tradition another step, making it into more of a light soup. "Bott bie has been in our family for at least several generations. My grandmother always prepared her bott bie using only rabbit, potatoes, and noodle dough, probably due to a combination of factors: economic hardship during the 1930s, wartime rationing, and living in a rural area where hunting was a popular outdoor activity. My mother prepares her bott bie with chicken, as obtaining chicken from a supermarket became quicker, and certainly more reliable, than obtaining a rabbit from a good shot. She also added carrots to the pot, to increase both the nutritional value and the visual appeal. My contribution to the family tradition is the addition of French herbs to the broth to increase the flavor appeal."

SERVES 6 TO 8

BROTH
- 3 quarts water
- 2½ pounds bone-in, skin-on chicken leg quarters, trimmed
- 1 tablespoon salt

NOODLES
- 2 cups all-purpose flour, plus more as needed
- 2 large eggs, lightly beaten
- 1–2 tablespoons water
- 2 teaspoons vegetable oil

SOUP
- 1 pound Yukon gold potatoes, peeled and cut into ½-inch pieces
- 3 carrots, peeled and sliced thin
- 1 onion, minced
- 1 celery rib, sliced thin
- 1 tablespoon chopped fresh parsley
- 2 teaspoons chopped fresh tarragon
  Salt and pepper

1. FOR THE BROTH: Bring the water, chicken legs, and salt to a boil in a large Dutch oven, skimming any foam from the surface. Reduce to a simmer and cook until the chicken is tender, 1 to 1½ hours. Transfer the chicken to a plate.

2. When the chicken is cool enough to handle, remove the meat from the bones and shred into bite-sized pieces, discarding the skin and bones. Let the broth settle for 5 minutes, then use a wide spoon to skim the fat off the surface. Reserve the meat and broth separately.

3. FOR THE NOODLES: While the chicken simmers, pulse the flour a few times in a food processor to aerate. Add the eggs, 1 tablespoon of the water, and the oil, and process until the dough resembles coarse sand and stays together when pinched, about 30 seconds. If the dough does not stay together when pinched, add water, 1 teaspoon at a time, until it does. If the dough sticks to the sides of the bowl, add flour, 1 tablespoon at a time, until it no longer sticks.

4. Turn the dough onto a clean counter, form into a ball, and knead by hand two or three times. Cut the dough in half, flatten each piece into a square, and cover with plastic wrap. Let the dough rest for 10 minutes.

5. Working with one piece at a time, roll the dough out on a lightly floured counter into a 7½-inch square with a ⅛-inch thickness. Cut the dough into 1-inch squares, spread in a single layer on a baking sheet, and dust with flour.

6. FOR THE SOUP: Return the reserved broth to a boil and add the noodles, one handful at a time, stirring frequently to prevent sticking. Reduce the heat to medium-low and cook the noodles for 25 minutes.

7. Add the potatoes, carrots, onion, and celery and continue to cook until the noodles and vegetables are tender, about 10 minutes longer.

8. Return the shredded chicken to the soup and cook until heated through, about 1 minute. Stir in the parsley and tarragon, season with salt and pepper to taste, and serve.

Notes from the Test Kitchen

The title of this recipe is a mouthful, but the dish is actually quite light and brothy, and once we understood the gist of Laura's take on bott bie stew, we became converts. The handmade noodles are minimally kneaded, which makes them easier to roll out, but also more fragile during cooking. We agree with Laura's advice that a long, gentle simmer is the key to tenderizing, and not destroying, the little squares. Laura's recipe required little change by us. The only small adjustments we made, in the name of user-friendliness, were substituting a little additional tarragon for the chervil called for in the original and letting the food processor do the dough mixing, rather than making it by hand.

PREPARING NOODLES FOR BOTT BIE

1. Cut the dough in half, flatten each piece into a square, cover with plastic wrap, and let rest for 10 minutes. Working with one piece at a time, roll the dough out on a lightly floured counter into a 7½-inch square with a ⅛-inch thickness.

2. With a pizza cutter or chef's knife, cut the dough into 1-inch squares, then spread the noodles in a single layer on a baking sheet and dust with flour.

Coke Oven Fried Chicken

DEBBIE FLEENOR | MONTEREY, TENNESSEE

"My grandparents lived in a coal camp in the 1940s. To help supplement their meager income, my grandmother would fry chicken for the miners' supper. When the oil lamps in the house were empty, she would fry her chicken outside, by the light of the coke ovens. Her fried chicken was so delicious that even the 'rich city folk' would come out to buy it. She gave away as many pieces as she sold, always catering to those who didn't have as much as she. My grandmother never had a pair of new shoes until she was in her forties, but she always had a smile, a helping hand, and a generous plate of fried chicken."

SERVES 4

- 2 cups buttermilk
- 3 tablespoons ground ginger
- 3 tablespoons ground sage
- 2 tablespoons salt
- 3 pounds bone-in, skin-on chicken pieces (split breasts cut in half, drumsticks, and/or thighs), trimmed
- 1¼ cups all-purpose flour
- 1 teaspoon onion powder
- 1 teaspoon sugar
- ½ teaspoon pepper
  Pinch baking soda
- 3–4 quarts vegetable oil

1. Stir the buttermilk, 1 tablespoon of the ginger, 1 tablespoon of the sage, and the salt together in a large bowl. Submerge the chicken completely in the buttermilk mixture, cover, and refrigerate for 1 hour.

2. Set a wire rack over a rimmed baking sheet. Whisk the remaining 2 tablespoons ginger, remaining 2 tablespoons sage, the flour, onion powder, sugar, pepper, and baking soda together in a shallow dish. Remove the chicken from the brine and, working with 3 pieces at a time, dredge in the flour mixture, shake off the excess, and transfer to the prepared wire rack. Refrigerate, uncovered, for 2 hours.

3. Adjust an oven rack to the middle position and heat the oven to 200 degrees.

4. Pour the oil into a large Dutch oven until it measures 2 inches deep. Heat the oil to 350 degrees over medium-high heat. Add half of the chicken pieces to the pot, skin-side down. Cover and cook, adjusting the heat as necessary to maintain an oil temperature of 325 degrees, until deep golden brown, 5 to 7 minutes. (After 2 minutes, check the chicken pieces for even browning and rearrange if some pieces are browning faster than others.)

5. Turn the chicken pieces over and continue to cook, uncovered, until deep golden brown and fully cooked (160 to 165 degrees for breasts and 175 degrees for thighs or drumsticks on an instant-read thermometer), 4 to 7 minutes longer. Drain the chicken briefly on a large paper towel–lined plate, then transfer to a clean wire rack set over a rimmed baking sheet and keep warm in the oven.

6. Return the oil to 350 degrees over medium-high heat and repeat with the remaining chicken pieces. Serve.

Notes from the Test Kitchen

Ginger and sage add a nice twist to this otherwise classic fried chicken. While Debbie's recipe had a flavorful crust, turning the buttermilk marinade into a brine of salt, powdered ginger, and sage seasoned the meat throughout. Air-drying the chicken after dredging it produced a crispier crust, while adding a pinch of baking soda lightened it up.

Louisiana Smothered Rabbit

VANESSA GERONDALE | HOUSTON, TEXAS

"My maternal grandparents were true Louisiana country people. They grew vegetables and raised chickens, goats, hogs, and cows. My grandfather hunted and we ate what he shot, including rabbits (and deer, squirrels, turtles, and alligators). This recipe is how my grandmother smothered all manner of wild meat, until it was falling-off-the-bone tender." With its cream-enriched mustard-wine sauce, Vanessa's rabbit recipe is about as flavorful as it is old-fashioned. She suggests serving over rice or egg noodles.

SERVES 4 TO 6

- 2 (3½- to 4-pound) rabbits, each rabbit cut into 7 pieces, thin membrane on the loin removed
  Salt and pepper
- ¼ cup vegetable oil
- 1 onion, halved and sliced thin
- 2 teaspoons minced fresh thyme
- 2 cups low-sodium chicken broth
- ½ cup dry white wine
- ½ cup water
- 3 tablespoons Dijon mustard
- ⅓ cup heavy cream
- 2 teaspoons fresh lemon juice
- 1 tablespoon chopped fresh tarragon

1. Adjust an oven rack to the lower-middle position and heat the oven to 300 degrees.

2. Pat the rabbit dry with paper towels and season with salt and pepper. Heat 2 tablespoons of the oil in a large Dutch oven over medium-high heat until just smoking. Add one-third of the rabbit pieces and cook until golden brown on both sides, 8 to 10 minutes, flipping halfway through. Transfer the rabbit to a plate. Return the pot to medium-high heat and repeat with the remaining rabbit pieces in two batches, using 1 tablespoon more oil for each batch.

3. Add the onion to the pot and cook over medium heat, stirring occasionally, until softened, 5 to 7 minutes. Stir in the thyme and cook until fragrant, about 30 seconds. Stir in the broth, wine, water, and mustard, scraping up any browned bits.

4. Return the forequarters, hindquarters, and necks, along with any accumulated juices, to the pot. Bring to a simmer, cover, and transfer to the oven. Cook the rabbit until the meat is tender, about 1½ hours.

5. Return the loin pieces, along with any accumulated juices, to the pot. Continue to cook until the rabbit is tender and an instant-read thermometer inserted into the center of the loins registers 145 degrees, about 10 minutes longer.

6. Transfer the rabbit to a serving platter and tent loosely with foil. Stir in the cream, bring the sauce to a simmer, and cook until thickened and reduced to about 1½ cups, about 10 minutes. Off the heat, stir in the lemon juice and season with salt and pepper to taste. Spoon the sauce over the rabbit, sprinkle with the tarragon, and serve.

Notes from the Test Kitchen

Though flavorful, ½ cup of braising liquid wasn't enough, so we added chicken broth. Vanessa's mustard rub interfered with browning, so we stirred it into the sauce. Searing the rabbit in a Dutch oven, then transferring it with the braising liquid to the oven for a slow braise helped streamline the process. It's easiest to have your butcher prepare the rabbit: two hindquarters, two forequarters, two loin pieces, and the neck. The membrane on the loin can be removed at home. Chicken thighs will also work: In step 4, cook the chicken until the thickest part of the thighs registers 175 degrees on an instant-read thermometer, about 1 hour, and skip step 5.

Duck Gumbo

HELEN PALMER ONCKEN | HOUSTON, TEXAS

"When she was fourteen, my grandmother, Bessie Brown Grant, moved from Clayton to Cushing, Texas, where her mother established a boarding house and served meals not only to her boarders, but also the locals. When her mother died, Grandmother Grant, who was by then married with three daughters, took over running the establishment. In 1926, the family moved to Nacogdoches, where Grandmother established the Grant Boarding House on Church Street. Later, Grandmother moved to Mound Street, where she continued having boarders and serving meals until she retired. I chose this duck recipe from the hundreds of recipes Mother had compiled throughout her lifetime. I still remember Daddy and his friends bringing their kill home and Mother and her friends helping clean the ducks and preparing them. They had some great times doing this! We now have three grown sons who enjoy cooking and grilling. At least once a year, we all get together in our kitchen and prepare this recipe."

SERVES 6

- 8 ounces salt pork, chopped
- 2 pounds bone-in, skin-on duck leg quarters, trimmed
  Salt and pepper
- 1 tablespoon vegetable oil, plus more as needed
- ½ cup all-purpose flour
- 2 onions, minced
- 2 celery ribs, chopped fine
- 1 red bell pepper, stemmed, seeded, and chopped fine
- 6 garlic cloves, minced
- 2 bay leaves
- 4 cups low-sodium chicken broth, warmed
- 1 (14.5-ounce) can diced tomatoes
- 1 pound fresh okra, trimmed and sliced ¼ inch thick
- 2 teaspoons filé powder

1. Cook the salt pork in a large Dutch oven over medium-low heat until crisp, about 10 minutes. Strain the salt pork and fat though a fine-mesh strainer into a liquid measuring cup and set aside. Discard the salt pork.

2. Pat the duck dry with paper towels and season with salt and pepper. Heat the 1 tablespoon vegetable oil in the pot over medium heat until shimmering. Add the duck, skin-side down, and lower the heat to medium-low. Cook, adjusting the heat as needed for the fat to maintain a constant but gentle simmer, until most of the fat is rendered and the skin is deep golden and crisp, 25 to 30 minutes. Flip the duck over and continue to cook until golden brown on the second side, 6 to 8 minutes longer. Transfer the duck to a plate.

(Continued on page 166)

3. Pour off the fat into the measuring cup with the salt pork fat. Add enough vegetable oil to the measuring cup to equal ½ cup. Heat the fat in the pot over medium heat until just smoking. Gradually stir in the flour with a wooden spoon, working out any lumps that form. Cook, stirring constantly and reaching into the edges of the pan, until the mixture has a toasty aroma and is deep reddish brown, about 20 minutes. (The roux will become thinner as it cooks. If it begins to smoke, remove the pan from the heat and stir the roux constantly to cool slightly.)

4. Add the onions, celery, bell pepper, and 1 teaspoon salt to the roux and cook, stirring occasionally, until the vegetables are softened, 8 to 10 minutes. Stir in the garlic and bay leaves and cook until fragrant, about 30 seconds.

5. Gradually stir in 1 cup of the warm broth, scraping up any browned bits. Stir in the remaining 3 cups broth and the tomatoes. Return the duck legs, along with any accumulated juices, to the pot. Bring to a simmer and cook until the duck legs are tender, 1 to 1½ hours.

6. Transfer the duck legs to a plate. When the duck is cool enough to handle, remove the meat from the bones and shred into bite-sized pieces; discard the skin and bones.

7. Meanwhile, simmer the gumbo for 30 minutes, then stir in the okra and shredded duck meat. Continue to cook until the okra is tender, about 30 minutes longer.

8. Discard the bay leaves. Off the heat, stir in the filé powder, cover, and let sit until thickened slightly, about 5 minutes. Season with salt and pepper to taste and serve.

Notes from the Test Kitchen

Gumbo is an old Creole-style Southern staple open to lots of interpretation, and this flavorful duck version does not disappoint. The original recipe used a whole duck (convenient if you just shot it), which we replaced with the more accessible option of duck leg quarters. And in lieu of poaching a whole duck stuffed with aromatics and vegetables to make stock (which we found had little flavor after the recipe's relatively short cooking time anyway), we instead used chicken broth. To create even more duck flavor, we seared the duck legs to render the fat, which we then used when making the roux. Because a dark brown roux is the heart and foundation of a good gumbo, we found it important to take our time (it took about 20 minutes) to reach the nice chocolaty brown color Helen indicated in her recipe. Make sure to stir the roux constantly to prevent burning.

Blue Ridge Baked Bean Burgoo

JANICE ELDER | CHARLOTTE, NORTH CAROLINA

"Having recently unearthed a file of index cards with recipes from my early days of marriage in the 1970s, I found it quite interesting seeing what, and how, I cooked at that time. Cooking on a budget was definitely the underlying theme, but we enjoyed sitting down as a family to dinner every night, even if the fare was economical. This one I remember as a particular family favorite—quick yet delicious." Though Janice hails from the Tar Heel State (North Carolina), her recipe stands as an institution in another Southern locale: Kentucky. Burgoo was a dish born of necessity, mixing together any ingredients available at the moment, whether hunted or harvested. Though once more commonly found, today burgoo is a mainstay in Kentucky alone. There it is now known as a thick, heady meat stew of tomatoes, corn, potatoes, chicken, and mutton. Janice's recipe, a riff on Kentucky's burgoo, is a vegetarian-friendly version that offers a mix of bell pepper, celery, onion, tomatoes, and the sweet tang of baked beans, topped with crunchy pecans. Serve this over rice for a filling dinner that you can put together quickly any night of the week.

SERVES 6

- 1 tablespoon vegetable oil
- 1 onion, minced
- 1 green bell pepper, stemmed, seeded, and chopped
- 1 celery rib, chopped
- 1 tablespoon chili powder
- 2 (16-ounce) cans baked beans
- 2 (14.5-ounce) cans stewed tomatoes
- 1¾ cups low-sodium chicken broth
  Salt and pepper
- 2 plum tomatoes, cored, seeded, and chopped
- ⅓ cup pecans, toasted and chopped fine

1. Heat the oil in a large Dutch oven over medium heat until shimmering. Add the onion, bell pepper, and celery and cook, stirring occasionally, until softened, 5 to 7 minutes. Stir in the chili powder and cook until fragrant, about 30 seconds. Stir in the beans, stewed tomatoes, and broth.

2. Bring to a simmer and cook, stirring often, until the sauce has thickened slightly, 10 to 15 minutes. Season with salt and pepper to taste.

3. Sprinkle individual portions with the plum tomatoes and pecans and serve.

Notes from the Test Kitchen

We appreciated Janice's Blue Ridge take on a Kentucky staple, opting for beans rather than the usual meat. Her homey recipe comes together in minutes and has a sweet-savory flavor we loved. Instead of adding the chili powder with the beans, broth, and tomatoes as Janice did, we found that adding it to the pan when sautéing the onions, pepper, and celery helped to deepen its flavor, rather than dilute it in all the liquid. Janice noted that she usually uses leftover homemade baked beans, and used canned beans in a pinch. For the sake of simplicity, we just went with the canned (our favorite brand is B&M Vegetarian Baked Beans). If you want to make this an entirely vegetarian dish, you can use vegetable broth rather than chicken broth.

Cincinnati Chili

THE EDITORS OF COOK'S COUNTRY

Most of us know chili as a meaty, spicy, thick red stew. That's the stuff with Southwestern roots—a far cry from what they serve up in Cincinnati. There, chili means a thin brown meat sauce with warm (not spicy) seasonings, like cinnamon, allspice, and cloves, and it's ladled over spaghetti or spooned onto hot dogs (locally referred to as Coneys). And let's not forget all the garnishes that top it off: beans, onions, oyster crackers, and, of course, a hefty pile of shredded cheese. Cincinnati chili was first served from a hot dog cart, a business that has since turned into a well-known local chain, Empress Chili, started by two Greek immigrants in 1922. Soon enough the one-of-a-kind chili became a local phenomenon that has since spawned numerous chili parlors—and even more fans. Serve our recipe over spaghetti with all the classic garnishes.

SERVES 6 TO 8

1	tablespoon vegetable oil
2	onions, minced
2	tablespoons tomato paste
2	tablespoons chili powder
1	tablespoon dried oregano
1½	teaspoons ground cinnamon
1	garlic clove, minced
	Salt and pepper
¼	teaspoon ground allspice
2	cups low-sodium chicken broth
2	cups tomato sauce
2	tablespoons cider vinegar
2	teaspoons dark brown sugar
1½	pounds 85 percent lean ground beef

1. Heat the oil in a Dutch oven over medium heat until shimmering. Add the onions and cook, stirring occasionally, until softened and browned around the edges, about 8 minutes. Stir in the tomato paste, chili powder, oregano, cinnamon, garlic, 1 teaspoon salt, ¾ teaspoon pepper, and allspice and cook until fragrant, about 30 seconds. Stir in the chicken broth, tomato sauce, vinegar, and sugar.

2. Add the beef, breaking up any large clumps with a wooden spoon. Bring to a simmer and cook until the chili is deep brown and thickened slightly, 15 to 20 minutes. Season with salt and pepper to taste and serve.

Notes from the Test Kitchen

Tender meat and just the right combination and balance of spices are the keys to great Cincinnati chili. Starting with the spices, we found recipes with unexpected choices like mace, ginger, nutmeg, and even chocolate, but in the end, a simple combination of cinnamon, allspice, chili powder, and oregano gave us the flavor we were after. Most area chili parlors get their beef ultra-tender by boiling it in water before adding it to the spiced liquid. To keep things simple, we just boiled our meat right in the sauce rather than separately. We also found that unlike a spicy bowl of red, this regional favorite will be on the table in minutes, not hours—another reason we couldn't help but love it.

Pivoto-Robinson Shrimp Creole

TINA ROBINSON | SANTA FE, TEXAS

"My ancestors settled in Texas in the 1830s. The old homestead served as a stagecoach stop, cattle-drive bed-down, schoolhouse, and gathering place for many social events. The food was raised, grown, or caught nearby and, being close to Galveston Bay, fresh fish and shrimp were favorite components. My mother would make large batches of shrimp Creole for her Junior Trivium Club annual fundraiser, and I helped peel and devein the shrimp. I have repeated the preparation many times. The aroma and the sight of the rich, chunky Creole ladled over a pile of white rice brings everyone to the table."

SERVES 10 TO 12

4	pounds large shrimp, peeled, shells reserved, and shrimp deveined
2½	cups water
½	cup vegetable oil
½	cup all-purpose flour
2	onions, minced
2	celery ribs, chopped fine
1	red bell pepper, stemmed, seeded, and chopped fine
	Salt
6	garlic cloves, minced
2	bay leaves
¼	teaspoon celery salt
	Pepper
⅛	teaspoon ground cloves
1½	cups tomato juice
1	(14.5-ounce) can stewed tomatoes
4	ripe tomatoes, cored, seeded, and chopped
¼	cup ketchup
2	tablespoons Worcestershire sauce
1	tablespoon hot sauce

1. Bring the reserved shrimp shells and water to a simmer in a large saucepan over medium-high heat and cook for 20 minutes. Strain the stock through a fine-mesh strainer and discard the shells. Set the stock aside to cool slightly.

2. Heat the oil in a Dutch oven over medium heat until just smoking. Gradually stir in the flour with a wooden spoon, working out any lumps that form. Cook, stirring constantly, and reaching into the edges of the pan, until the mixture has a toasty aroma and is deep reddish brown, about 20 minutes. (The roux will become thinner as it cooks; if it begins to smoke, remove the pan from the heat and stir the roux constantly to cool slightly.)

3. Add the onions, celery, bell pepper, and 1 teaspoon salt to the roux and cook, stirring occasionally, until the vegetables are softened, 8 to 10 minutes. Stir in the garlic, bay leaves, celery salt, ¼ teaspoon pepper, and cloves and cook until fragrant, about 30 seconds.

4. Gradually stir in 1 cup of the reserved shrimp stock. Stir in the remaining stock, the tomato juice, stewed tomatoes, chopped tomatoes, ketchup, Worcestershire sauce, and hot sauce. Bring to a simmer and cook until thickened, about 2 hours.

5. Stir in the shrimp and cook until just cooked through, 3 to 5 minutes. Discard the bay leaves and season with salt and pepper to taste. Serve.

Notes from the Test Kitchen

The original recipe served 50 people, so we scaled it down to serve 10 to 12, perfect for a small gathering. While it took Tina 1 hour to make her roux, in 20 minutes ours was a deep chocolate color (stir it constantly to prevent burning). The shrimp only needed about 5 minutes (rather than 20 minutes) to cook. This is a spicy Creole, so adjust the hot sauce as needed.

Chesapeake Partan Bree

CAMILLA SAULSBURY | NACOGDOCHES, TEXAS

"My father grew up in the Eastern Shore area of Maryland, along the Chesapeake Bay; his family has been living there since the 1600s. His mother was a phenomenal cook and was particularly proud of her Scottish-American and Irish-American roots. She combined the two by making a wide range of dishes that were passed down from her mother and grandmother (and even further back than that). One of her specialties: partan bree. *Partan* is the Scottish word for a crab, and *bree* is a liquid in which something edible has been boiled and left to soak. It's a famous Scottish soup that was brought over by Scottish settlers, including my ancestors, and was very popular in coastal areas on the east coast of the United States. My grandmother's version had two incredible regional additions that were in abundance when she was alive: fresh morels and Chesapeake Bay crab. My dad made this throughout my childhood, and even though he moved to the San Francisco Bay Area after college, he was still able to get fantastic crab and fresh produce to carry on the tradition of this great Scottish-American soup. I've made a few little tweaks to the recipe over the years, but it is very close to my grandmother's original version (according to my dad, who is the only person who has tasted both). I love to serve this to friends and acquaintances of all kinds, in part to disprove the notion that Scottish cooking is bland, tasteless, and uninspired. Everyone loves it! And it's easy enough that I can make it for weeknight suppers as easily as for special occasions. A final note: the best thing to eat with this soup is Maryland beaten biscuits. They are shaped like little eggs and are pure heaven."

SERVES 8

- 1¼ cups water
- ¾ cup long-grain white rice, rinsed until the water runs clear
- Salt
- 8 ears corn, husks and silk removed
- 4 cups low-sodium chicken broth
- 3 cups heavy cream
- 8 slices bacon, chopped
- 8 ounces morel mushrooms, sliced thin, or shiitake mushrooms, stemmed and sliced thin
- 1½ tablespoons minced fresh thyme
- 2 tablespoons whiskey
- 2 tablespoons unsalted butter
- 3 leeks, white and light green parts only, chopped fine
- 2 celery ribs, chopped fine
- 1 pound crabmeat, picked over for shells
- Pepper
- 3 tablespoons minced fresh chives

1. Bring the water, rice, and a pinch salt to a boil in a medium saucepan over medium heat. Reduce the heat to low, cover, and cook until all the water is absorbed, about 15 minutes. Off the heat, remove the lid and place a clean kitchen towel folded in half over the saucepan. Replace the lid and let sit.

2. Stand the corn upright inside a bowl and carefully cut the kernels from 5 ears of the corn using a paring knife. Grate the remaining 3 ears corn on the large holes of a box grater into a separate bowl. Scrape any remaining pulp from the cobs into the bowl with the grated corn using the back of a butter knife. (Do not discard the cobs.)

3. Combine the cobs, broth, and cream in a large saucepan, bring to a simmer, and cook for 5 minutes. Cover and let steep off the heat for 20 minutes, then discard the cobs.

4. Meanwhile, cook the bacon in a large Dutch oven over medium-low heat until crisp, about 10 minutes. Using a slotted spoon, transfer the bacon to a paper towel–lined plate.

5. Pour off all but 3 tablespoons of the bacon fat and return the pot to medium-high heat until shimmering. Add the mushrooms and cook, stirring occasionally, until they have released their juices and are brown around the edges, 7 to 10 minutes. Stir in the thyme and cook until fragrant, about 30 seconds. Stir in the whiskey and cook until evaporated, about 30 seconds. Transfer the mushroom mixture to a bowl and cover to keep warm.

6. Melt the butter in the pot over medium heat. Add the leeks, celery, and ½ teaspoon salt and cook, stirring occasionally, until softened, 5 to 7 minutes. Stir in the broth mixture and grated corn, scraping up any browned bits. Bring to a simmer and cook until the flavors have combined, about 5 minutes.

7. Stir in the corn kernels and rice and continue to cook until the kernels are crisp-tender, about 3 minutes. Stir in the reserved mushroom mixture and crabmeat and cook until heated through, about 1 minute. Season with salt and pepper to taste. Sprinkle individual portions with the reserved bacon and the chives and serve.

Notes from the Test Kitchen

Tasters were unanimous that this old Maryland crab soup with corn needed only the smallest of tweaks—it was near-perfect. To save us from one more pan to clean, rather than sauté the mushrooms in a separate pan, we just cooked them in the same pot we were using, after we'd cooked the bacon and before the leeks and celery. Camilla uses sublime fresh morels in her soup, but these specialty mushrooms can be difficult to find. We discovered that shiitake mushrooms, stemmed and sliced thin, are a fine substitute if you can't find morels.

Char's Maine Fish Chowder

CHARLENE CHAMBERS | ORMOND BEACH, FLORIDA

"Years ago, when my husband, Jere, and I used to vacation in a lovely cabin in Maine on Moosehead Lake, I would make this chowder with fresh fish we picked up in Camden on our way up. This was our private getaway cabin where the two of us could reconnect while our children were at camp for two weeks. It was heaven—and so was the food I cooked with the fresh seafood and fresh vegetables!" Like most of the fish chowders you'll find along Route 1 running down the coast of Maine, Charlene's fish chowder is a brothy, milky—and flour-free—chowder. Unlike a thicker style of chowder (think Boston-style clam chowder), this looser soup lets the fish (and the bacon cooked with it) take center stage. You might not have a cabin in Maine to escape to, but this fish chowder will bring the Down East flavors right into your own kitchen.

SERVES 4 TO 6

- 8   slices bacon, chopped
- 3   onions, minced
-     Salt
- ½   cup dry white wine
- 3   (8-ounce) bottles clam juice
- 1½ pounds red potatoes, scrubbed and cut into ½-inch pieces
- 2   teaspoons minced fresh thyme
- 2   bay leaves
- 5   cups whole milk
- 2   pounds haddock or cod fillets, cut into 1-inch chunks
- 2   tablespoons unsalted butter, cut into ½-inch pieces
-     Pepper

1. Cook the bacon in a large Dutch oven over medium-low heat until crisp, about 10 minutes. Using a slotted spoon, transfer the bacon to a paper towel–lined plate.

2. Pour off all but 2 tablespoons of the bacon fat and return the pot to medium heat until shimmering. Add the onions and ¾ teaspoon salt and cook, stirring occasionally, until softened, 5 to 7 minutes.

3. Add the wine and cook until almost evaporated, 1 to 2 minutes. Stir in the clam juice, scraping up any browned bits. Stir in the potatoes, thyme, and bay leaves. Bring to a simmer and cook until the potatoes are almost tender, 10 to 15 minutes.

4. Stir in the milk and fish and cook over medium-high heat until the milk is hot and tiny bubbles begin to appear around the edge of the pot (do not simmer or boil) and the fish is just cooked through, 8 to 12 minutes.

5. Discard the bay leaves. Stir in the butter and season with salt and pepper to taste. Stir in the reserved bacon and serve.

Notes from the Test Kitchen

This simple, brothy chowder had a freshness about it that we could all appreciate. Charlene used 8 cups of milk and one bottle of clam juice in her original recipe, which tasters found to be a bit too milky, so to get more fish flavor we settled on 5 cups of milk and three bottles of clam juice. Adding ½ cup of dry white wine helped to cut the richness and round out the flavors.

Long Island Clam Pie

JOAN CARMAN | STUART, FLORIDA

"We lived on the South Shore of Long Island, where we could tread for hard clams any time we wanted. When we got tired of clams on the half-shell, clam chowder, clam fritters, and linguine and clam sauce, my mother-in-law would say, 'How about a clam pie?' 'Yes!' we would shout." Historically, Long Islanders have always been enthusiastic about clams, even when eighteenth-century northern New Englanders thought of them disparagingly. Clam pie became a particular specialty of the area, specifically of East Hampton's Bonacker culture, the families of working-class pioneers who came over from England. Basically clams and potatoes baked in a pie crust, it was certainly a thrifty family meal. Though made long before, the first recipe for clam pie appeared in print in 1896, in the cookbook *The Lady's Village Improvement Society of East Hampton*. In modern times the Long Islanders' love of clam pie has remained strong—every edition of that cookbook has continued to have at least one East Hampton clam pie recipe. The 1955 edition had a whopping four!

SERVES 8

CRUST

2½	cups all-purpose flour
1	teaspoon salt
8	tablespoons vegetable shortening, cut into ¼-inch pieces and chilled
12	tablespoons (1½ sticks) unsalted butter, cut into ¼-inch pieces and chilled
6–8	tablespoons ice water

FILLING

8	slices bacon, chopped
1	onion, minced
½	teaspoon salt
1	teaspoon minced fresh thyme
¼	teaspoon pepper
2	tablespoons all-purpose flour
1	(8-ounce) bottle clam juice
¾	cup heavy cream
1	pound Yukon gold potatoes, peeled and sliced ¼ inch thick
1	pound chopped clams, drained (about 2 cups)

1. FOR THE CRUST: Process the flour and salt together in a food processor until combined. Scatter the shortening over the top and process until the mixture resembles coarse cornmeal, about 10 seconds. Scatter the butter pieces over the top and pulse the mixture until it resembles coarse crumbs, about 10 pulses. Transfer the mixture to a bowl.

2. Sprinkle 6 tablespoons of the ice water over the mixture. Stir and press the dough together, using a stiff rubber spatula, until the dough sticks together. If the dough does not come together, stir in the remaining water, 1 tablespoon at a time, until it does.

3. Divide the dough into two even pieces. Turn each piece of dough onto a sheet of plastic wrap and flatten each into a 4-inch disk. Wrap each piece tightly in the plastic wrap and refrigerate for at least 1 hour, or up to 2 days. Before rolling out the dough, let it sit on the counter to soften slightly, about 10 minutes.

4. FOR THE FILLING: Cook the bacon in a large saucepan over medium-low heat until crisp,

(Continued on page 176)

about 10 minutes. Using a slotted spoon, transfer the bacon to a paper towel–lined plate. Add the onion and salt to the pot and cook, stirring occasionally, until softened, 5 to 7 minutes. Stir in the thyme and pepper and cook until fragrant, about 30 seconds. Stir in the flour and cook for 1 minute. Slowly stir in the clam juice and cream, scraping up any browned bits.

5. Add the potatoes, bring to a simmer, and cook until just tender, 10 to 15 minutes. Transfer the filling to a bowl and refrigerate until cooled slightly, about 45 minutes.

6. TO ASSEMBLE AND BAKE: While the filling cools, adjust an oven rack to the lowest position, place a foil-lined rimmed baking sheet on the rack, and heat the oven to 425 degrees.

7. Roll one disk of dough on a lightly floured counter to a 12-inch circle, about ⅛ inch thick. Fit the dough into a 9-inch deep-dish pie plate, letting the excess dough hang over the edge; cover and refrigerate for 30 minutes. Roll out the second disk of dough to a 12-inch circle on a lightly floured counter, then transfer to a parchment-lined baking sheet; cover and refrigerate for 30 minutes.

8. When the filling has cooled, gently fold in the clams and reserved bacon. Pour the filling into the dough-lined pie plate and gently pack

the potatoes into an even layer, removing any air pockets. Loosely roll the second dough circle around the rolling pin and gently unroll it over the pie. Trim, fold, and crimp the edges, then cut eight vent holes in the top.

9. Place the pie on the heated baking sheet and bake until the crust is golden, about 30 minutes. Reduce the oven temperature to 375 degrees, rotate the baking sheet, and continue to bake until the filling is bubbling and the crust is deep golden brown, 25 to 35 minutes longer. Cool the pie on a wire rack to room temperature, about 2 hours, before serving.

Notes from the Test Kitchen

This classic clam pie recipe is essentially clam chowder baked in a pie shell. Joan used milk combined with the juice left over from shucking the clams as the base for her filling, but we felt the recipe would stay more consistent from one batch to the next if we just stuck with 1 bottle of clam juice. We also replaced the milk with cream to prevent the filling from curdling, which can often happen when cooking milk for a long time. We swapped out the savory called for in the original recipe for easier-to-find thyme and used our test-kitchen method of baking the pie on a preheated baking sheet to ensure a crisp, golden crust.

MAKING A DOUBLE-CRUST PIE

1. After pouring the filling into the dough-lined pie plate, loosely roll the top crust around the rolling pin, then gently unroll it over the filled pie crust bottom.

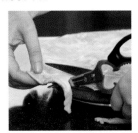

2. Trim all but ½ inch of the dough overhanging the edge of the pie plate with scissors, then press the top and bottom crusts together and tuck the edges underneath.

3. Crimp the dough evenly around the edge of the pie, using the index finger of one hand and the thumb and index finger of the other.

4. Cut eight 2-inch slits in the center of the top crust with a paring knife, then move the pie to the oven to bake.

Grandma Taylor's Crab Cakes

WILLIAM AND LIBBY HOOVER | LAS VEGAS, NEVADA

This Hoover family recipe is claimed by Libby's side of the family, contributed by her Grandmother Taylor. The recipe comes from Chincoteague Island, Virginia, on the state's Eastern Shore. Located on the Chesapeake Bay, Chincoteague is right in the middle of a region well known for its culinary tradition—all things crab. With only a cup of bread crumbs to a full pound of crab, this recipe, unlike a lot of filler-heavy recipes, promises fresh, meaty, tender cakes that emphasize the star ingredient. Though Worcestershire sauce and dry mustard are not unusual inclusions in Chesapeake crab cake recipes, the ginger is an addition that lends a unique flavor, making this family recipe even more of a standout.

SERVES 4

- 4 tablespoons (½ stick) unsalted butter
- 1 small onion, minced
- 1 pound crabmeat, picked over for shells
- 2 slices hearty white sandwich bread, torn into large pieces and pulsed in a food processor to crumbs
- ¼ cup chopped fresh parsley
- 1 teaspoon dry mustard
- ¾ teaspoon Worcestershire sauce
- ½ teaspoon salt
- ¼ teaspoon pepper
- ¼ teaspoon ground ginger
- 1 large egg, lightly beaten
- ¼ cup all-purpose flour
- ¼ cup vegetable oil
- 1 lemon, cut into wedges

1. Melt the butter in a medium skillet over medium heat. Add the onion and cook, stirring occasionally, until softened, 5 to 7 minutes. Set aside to cool to room temperature.

2. Gently toss the onion, crabmeat, bread crumbs, parsley, mustard, Worcestershire sauce, salt, pepper, and ginger together in a bowl. Gently fold in the egg.

3. Divide the crab mixture into four equal portions and shape each into a 3-inch-wide patty. Transfer the patties to a plastic wrap–lined plate. Cover with plastic wrap and refrigerate until firm, about 30 minutes.

4. Spread the flour in a shallow dish. Coat the crab cakes lightly with the flour. Heat the oil in a large nonstick skillet over medium heat until shimmering. Gently lay the crab cakes in the skillet and cook until crisp and light golden brown on both sides, 8 to 10 minutes, flipping halfway through. Serve with the lemon wedges.

Notes from the Test Kitchen

Bursting with fresh meaty crab, these cakes kept our test-kitchen tasters coming back for more. We didn't find any need to change her combination of seasonings, but to combat cakes that were too wet, we reduced the eggs from two to one. We also swapped the cracker-meal coating in the original recipe for flour to coat the cakes before frying. We found that cracker meal didn't add anything unique, and flour is a much more convenient choice.

Great-Grandma's Corn Fritters

SALLY NASH | FALLS CHURCH, VIRGINIA

"These fritters are unlike most; they are light, airy, and delicate. My great-grandmother was a cook at an inn in Pennsylvania and these were one of her specialties. My grandmother made them every year for my mother on her birthday, and my mom and I recently rediscovered them together and made them for the family." What makes these fritters so light? Sally incorporates beaten egg whites, making them more like little fluffy corn pancakes than heavy fried fritters. Corn fritters are often tied historically to New England and the mid-Atlantic, as even the earliest immigrants were making such fritters (then called corn oysters), since corn was readily available. The fresh flavor of Sally's fritters makes them perfect for any summertime spread.

SERVES 6 TO 8

8 ears corn, husks and silk removed
3 large eggs, separated
2 tablespoons all-purpose flour
¾ teaspoon salt
¼ teaspoon pepper
  Pinch cream of tartar
1 teaspoon sugar
6 tablespoons vegetable oil
2 tablespoons minced fresh chives

1. Adjust an oven rack to the middle position and heat the oven to 200 degrees. Set a wire rack over a rimmed baking sheet and set aside.

2. Grate each ear of corn over the large holes of a box grater into a bowl. Using the back of a butter knife, scrape any remaining milk from the cobs into the bowl.

3. Whisk the egg yolks, flour, salt, and pepper into the corn mixture. In a medium bowl, whip the egg whites and cream of tartar with an electric mixer on medium-low speed until foamy. Increase the speed to medium-high, gradually add the sugar, and whip until the whites form stiff peaks, 1 to 3 minutes. Gently fold the whipped egg whites into the batter until combined.

4. Heat 1 tablespoon of the oil in a large nonstick skillet over medium-high heat until shimmering. Drop 6 heaping tablespoons of batter into the oil, then flatten each into a 2½-inch-diameter circle with the back of the spoon. Cook until puffed and golden brown on both sides, about 2 minutes, flipping halfway through. Transfer the fritters to a paper towel–lined plate, then transfer to the prepared wire rack and keep warm in the oven. Repeat with the remaining oil and the remaining batter in five batches. Sprinkle with the chives and serve.

Notes from the Test Kitchen

These feather-light corn fritters were different than any we had ever tasted, more crepe or pancake than traditional fritter. We did add a pinch of cream of tartar and a teaspoon of sugar to the whites to help stabilize them and create a more reliable batter. The sugar also helped bring out the corn's sweetness. We found that an extra tablespoon of flour added needed structure. Wanting a bit more corn flavor, we increased the amount of corn from the recommended four to five ears up to eight ears. While Sally's original recipe used clarified butter to fry her fritters, we found vegetable oil to be a fine, and easier, option. With a little extra salt (we added ¼ teaspoon more) and a sprinkling of fresh chives, these corn fritters disappeared as fast as we could make them.

Baked Boston Brown Bread

MARIANNA VAN ERP | MOUNTAIN VIEW, CALIFORNIA

Robust, dense, and slightly sweet, Boston brown bread isn't often seen once you've ventured much beyond the boundaries of Boston. Traditionally, Boston brown bread is steamed in an old coffee can, but Marianna's recipe is a bit more home cook–friendly because the bread is baked in a loaf pan. "This recipe came from my mother, who studied at the New England Conservatory of Music in Boston. In the 1930s and 1940s our family had this with Boston baked beans, our traditional Saturday night supper. It is worth making just for little cream cheese sandwiches." Once you taste it, you'll find this regional favorite is easy to love.

MAKES ONE 8-INCH LOAF

2	cups stone-ground graham flour
⅓	cup all-purpose flour
⅓	cup packed light brown sugar
1	teaspoon salt
1¼	cups buttermilk
⅓	cup molasses
1	large egg
¾	cup raisins
1	teaspoon baking soda
⅓	cup boiling water

1. Adjust an oven rack to the middle position and heat the oven to 350 degrees. Grease an 8½ by 4½-inch loaf pan and set aside.

2. Whisk the flours, sugar, and salt together in a bowl. Whisk the buttermilk, molasses, and egg together in a separate bowl. Gradually stir the buttermilk mixture into the flour mixture until combined. Stir in the raisins. Stir the baking soda into the boiling water until dissolved, then stir into the batter until just incorporated.

3. Scrape the batter into the prepared pan and smooth the top. Bake until a skewer inserted into the center of the loaf comes out clean, 50 to 60 minutes, rotating the pan halfway through.

4. Cool the loaf in the pan for 10 minutes. Run a small knife around the edge of the pan to loosen, then turn out onto a wire rack and cool for 1 hour before serving.

Notes from the Test Kitchen

We found this a welcome, simple version of old-fashioned Boston brown bread that produced a moist and flavorful loaf. Though Marianna's recipe called for using either an 8 by 4-inch or a 9 by 5-inch pan, we found there was just too much batter and it bubbled up and over the sides of either pan during cooking. We opted to use a standard 8½ by 4½-inch loaf pan and scaled down a few of the ingredients, which guaranteed an evenly cooked, perfect loaf every time. Graham flour is simply coarsely ground whole wheat flour; you can substitute whole wheat flour if you can't find graham flour.

VANILLA WAFER CAKE

Sweet Endings

Vanilla Wafer Cake **184**

One-Egg Cake **185**

Boiled Cake **186**

Ma Sapp's Gingerbread **187**

Lemon Pudding Cake **188**

Maine Blueberry Grunt **191**

Grandma Newman's Rice Pudding **192**

Jefferson Davis Pie **193**

Single-Crust Pie Dough **194**

Egg Pie **195**

French Silk Chocolate Pie **196**

Fruitcake **198**

Vanilla Wafer Cake

CYNTHIA STILLEY | SAN MARINO, CALIFORNIA

When we see vanilla wafers in an ingredient list, it's usually to make a pie crust or to layer in a banana pudding or other trifle-like dessert. So we were a little surprised when we came across Cynthia's recipe, which came from her mother-in-law, Roberta Stilley, since it turns to this favorite little cookie to make not one of the usual suspects, but rather, a cake. Cynthia grinds the wafers and uses them instead of flour, a twist that lends a sweet, vanilla-infused flavor that makes her coconut- and pecan-studded cake truly irresistible. You'll find it's great not only for dessert, but also as a treat served with mid-morning or afternoon coffee or tea. If you buy the vanilla wafers packaged in boxes, you'll need to buy two boxes (they are also sold in one-pound bags).

SERVES 12

- 1 pound (7 cups) vanilla wafer cookies, broken into rough pieces
- ¼ teaspoon salt
- 1¼ cups sugar
- 12 tablespoons (1½ sticks) unsalted butter, softened
- 6 large eggs
- ½ cup whole milk
- 2 cups sweetened shredded coconut
- 1 cup pecans, toasted and chopped

1. Adjust an oven rack to the middle position and heat the oven to 300 degrees. Grease a 9-inch springform pan and set aside.

2. Process half of the cookies in a food processor to fine crumbs, about 1 minute. Transfer the crumbs to a bowl. Repeat with the remaining cookies. Stir in the salt and set aside.

3. In a large bowl, beat the sugar and butter together with an electric mixer on medium-high speed until light and fluffy, 3 to 6 minutes. Beat in the eggs, one at a time, until incorporated, scraping down the bowl and beaters as needed. Reduce the mixer speed to low and add one-third of the cookie crumbs followed by ¼ cup of the milk. Repeat with half of the remaining cookie crumbs and the remaining ¼ cup milk,

and finish with the remaining cookie crumbs. Fold in the coconut and pecans.

4. Give the batter a final stir with a rubber spatula to make sure it is thoroughly combined. Scrape the batter into the prepared pan, smooth the top, and gently tap the pan on the counter to settle the batter. Bake until the cake is golden brown and a toothpick inserted in the center comes out with a few moist crumbs attached, 1 hour 20 minutes to 1 hour 40 minutes, rotating the pan halfway through.

5. Cool the cake in the pan for 15 minutes. Run a small knife around the edge of the cake, then remove the sides of the pan. Cool the cake on a wire rack to room temperature, 2 to 3 hours, before serving.

Notes from the Test Kitchen

Cynthia's one-of-a-kind recipe produces an incredibly moist, flavorful cake. A test-kitchen favorite from the get-go, the combination of wafer cookies, coconut, and pecans makes for a cake somewhere between coffee cake and tea cake. To pack in as much vanilla-wafer flavor as we could, we doubled the amount of cookies Cynthia called for. We also lowered the amount of sugar and butter, changes that brought it all into balance.

One-Egg Cake

ALICE LUHRING | SYCAMORE, OHIO

"My mother, born in 1902, made this cake for many years. It was baked in the summer when we would go out looking for wild strawberries. Mom would make it in two round cake pans, then she would cut the berries in half and put them all over the cake. It was such a treat. My kids grew up on this recipe and now all of my daughters and daughters-in-law have learned to bake it." The popularity of the one-egg cake peaked in the twenties and thirties (likely because egg prices had gone up), so it's not surprising it was a recipe in Alice's mother's repertoire. We came across many recipes in our research for cakes made with a single egg, and while fillings and frostings differ over the years (it could be filled with jam, frosted with boiled icing, or served with berries and cream or milk), there is always a theme of economy, simplicity, and adaptability to the seasons. And it doesn't hurt that this cake just plain tastes good.

SERVES 8 TO 10

- 2 cups all-purpose flour
- 2 teaspoons baking powder
- ¼ teaspoon salt
- 1 cup sugar
- 10 tablespoons (1¼ sticks) unsalted butter, softened
- 1 large egg
- 2 teaspoons vanilla extract
- ½ cup whole milk

1. Adjust an oven rack to the middle position and heat the oven to 350 degrees. Grease and flour two 8-inch cake pans, line the bottoms with parchment paper, and set aside.

2. Whisk the flour, baking powder, and salt together in a bowl. In a large bowl, beat the sugar and butter together with an electric mixer on medium-high speed until light and fluffy, 3 to 6 minutes. Beat in the egg and vanilla until incorporated, scraping down the bowl and beaters as needed. Reduce the mixer speed to low and add one-third of the flour mixture followed by ¼ cup of the milk. Repeat with half of the remaining flour mixture and the remaining ¼ cup milk, and finish with the remaining flour mixture (the batter will be quite thick).

3. Give the batter a final stir with a rubber spatula to make sure it is thoroughly combined. Scrape the batter into the prepared pans, smooth to cover the bottom of each pan, and gently tap the pans on the counter to settle the batter. Bake until the cakes are golden brown and a toothpick inserted in the center comes out with a few moist crumbs attached, 20 to 25 minutes, rotating the pans halfway through.

4. Cool the cakes in the pans for 10 minutes. Run a small knife around the edge of the cakes, then flip them out onto a wire rack. Peel off the parchment paper, flip the cakes right side up, and cool to room temperature, 2 to 3 hours, before serving.

Notes from the Test Kitchen

We liked that this cake could be thrown together with ingredients we almost always have on hand. No matter how it's going to be served—with fruit as Alice does, or jam, or as a plain snacking cake—its success relies on its simplicity. We did put more emphasis on the vanilla flavor for depth, doubling the amount of vanilla extract that Alice called for, and we increased the butter by 2 tablespoons for added richness and a moister crumb.

Boiled Cake

JOAN ANDERSON | MESA, ARIZONA

"I grew up in rural North Dakota, and desserts were part of every dinner and supper. My family ate boiled cake for dessert at many meals. This recipe is from one of our neighbors who was known as a great baker." Whether you know it as boiled cake, Canadian cake, Hoover cake, cowboy cake, or otherwise, this dessert was once widely popular for its thrift, portability, and versatility (the earliest recipe we found was printed in 1908). The name comes from the fact that the spices, fruits, sugar, butter, and water are boiled together until the sugar dissolves, then flour is folded in and the cake is baked. In later years nuts were added. Made without eggs or milk, it's economical, and the spices and dried fruits are easily adaptable to what is on hand. But you'll find boiled cake is worth making simply because it tastes so good.

SERVES 9

- 12 tablespoons (1½ sticks) unsalted butter
- 2 teaspoons ground cinnamon
- ½ teaspoon ground nutmeg
- ¼ teaspoon ground cloves
- ¼ teaspoon ground ginger
- 1 cup granulated sugar
- 1 cup water
- 1 cup raisins
- ½ teaspoon salt
- 1 teaspoon vanilla extract
- 2 cups all-purpose flour
- ½ teaspoon baking powder
- ½ teaspoon baking soda
- ½ cup pecans or walnuts, toasted and chopped
  Confectioners' sugar

1. Adjust an oven rack to the middle position and heat the oven to 350 degrees. Grease an 8-inch square baking pan, line the bottom with parchment paper, and set aside.

2. Melt the butter in a saucepan over medium heat. Stir in the cinnamon, nutmeg, cloves, and ginger and cook until fragrant, about 30 seconds. Stir in the granulated sugar, water, raisins, and salt. Bring to a simmer and cook until the sugar dissolves, about 5 minutes. Off the heat, stir in the vanilla and set the mixture aside to cool to room temperature.

3. Whisk the flour, baking powder, and baking soda together in a bowl. Stir the flour mixture into the cooled batter to combine. Stir in the nuts.

4. Give the batter a final stir with a rubber spatula to make sure it is thoroughly combined. Scrape the batter into the prepared pan, smooth the top, and gently tap the pan on the counter to settle the batter. Bake the cake until a toothpick inserted in the center comes out with a few moist crumbs attached, 30 to 35 minutes, rotating the pan halfway through.

5. Cool the cake in the pan for 10 minutes. Run a small knife around the edge of the cake, then flip it out onto a wire rack. Peel off the parchment paper, flip the cake right side up, and cool to room temperature, 2 to 3 hours. Sprinkle with confectioners' sugar before serving.

Notes from the Test Kitchen

We happily added Joan's recipe to our file of great snack cakes. We did prefer butter's flavor to shortening, and blooming the spices in the melted butter boosted their flavor. A teaspoon of vanilla lent nice depth. We switched from a 13 by 9-inch pan to an 8-inch square pan for a thicker, moister cake.

Ma Sapp's Gingerbread

CYNTHIA HUTCHINS | CONROE, TEXAS

"Annie Wilson Sapp, my great-grandmother, was widowed in November of 1900 and left with four children to support and a farm in Shelby County, Texas. Annie rented out most of her land to other farmers and lived a very conservative and practical life. It was a hard life, but with faith and trust she never looked back. This is a very simple, but wonderful, recipe of hers that has been passed down through the years. I make pans and pans of this at Christmas for friends and family. When I am making Ma Sapp's gingerbread, I can share memories of my own childhood with my grandchildren and remind them of their heritage and the strength of our roots."

SERVES 15 TO 18

2	cups all-purpose flour
2½	teaspoons ground ginger
1½	teaspoons ground cinnamon
1½	teaspoons baking soda
1	teaspoon ground allspice
½	teaspoon salt
1¼	cups boiling water
1	cup molasses
1	cup granulated sugar
¾	cup vegetable oil
3	large eggs
	Confectioners' sugar

1. Adjust an oven rack to the middle position and heat the oven to 350 degrees. Grease and flour a 13 by 9-inch baking pan and set aside.

2. Whisk the flour, ginger, cinnamon, baking soda, allspice, and salt together in a bowl. In a large bowl, whisk the boiling water, molasses, granulated sugar, and oil together. Whisk in the eggs, one at a time, until incorporated. Whisk in the flour mixture until the batter is combined (the mixture will be very thin), 2 to 4 minutes.

3. Give the batter a final stir with a rubber spatula to make sure it is thoroughly combined. Pour the batter into the prepared pan. Bake the gingerbread until a toothpick inserted in the center comes out with a few moist crumbs attached, 30 to 35 minutes, rotating the pan halfway through.

4. Cool the gingerbread to room temperature in the pan on a wire rack, 2 to 3 hours. Sprinkle with confectioners' sugar before serving.

Notes from the Test Kitchen

We found Cynthia's gingerbread to be ultra moist, and it was a quick and foolproof recipe that didn't need much work. Tasters thought it was a touch too oily, so we reduced the oil from 1 cup to ¾ cup, and for even more ginger flavor we went up from 1 heaping teaspoon of ground ginger to 2½ teaspoons.

Lemon Pudding Cake

THE EDITORS OF COOK'S COUNTRY

This near-forgotten dessert, with its seemingly magical formation of layers—airy and soufflé-like on top, dense, lemony custard below—had us set on reviving it. The recipe has roots in flour puddings, like the 1796 recipe from *American Cookery* made with cinnamon, nutmeg, and whole eggs. Eventually lemon replaced the spices, beaten egg whites became favored, and by the nineteenth century, "sponge pudding" recipes relying on a water bath appeared, allowing steady, low heat to prevent the mixture from scrambling and giving the dessert enough time to split in two. Starting with simply butter, sugar, milk, eggs, flour, and lemon juice, we developed this recipe with a rich, creamy pudding, delicate tender cake, and bright, balanced lemon flavor.

SERVES 8

- ¼ cup all-purpose flour
- 2 teaspoons cornstarch
- 1¼ cups granulated sugar
- 5 tablespoons unsalted butter, softened
- 2 tablespoons grated lemon zest and ½ cup fresh lemon juice (4 lemons)
- 5 large eggs, separated
- 1¼ cups whole milk, room temperature
- Pinch cream of tartar
- Confectioners' sugar

1. Adjust an oven rack to the lowest position and heat the oven to 325 degrees. Grease an 8-inch square baking dish. Place a kitchen towel in the bottom of a roasting pan, arrange the prepared baking dish on the towel, and set aside.

2. Whisk the flour and cornstarch together in a bowl. In a large bowl, beat ½ cup of the granulated sugar, the butter, and lemon zest together on medium-high speed until light and fluffy, 3 to 6 minutes. Beat in the egg yolks, one at a time, until incorporated. Reduce the mixer speed to low, add the flour mixture, and beat until incorporated. Slowly add the lemon juice and milk and mix until just combined.

3. In a medium bowl, whip the egg whites and cream of tartar with the electric mixer on medium-low speed until foamy. Increase the speed to medium-high and gradually whip in the remaining ¾ cup granulated sugar until the whites form stiff peaks, 1 to 3 minutes.

4. Whisk one-third of the egg whites into the batter, then gently fold in the remaining egg whites, one spoonful at a time, until well combined. Spoon the batter into the prepared baking dish.

5. Place the roasting pan in the oven and carefully pour enough boiling water into the pan to come halfway up the sides of the baking dish. Bake until the surface is golden brown and the edges are set (the center should jiggle slightly when gently shaken), about 1 hour.

6. Remove the baking dish from the water bath, transfer to a wire rack, and cool for at least 1 hour. Dust the cake with confectioners' sugar and serve.

Notes from the Test Kitchen
The best recipe we found creamed butter with sugar, added egg yolks and flour, poured in milk and lemon juice, then folded in beaten egg whites. We doubled the lemon juice in that recipe, and grated zest lent even more lemon flavor. Cornstarch firmed up our custard, while beating sugar into the egg whites helped stabilize them.

Maine Blueberry Grunt

THE EDITORS OF COOKS COUNTRY

Unlike a cobbler or crisp, a grunt cooks start to finish on the stovetop. Stewed, spiced berries are topped with dollops of biscuit dough, covered, and cooked until the dumplings are done. The technique can be traced to 1807, when recipes cooked sweetened dumpling dough in water to make quick "puddings." It eventually evolved into the grunt, a name given for the sound the fruit made as it bubbled beneath the dumplings. Blueberry grunts are particularly popular in New England and Nova Scotia, and after one bowlful at a Maine diner, we were set on developing our own.

SERVES 12

FILLING
- 8 cups fresh blueberries
- ½ cup sugar
- 2 tablespoons water
- 1 teaspoon grated lemon zest and 1 tablespoon fresh lemon juice
- ½ teaspoon ground cinnamon
- 1 teaspoon cornstarch

TOPPING
- ¾ cup buttermilk
- 6 tablespoons (¾ stick) unsalted butter, melted and cooled
- 1 teaspoon vanilla extract
- 2¼ cups all-purpose flour
- ½ cup sugar
- 1½ teaspoons baking powder
- ½ teaspoon baking soda
- ½ teaspoon salt
- ½ teaspoon ground cinnamon

1. FOR THE FILLING: Cook 4 cups of the blueberries, the sugar, water, lemon zest, and cinnamon in a Dutch oven over medium-high heat, stirring occasionally, until the mixture is thick and jam-like, 10 to 12 minutes. Whisk the lemon juice and cornstarch together in a small bowl, then stir into the blueberry mixture. Stir in the remaining 4 cups blueberries and cook until heated through, about 1 minute. Cover to keep warm and let sit off the heat.

2. FOR THE TOPPING: Combine the buttermilk, melted butter, and vanilla in a measuring cup. Whisk the flour, 6 tablespoons of the sugar, the baking powder, baking soda, and salt together in a large bowl. Slowly stir the buttermilk mixture into the flour mixture until a dough forms.

3. Using a small ice cream scoop or two large spoons, spoon golf ball–sized dumplings on top of the warm berry mixture (you should have 14 dumplings). Wrap the lid of the Dutch oven with a clean kitchen towel (keeping the towel away from the heat source) and cover the pot. Simmer gently until the dumplings have doubled in size and a toothpick inserted into the center comes out clean, 16 to 22 minutes.

4. Combine the cinnamon and the remaining 2 tablespoons sugar in a bowl. Uncover the pot and sprinkle the dumplings evenly with the cinnamon sugar. Serve.

Notes from the Test Kitchen
A grunt usually has a loose filling so it can soak into the dumplings, but we felt this just led to soggy dumplings. We cooked half the berries to a jam-like consistency and stirred in the other half. We chose buttermilk, instead of milk, to make the dumplings tangy and light. Condensation dripping from the pot's lid caused soggy-topped dumplings, so we put a kitchen towel under the lid to soak up the liquid.

Grandma Newman's Rice Pudding

E.H. NEWMAN | TORRANCE, CALIFORNIA

Since the earliest colonial times, rice pudding has been in the American cooking repertoire (it actually goes back to ancient times). It was so common in our country's early days that a whopping six recipes for it appeared in Amelia Simmons' 1796 cookbook *American Cookery* alone (this was the first cookbook written by an American for Americans). Grandma Newman's recipe, like one of Amelia's, is made without eggs. The additions of sugar, spices, and raisins turn basic rice pudding, which in ancient times was a prescription for stomach ailments, into a deliciously simple and appealing dessert. Grandma adds a twist by making a "brûléed" topping, a layer of caramelized sugar on top that adds a toasty-sweet flavor and crunch that makes this comfort-food favorite even better.

SERVES 6

- 2 cups whole milk
- 1¼ cups heavy cream
- ¼ cup granulated sugar
- 2 teaspoons vanilla extract
- ½ teaspoon ground cinnamon
- ¼ teaspoon ground nutmeg
- ¼ teaspoon salt
- ½ cup long-grain white rice
- ¼ cup raisins (optional)
- ¼ cup packed light brown sugar

1. Adjust an oven rack to the upper-middle position and heat the oven to 350 degrees. Grease a 2-quart broiler-safe shallow baking dish and set aside.

2. Whisk the milk, cream, granulated sugar, vanilla, cinnamon, nutmeg, and salt together in a bowl. Stir in the rice and raisins (if using), then pour into the prepared baking dish.

3. Place the baking dish on a foil-lined rimmed baking sheet and bake until the rice is tender and the liquid is thick and creamy, about 1 hour, stirring every 20 minutes.

4. Remove the pudding from the oven and turn on the broiler. Gently stir the pudding, then smooth the top. Sprinkle the brown sugar evenly over the top of the pudding. Broil until the sugar melts and begins to forms a crust, about 2 minutes. Cool for 5 minutes. Serve warm or at room temperature.

Notes from the Test Kitchen

We loved the crackly, caramelized sugar topping on this rice pudding, which lent a touch of elegance to a homey classic. We did tweak the ratios in the original recipe, doubling the amount of rice to give us a better ratio of grains to custard and a heartier pudding, and for richer flavor we substituted cream for some of the milk. We also toned down the sweetness by reducing the sugar. Decreasing the cooking time by about 45 minutes ensured that the rice still had some bite. The original turned to an ice bath when cooking the topping under the broiler, but we found this step unnecessary.

Jefferson Davis Pie

THE EDITORS OF COOK'S COUNTRY

It's said that the true measure of a Southern historical figure's status is a namesake dessert. Confederate president Jefferson Davis has a pie—a spiced brown sugar custard accented with dried fruits and nuts. Despite its promise, test recipes baked up with saccharine, loose fillings and soggy crusts, with bits of fruits and nuts detracting from the smooth custard. We set out to reinvent this little known Dixie delight. The results? A well-balanced pie with a layer of flavorful fruit filling beneath smooth, creamy custard.

SERVES 8

PIE

- ½ cup raisins
- ½ cup chopped dates
- ½ cup pecans, toasted and chopped
- 1 recipe Single-Crust Pie Dough (page 194), chilled in freezer
- 3 tablespoons all-purpose flour
- 1 teaspoon ground cinnamon
- ½ teaspoon salt
- ¼ teaspoon ground allspice
- 1 cup packed light brown sugar
- 8 tablespoons (1 stick) unsalted butter, softened
- 5 large egg yolks
- 1¼ cups heavy cream

BOURBON WHIPPED CREAM

- 1 cup heavy cream
- 2 tablespoons bourbon
- 1½ tablespoons light brown sugar
- ½ teaspoon vanilla extract

1. FOR THE PIE: Adjust an oven rack to the lowest position and heat the oven to 325 degrees.

2. Pulse the raisins, dates, and pecans together in a food processor until finely ground. Remove the prepared pie shell from the freezer. Transfer the mixture to the chilled pie shell and gently press into an even layer.

3. Whisk the flour, cinnamon, salt, and allspice together in a bowl. Beat the sugar and butter together in a bowl with an electric mixer on medium-low speed until just combined,

about 1 minute. Beat in the egg yolks, one at a time, until incorporated. Beat in the flour mixture and cream until just combined, scraping down the bowl and beaters as needed.

4. Give the filling a final stir with a rubber spatula to make sure it is thoroughly combined. Pour the filling over the fruit and nuts in the pie shell and bake until the surface is deep brown and the center jiggles slightly when the pie is shaken, 55 minutes to 1 hour 5 minutes.

5. Cool the pie to room temperature on a wire rack, 2 to 3 hours.

6. FOR THE BOURBON WHIPPED CREAM: While the pie cools, in a bowl, whip the cream, bourbon, sugar, and vanilla together with an electric mixer on medium-low speed until frothy, about 1 minute. Increase the speed to high and continue to whip until the cream forms stiff peaks, 1 to 3 minutes. Cover and refrigerate until ready to serve. Serve individual portions of the pie with a spoonful of the whipped cream.

Notes from the Test Kitchen

For the right balance of spice and sweet, we cut the typical amount of sugar in half. Heavy cream instead of milk lent a silkier texture and richer flavor. This pie usually starts at a high temperature and finishes more moderately, but we found a slightly longer bake in a gentle 325-degree oven cooked the pie more evenly. Grinding the fruits and nuts and pressing this mixture into the bottom of the raw crust before pouring the custard over created two distinct layers that gave our pie appealing flavor and texture in every bite.

Single-Crust Pie Dough

MAKES ENOUGH FOR ONE 9-INCH PIE

- 1¼ cups all-purpose flour
- 1 tablespoon sugar
- ½ teaspoon salt
- 3 tablespoons vegetable shortening, cut into ¼-inch pieces and chilled
- 4 tablespoons (½ stick) unsalted butter, cut into ¼-inch pieces and chilled
- 4–6 tablespoons ice water

1. Process the flour, sugar, and salt together in a food processor until combined. Scatter the shortening over the top and process until the mixture resembles coarse cornmeal, about 10 pulses. Scatter the butter pieces over the top and pulse the mixture until it resembles coarse crumbs, about 10 pulses. Transfer the mixture to a bowl.

2. Sprinkle 4 tablespoons of the ice water over the mixture. Stir and press the dough together, using a stiff rubber spatula, until the dough sticks together. If the dough does not come together, stir in the remaining water, 1 tablespoon at a time, until it does.

3. Turn the dough onto a sheet of plastic wrap and flatten into a 4-inch disk. Wrap the dough tightly in the plastic wrap and refrigerate for at least 1 hour, or up to 2 days. Before rolling out the dough, let it sit on the counter to soften slightly, about 10 minutes.

4. Roll the dough on a lightly floured counter to a 12-inch circle, about ⅛ inch thick. Fit the dough into a 9-inch pie plate, letting the excess dough hang over the edge. Following the photos, trim, fold, and crimp the edges. Freeze the unbaked pie crust until firm, about 30 minutes, before filling or baking.

Notes from the Test Kitchen

Traditional pie dough recipes call for either butter or shortening. Butter makes for the richest, most flavorful crust, but butter crusts can be difficult to prepare. Shortening lacks the flavor of butter, but makes the dough easy to work with and the crust exceptionally flaky. We found that combining the two fats gives you the best of both worlds: flavor and easy handling.

ROLLING AND FITTING PIE DOUGH

1. Loosely roll the dough around the rolling pin. Then gently unroll the dough over the pie plate.

2. Lift the dough around the edges and gently press it down into the corners of the pie plate.

3. Trim the dough to within ½ inch of the pie plate. Tuck the dough underneath itself to form a rim that sits above the pie plate.

4. Use the index finger of one hand and the thumb and index finger of the other to create a crimped edge.

Egg Pie

KARLA KELLEY | WASHINGTON, D.C.

"My grandmother always made this pie for any family gathering. It is a simple recipe and she always said it was a recipe that evolved through the hard times because it is just sugar, milk, butter, and eggs. Because homes usually have these ingredients on hand, you can always make something sweet." Though we only found one sweet pie going under the name "egg pie" in our research (we did find several savory ones), Karla's dessert mirrors the traditional recipes for custard pies, which began appearing in America in the early 1800s. With a hint of lemon and vanilla, her ultra-creamy custard pie is simple yet satisfying, a perfect choice for taking care of just about anyone's sweet tooth.

SERVES 8

1   recipe Single-Crust Pie Dough (page 194), chilled in freezer
1 ¾   cups sugar
¾   cup whole milk
6   large eggs
6   tablespoons (¾ stick) unsalted butter, melted and cooled
2   tablespoons all-purpose flour
1   teaspoon vanilla extract
½   teaspoon grated lemon zest and 1 tablespoon fresh lemon juice

1. Adjust an oven rack to the middle position and heat the oven to 375 degrees.

2. Remove the prepared pie shell from the freezer. Line the chilled pie crust with a double layer of foil, covering the edges to prevent burning, and fill with pie weights or pennies. Bake until the pie dough looks dry and is light golden brown in color, 25 to 30 minutes. Remove the weights and foil and continue to bake until the crust is just beginning to brown, 5 to 10 minutes. Set aside to cool to room temperature.

3. Lower the oven temperature to 350 degrees. Whisk the sugar, milk, eggs, melted butter, flour, vanilla, lemon zest, and lemon juice together in a bowl.

4. Pour the filling into the cooled crust and bake until the surface is light golden brown and the center jiggles slightly when the pie is shaken, 40 to 45 minutes. Cool the pie to room temperature on a wire rack, 2 to 3 hours, before serving.

Notes from the Test Kitchen

Tasters were immediately impressed by this pie's smooth, creamy custard made with just a few kitchen staples. However, tasters wanted more of the custard, so we scaled up the amount of filling, and to ensure a crisp crust we parbaked it before adding the filling. Karla's recipe called for lemon extract, but we preferred the fresher flavor of fresh lemon zest and juice. Be careful not to overcook the pie, or it will curdle and lose its smooth, creamy texture.

French Silk Chocolate Pie

THE EDITORS OF COOK'S COUNTRY

Don't let the name fool you: this pie was "born" in America. Maryland's Betty Cooper won $1,000 for this from-scratch icebox pie in 1951's Pillsbury Bake-Off (the exotic name reflects the international curiosity of postwar America). Betty whipped together butter, sugar, three ounces of unsweetened chocolate, and raw eggs until the mixture was light and fluffy, then poured the filling into a prebaked crust and chilled until firm. It was an instant hit, but today few make the original recipe, likely because it calls for raw eggs and, by today's standards, barely tastes like chocolate. Here we reintroduce homemade French Silk Chocolate Pie, one that remains true to the eggy richness of the original and has a chocolaty flavor we can all get excited about.

SERVES 8

- 1 recipe Single-Crust Pie Dough (page 194), chilled in freezer
- 1 cup heavy cream, chilled
- 3 large eggs
- ¾ cup sugar
- 2 tablespoons water
- 8 ounces bittersweet chocolate, melted and cooled
- 1 tablespoon vanilla extract
- 8 tablespoons (1 stick) unsalted butter, cut into ½-inch pieces and softened

1. Adjust an oven rack to the lower-middle position and heat the oven to 375 degrees.

2. Remove the prepared pie shell from the freezer. Line the chilled pie crust with a double layer of foil, covering the edges to prevent burning, and fill with pie weights or pennies. Bake until the pie dough looks dry and is light in color, 20 to 25 minutes. Remove the weights and foil and continue to bake until the crust is deep golden brown, 10 to 15 minutes. Set aside to cool to room temperature.

3. In a medium bowl, whip the cream with an electric mixer on medium-low speed until frothy, about 1 minute. Increase the speed to high and continue to whip until the cream forms stiff peaks, 1 to 3 minutes. Cover and refrigerate until needed.

4. Combine the eggs, sugar, and water in a large heatproof bowl set over a medium saucepan filled with ½ inch barely simmering water (don't let the bowl touch the water). Beat with an electric mixer on medium speed until the egg mixture is thickened and registers 160 degrees, 7 to 10 minutes. Off the heat, continue to beat the egg mixture until fluffy and cooled to room temperature, about 8 minutes longer.

5. Add the cooled chocolate and vanilla to the egg mixture and beat until incorporated. Beat in the butter, a few pieces at a time, until well combined. Using a spatula, fold in the whipped cream until no streaks of white remain. Scrape the filling into the cooled pie shell and refrigerate until set, at least 3 hours, and up to 24 hours. Serve.

Notes from the Test Kitchen

To avoid the off-flavor from egg substitutes, we stuck with real eggs and cooked our filling on the stovetop like a custard. The original recipe called for unsweetened chocolate, but we preferred bold but balanced bittersweet—8 ounces of it. Cutting the original's 2 sticks of butter in half made the filling less dense and more satiny, but the real key was folding whipped cream, usually a topping, into the filling. This pie was light, rich, thick, and chocolaty all at once. Garnish with more whipped cream.

Fruitcake

DAN HENDERSON | SUNNYVALE, CALIFORNIA

Fruitcake might not be a dessert you see year-round, but it certainly is about as old-fashioned as a recipe can get. And for that reason, we just couldn't pass up including a great fruitcake in this collection. Each holiday season, it becomes the proud focus of countless home cooks, as they pull out the family recipes passed down from grandparents and parents that have been made year after year. Neighbors, friends, families, teachers, and coworkers welcome the gift of fruitcake not just as a dessert but as a favorite snack. And while this traditional holiday cake gets a fair amount of flak, we feel pretty sure that the problem is that most people just haven't had a good fruitcake. Dan would probably agree. "I never understood while I was growing up in the fifties and sixties why people always made fun of fruitcake. I couldn't wait for Christmas because it meant my grandmother would make this wonderful fruitcake recipe, which she inherited from her father, who was a baker in Germany before World War I." Dan's grandmother's recipe is packed with candied fruit, raisins, and nuts (including Brazil nuts and almonds in addition to the more commonly found pecans and walnuts), while spices and brandy both help punch up the flavor. The unusual addition of several cups of applesauce adds even more fruity flavor and ensures that the cake is moist. This recipe makes five hefty loaves, enough for you to keep one and share the rest—just as it should be in the spirit of the holidays. To save time since it's such a large amount of nuts, for this recipe we use pecans sold in pieces rather than whole pecans that we chop ourselves.

MAKES FIVE 8-INCH LOAVES

1 pound raisins
1 cup currants
2 pounds candied fruit mix
1 pound chopped dates
1 pound walnut pieces, toasted
1 pound Brazil nuts, toasted and chopped
1 pound sliced almonds, toasted
2 cups pecan pieces, toasted
4½ cups all-purpose flour
4 teaspoons baking soda

1 teaspoon salt
1 tablespoon ground cinnamon
2 teaspoons ground nutmeg
2 teaspoons ground allspice
½ teaspoon ground mace
3 cups unsweetened applesauce
¾ cup brandy
1½ cups granulated sugar
¾ cup packed dark brown sugar
16 tablespoons (2 sticks) unsalted butter, softened
¼ cup molasses
3 large eggs

1. Adjust the oven racks to the upper-middle and lower-middle positions and heat the oven to 275 degrees. Grease five 8½ by 4½-inch loaf pans and set aside.

2. Cover the raisins and currants with boiling water in a bowl. Let sit for 5 minutes, then drain the fruit and transfer to a very large bowl. Stir in the candied fruit, dates, and nuts and set aside.

3. Whisk the flour, baking soda, salt, cinnamon, nutmeg, allspice, and mace together in a bowl. Whisk the applesauce and the brandy together in another bowl. In a large bowl, beat the sugars and butter together with an electric mixer on medium-high speed until light and fluffy, 3 to 6 minutes. Beat in the molasses, then the eggs, one at a time, until incorporated.

4. Reduce the mixer speed to medium-low and add one-quarter of the flour mixture, followed by one-third of the applesauce mixture. Repeat twice more, adding one-quarter of the flour and one-third of the applesauce mixture each time, then finish with remaining one-quarter flour mixture. Increase the mixer speed to medium and beat until the batter is uniform, scraping down the bowl and beaters as needed. Fold the batter into the fruit-nut mixture. (Use your hands if necessary.)

5. Give the batter a final stir with a rubber spatula to make sure it is thoroughly combined. Spoon the batter evenly into the prepared loaf pans and smooth the tops. Arrange the loaf pans on two baking sheets (three on one sheet, two on another) and bake until the edges of the cakes begin to pull away from the sides of the pans and the centers are firm to the touch, about 2½ hours, switching and rotating the baking sheets halfway through.

6. Cool the cakes in the pans for 10 minutes. Run a small knife around the edge of the cakes, then flip them out onto a wire rack. Flip the cakes right side up and cool to room temperature, 2 to 3 hours, before serving. (The fruitcakes can be wrapped tightly with plastic wrap and stored at room temperature for up to 1 week or in the freezer for up to 1 month.)

Notes from the Test Kitchen

Dan's moist, dense loaves converted many of the test kitchen's former fruitcake haters to fans. We made a few tweaks to the original—some for flavor, some for ease of preparation. Tasters preferred the fruitcake with less sugar (1½ cups rather than 2 cups) and more brandy—Dan's original had just 2 tablespoons, which we raised all the way to ¾ cup. We cut out some of the more difficult-to-find dried fruits, namely pineapple and cherries, since we thought the raisins, currants, dates, and candied fruit mix (which you can find in the baking aisle at the supermarket) were sufficient. Switching from bread flour to all-purpose flour gave us a lighter loaf. This recipe makes a lot of batter, so if you don't have a very large bowl, divide the batter among a few smaller bowls when mixing it together.

Conversions & Equivalencies

SOME SAY COOKING IS A SCIENCE AND AN ART. We would say that geography has a hand in it, too. Flour milled in the United Kingdom and elsewhere will feel and taste different from flour milled in the United States. So we cannot promise that the loaf of bread you bake in Canada or England will taste the same as a loaf baked in the States, but we can offer guidelines for converting weights and measures. We also recommend that you rely on your instincts when making our recipes. Refer to the visual cues provided. If the bread dough hasn't "come together in a ball," as described, you may need to add more flour—even if the recipe doesn't tell you to. You be the judge.

The recipes in this book were developed using standard U.S. measures following U.S. government guidelines. The charts below offer equivalents for U.S., metric, and Imperial (U.K.) measures. All conversions are approximate and have been rounded up or down to the nearest whole number.

EXAMPLE:

1 teaspoon	=	5 milliliters (rounded up from 4.9292 milliliters)
1 ounce	=	28 grams (rounded down from 28.3495 grams)

VOLUME CONVERSIONS

U.S.	METRIC
1 teaspoon	5 milliliters
2 teaspoons	10 milliliters
1 tablespoon	15 milliliters
2 tablespoons	30 milliliters
¼ cup	59 milliliters
⅓ cup	79 milliliters
½ cup	118 milliliters
¾ cup	177 milliliters
1 cup	237 milliliters
1¼ cups	296 milliliters
1½ cups	355 milliliters
2 cups (1 pint)	473 milliliters
2½ cups	592 milliliters
3 cups	710 milliliters
4 cups (1 quart)	0.946 liter
1.06 quarts	1 liter
4 quarts (1 gallon)	3.8 liters

WEIGHT CONVERSIONS

OUNCES	GRAMS
½	14
¾	21
1	28
1½	43
2	57
2½	71
3	85
3½	99
4	113
4½	128
5	142
6	170
7	198
8	227
9	255
10	283
12	340
16 (1 pound)	454

CONVERSIONS FOR INGREDIENTS COMMONLY USED IN BAKING

Baking is an exacting science. Because measuring by weight is far more accurate than measuring by volume, and thus more likely to achieve reliable results, in our recipes we provide ounce measures in addition to cup measures for many ingredients. Refer to the chart below to convert these measures into grams.

INGREDIENT	OUNCES	GRAMS
1 cup all-purpose flour*	5	142
1 cup whole wheat flour	5½	156
1 cup granulated (white) sugar	7	198
1 cup packed brown sugar (light or dark)	7	198
1 cup confectioners' sugar	4	113
1 cup cocoa powder	3	85
4 tablespoons butter† (½ stick, or ¼ cup)	2	57
8 tablespoons butter† (1 stick, or ½ cup)	4	113
16 tablespoons butter† (2 sticks, or 1 cup)	8	227

* U.S. all-purpose flour, the most frequently used flour in this book, does not contain leaveners, as some European flours do. These leavened flours are called self-rising or self-raising. If you are using self-rising flour, take this into consideration before adding leavening to a recipe.

† In the United States, butter is sold both salted and unsalted. We generally recommend unsalted butter. If you are using salted butter, take this into consideration before adding salt to a recipe.

OVEN TEMPERATURES

FAHRENHEIT	CELSIUS	GAS MARK (IMPERIAL)
225	105	¼
250	120	½
275	130	1
300	150	2
325	165	3
350	180	4
375	190	5
400	200	6
425	220	7
450	230	8
475	245	9

CONVERTING TEMPERATURES FROM AN INSTANT-READ THERMOMETER

We include doneness temperatures in many of the recipes in this book. We recommend an instant-read thermometer for the job. Refer to the above table to convert Fahrenheit degrees to Celsius. Or, for temperatures not represented in the chart, use this simple formula: Subtract 32 degrees from the Fahrenheit reading, then divide the result by 1.8 to find the Celsius reading.

EXAMPLE:
"Roast until the thickest part of a chicken thigh registers 175 degrees on an instant-read thermometer." To convert:

175°F – 32 = 143
143 ÷ 1.8 = 79°C (rounded down from 79.44)

Index

NOTE: *Italicized* page references indicate recipe photographs.

A

Apple(s)
"Candied," in Cinnamon Syrup, **105**
and Sauerkraut Pork Chops, **51**
Aunt Cho's Chicken with Vinegar and Onions, **140**
Aunt Fanny's Pasta Soup with Little Meatballs,
106, 116
Aunt Nina's Breadballs and Sauce, **142–44,** *143*

B

Baked Boston Brown Bread, **180,** *181*
Baked Eggplant Casserole, **20**
Bean(s)
Baked, Burgoo, Blue Ridge, **167**
Black and White Chicken Chili, *88,* **90**
Easy Bird's Nest, *150,* **151**
Grandma's Borscht, **127**
Pork Chop Scallop, **53**
Beef
Aunt Fanny's Pasta Soup with Little Meatballs,
106, 116
Barbecue, Grandma Wooly's, *62,* **63**
Braciole with Neapolitan Sauce, **117–18**
Chili Balls, **68**
Cincinnati Chili, *168,* **169**
Cornbread Meatloaf, *98,* **99**
Grandma's Borscht, **127**
Grandma's Enchiladas, **14–16,** *15*
Hamburger Potato Roll, **76–77**
Johnny Marzetti, **78**
Kids' Favorite Shepherd's Pie, **97**
Kotlety, **113**
The Meatloaf with the Frosting, **64–65**
Meat-za Pie, **145**
Mrs. Rockefeller's Meatloaf, **74–75**
New England Boiled Dinner, **158,** *159*

Beef *(cont.)*
Outrageous Gulyás, **129**
Papa's Lasagna, **21–23,** *22*
Potatoes, and Onions, Savory Strudel with, **111–12**
Pot Roast Soup, **146**
Preacher's Delight, **12**
Prune Meat, **128**
Roast, and Gravy, Classic, *30,* **56**
Salmagundi Bake, **13**
Shall's Classic Lasagna, **122–25,** *123*
Sicilian Meatloaf, *114,* **115**
Steak, Saucy Mustard, **61**
Stew, Horseradish, **59**
Sunday Sugo, *66,* **67**
Sunday Tomato Sauce with Meatballs, **69**
Sweet and Sour Meatballs, **70**
Tenders, Deviled, **60**
Tia's Coffee Pot Roast, **57–58**
Traditional Upper Peninsula Pasties, **108–10,** *109*
Yankee Pot Roast Supper, **157**
see also Veal
Beets
Grandma's Borscht, **127**
New England Boiled Dinner, **158,** *159*
Black and White Chicken Chili, *88,* **90**
Blueberry Grunt, Maine, *190,* **191**
Blue Ridge Baked Bean Burgoo, **167**
Boiled Cake, **186**
Borscht, Grandma's, **127**
Boston Brown Bread, Baked, **180,** *181*
Bourbon Whipped Cream, **193**
Braciole with Neapolitan Sauce, **117–18**
Bread, Boston Brown, Baked, **180,** *181*
Breadballs and Sauce, Aunt Nina's, **142–44,** *143*
Bread Crumbs, Pasta with (Nonni's Pasta Mollica), **119**
Bubie Alte's Lukshen Kugel, **126**

C

Cabbage
    Apple and Sauerkraut Pork Chops, **51**
    Grandma's Borscht, **127**
    New England Boiled Dinner, **158**, *159*
Cakes
    Boiled, **186**
    Fruitcake, **198–99**
    Lemon Pudding, **188**, *189*
    Ma Sapp's Gingerbread, **187**
    One-Egg, **185**
    Vanilla Wafer, *182*, *184*
"Candied" Apples in Cinnamon Syrup, **105**
Carrots
    Chicken in a Pot, **43–45**, *44*
    Horseradish Beef Stew, **59**
    New England Boiled Dinner, **158**, *159*
    Tia's Coffee Pot Roast, **57–58**
    Yankee Pot Roast Supper, **157**
Char's Maine Fish Chowder, **174**
Cheddar Cheese
    Chicken Tetrazzini (à la Aunt Leah), **9–10**, *11*
    Creamy Potato Puff, **104**
    Glop, **100**
    Kids' Favorite Shepherd's Pie, **97**
    Martini Mac and Cheese, **24**, *25*
    Meat-za Pie, **145**
    Preacher's Delight, **12**
    Snowed-In Potato Hot Dish, **149**
    Tuna-Tater Bake, **148**
Cheese
    Aunt Nina's Breadballs and Sauce, **142–44**, *143*
    Baked Eggplant Casserole, **20**
    Braciole with Neapolitan Sauce, **117–18**
    Bubie Alte's Lukshen Kugel, **126**
    Chicken Tetrazzini (à la Aunt Leah), **9–10**, *11*
    Creamy Potato Puff, **104**
    Delicate Manicotti, **120–21**
    Fluffy Ham and Grits, **18**
    Frenchees, **86**, *87*
    Funeral Potatoes with Ham, **17**
    Glop, **100**
    Grandma's Enchiladas, **14–16**, *15*
    Johnny Marzetti, **78**
    Martini Mac and, **24**, *25*

Cheese *(cont.)*
    Mom's Hominy, **19**
    Nonni's Pasta Mollica (Pasta with Bread Crumbs), **119**
    Papa's Lasagna, **21–23**, *22*
    Pork Chop Scallop, **53**
    Preacher's Delight, **12**
    Saltine Lasagna, **134**, *141*
    Screaming Noodles, **102**, *103*
    Shall's Classic Lasagna, **122–25**, *123*
    Sicilian Meatloaf, *114*, **115**
    see also Cheddar Cheese
Chesapeake Partan Bree, **152**, **172–73**
Chicken
    à la King, WWII, **136**
    Bott Bie, Pennsylvania Dutch Slippery, **160–61**
    Chili, Black and White, **88**, **90**
    Crunchy, **91**
    and Dumplings Casserole, Home Ranch, *1*, **2–3**
    Fricassee, **34–35**
    Fried, Coke Oven, **162**, *163*
    Granny's Tamale Pie, **6**, **7–8**
    Hunter's, **40**, *41*
    International Dateline, **92**, *93*
    'n' Dumplings, **39**
    Oh My God (Chicken Fricassee with Heads of Garlic), **36–38**, *37*
    Olive Martini, **94**
    Pan-Fried, with Milk Gravy, **32–33**
    Pan Pie, Creamy, **4–5**
    Paprikash, **130–31**
    in a Pot, **43–45**, *44*
    and Rice Dish, Mom's, **137**
    Roast, with Orange Cream Gravy, **42**
    Tetrazzini (à la Aunt Leah), **9–10**, *11*
    Vesuvio, **82**, *83*
    with Vinegar and Onions, Aunt Cho's, **140**
    and Waffles, Creamy, **138–39**
Chili, Chicken, Black and White, **88**, *90*
Chili, Cincinnati, *168*, *169*
Chocolate Pie, French Silk, **196**, *197*
Chowder, Char's Maine Fish, **174**
Cincinnati Chili, *168*, *169*
Clam Pie, Long Island, **175–76**
Classic Roast Beef and Gravy, *30*, **56**

Coconut
  Vanilla Wafer Cake, *182, 184*
Coffee Pot Roast, Tia's, **57–58**
Coke Oven Fried Chicken, **162,** *163*
Corn
  Black and White Chicken Chili, **88, 90**
  Chesapeake Partan Bree, *152,* **172–73**
  Fritters, Great-Grandma's, *178, 179*
  Granny's Tamale Pie, **6, 7–8**
  Kids' Favorite Shepherd's Pie, **97**
  Pie, **27–29,** *28*
  and Pork Chops, Lorraine's, **95**
  Salmagundi Bake, **13**
Cornbread Meatloaf, **98, 99**
Cornish Game Hens with Rice Stuffing, **48–50,** *49*
Crab(meat)
  Cakes, Grandma Taylor's, **177**
  Chesapeake Partan Bree, *152,* **172–73**
Creamy Chicken and Waffles, **138–39**
Creamy Chicken Pan Pie, **4–5**
Creamy Potato Puff, **104**
Crispy Iowa Skinnies, **156**
Crunchy Chicken, **91**

D

Dates
  Fruitcake, **198–99**
  International Dateline Chicken, **92,** *93*
  Jefferson Davis Pie, **193**
Delicate Manicotti, **120–21**
Desserts
  Bubie Alte's Lukshen Kugel, **126**
  Egg Pie, **195**
  French Silk Chocolate Pie, **196,** *197*
  Grandma Newman's Rice Pudding, **192**
  Jefferson Davis Pie, **193**
  Maine Blueberry Grunt, *190, 191*
  see also Cakes
Deviled Beef Tenders, **60**
Dr Pepper–Glazed Ham, **54,** *55*
Duck Gumbo, **165–66**

E

Easy Bird's Nest, *150, 151*
Eggplant Casserole, Baked, **20**
Egg(s)
  Easy Bird's Nest, *150, 151*
  Green Mountain Surprise, **101**
  Pie, **195**
Enchiladas, Grandma's, **14–16,** *15*

F

Fish
  Chowder, Char's Maine, **174**
  Salmon Loaf, **147**
  Salmon Wiggle, **84**
  Tuna-Tater Bake, **148**
  see also Shellfish
Fluffy Ham and Grits, **18**
French Silk Chocolate Pie, **196,** *197*
Fritters, Corn, Great-Grandma's, *178, 179*
Fruits
  Fruitcake, **198–99**
  see also specific fruits
Funeral Potatoes with Ham, **17**

G

Garlic
  Heads of, Chicken Fricassee with (Oh My God
    Chicken), **36–38,** *37*
  Hunter's Chicken, **40,** *41*
Gingerbread, Ma Sapp's, **187**
Glop, **100**
Grains
  Fluffy Ham and Grits, **18**
  Granny's Tamale Pie, **6, 7–8**
  see also Rice
Grandma Newman's Rice Pudding, **192**
Grandma's Borscht, **127**
Grandma's Enchiladas, **14–16,** *15*
Grandma Taylor's Crab Cakes, **177**
Grandma Wooly's Beef Barbecue, **62, 63**
Granny's Tamale Pie, **6, 7–8**
Great-Grandma's Corn Fritters, *178, 179*
Green Beans
  Easy Bird's Nest, *150, 151*
  Pork Chop Scallop, **53**

Green Mountain Surprise, **101**

Greens. *See* Cabbage; Spinach

Grits, Fluffy Ham and, **18**

Gumbo, Duck, **165–66**

H

Ham

    Country, Quilt-Top, **154–55**

    Dr Pepper–Glazed, **54, 55**

    Funeral Potatoes with, **17**

    and Grits, Fluffy, **18**

    Sicilian Meatloaf, *114*, **115**

Hamburger Potato Roll, **76–77**

Home Ranch Chicken and Dumplings Casserole,
    1, 2–3

Hominy, Mom's, **19**

Horseradish Beef Stew, **59**

Hunter's Chicken, **40,** *41*

I

International Dateline Chicken, **92, 93**

Italian Pesto Lamb, **132,** *133*

J

Jefferson Davis Pie, **193**

Johnny Marzetti, **78**

K

Kids' Favorite Shepherd's Pie, **97**

Kotlety, **113**

Kugel, Lukshen, Bubie Alte's, **126**

L

Lamb

    Baked Eggplant Casserole, **20**

    Italian Pesto, **132,** *133*

    Shanks, Loekie's, **71**

Lasagna, Papa's, **21–23,** *22*

Lasagna, Saltine, *134*, **141**

Lasagna, Shall's Classic, **122–25,** *123*

Lemon Pudding Cake, **188,** *189*

Loekie's Lamb Shanks, **71**

Long Island Clam Pie, **175–76**

Lorraine's Pork Chops and Corn, **95**

Louisiana Smothered Rabbit, **164**

M

Mac and Cheese, Martini, **24, 25**

Main dishes (meat)

    Apple and Sauerkraut Pork Chops, **51**

    Baked Eggplant Casserole, **20**

    Braciole with Neapolitan Sauce, **117–18**

    Chili Balls, **68**

    Cincinnati Chili, *168*, **169**

    Classic Roast Beef and Gravy, *30*, **56**

    Cornbread Meatloaf, **98, 99**

    Crispy Iowa Skinnies, **156**

    Deviled Beef Tenders, **60**

    Dr Pepper–Glazed Ham, **54, 55**

    Fluffy Ham and Grits, **18**

    Funeral Potatoes with Ham, **17**

    Grandma's Borscht, **127**

    Grandma's Enchiladas, **14–16,** *15*

    Grandma Wooly's Beef Barbecue, **62, 63**

    Hamburger Potato Roll, **76–77**

    Horseradish Beef Stew, **59**

    Italian Pesto Lamb, **132,** *133*

    Kids' Favorite Shepherd's Pie, **97**

    Kotlety, **113**

    Loekie's Lamb Shanks, **71**

    Louisiana Smothered Rabbit, **164**

    The Meatloaf with the Frosting, **64–65**

    Meat-za Pie, **145**

    Mock Chicken Legs, **79–81,** *80*

    Mrs. Rockefeller's Meatloaf, **74–75**

    New England Boiled Dinner, **158,** *159*

    Orange Pork Chops, **52**

    Outrageous Gulyás, **129**

    Pork Chop Scallop, **53**

    Pot Roast Soup, **146**

    Prune Meat, **128**

    Quilt-Top Country Ham, **154–55**

    Salmagundi Bake, **13**

    Saucy Mustard Beef Steak, **61**

    Savory Strudel with Beef, Potatoes, and Onions,
        111–12

    Sicilian Meatloaf, *114*, **115**

    Southern Braised Pork Chops 'n' Gravy, **96**

    Sunday Sugo, **66, 67**

    Sunday Tomato Sauce with Meatballs, **69**

    Sweet and Sour Meatballs, **70**

Main dishes (meat) *(cont.)*

Tia's Coffee Pot Roast, **57–58**

Traditional Upper Peninsula Pasties, **108–10**, *109*

Yankee Pot Roast Supper, **157**

Main dishes (pasta and grains)

Chicken Tetrazzini (à la Aunt Leah), **9–10**, *11*

Delicate Manicotti, **120–21**

Easy Bird's Nest, *150, 151*

Glop, **100**

Green Mountain Surprise, **101**

Johnny Marzetti, **78**

Papa's Lasagna, **21–23**, *22*

Preacher's Delight, **12**

Shall's Classic Lasagna, **122–25**, *123*

Main dishes (poultry)

Aunt Cho's Chicken with Vinegar and Onions, **140**

Black and White Chicken Chili, *88*, **90**

Chicken Fricassee, **34–35**

Chicken in a Pot, **43–45**, *44*

Chicken 'n' Dumplings, **39**

Chicken Paprikash, **130–31**

Chicken Vesuvio, **82**, *83*

Coke Oven Fried Chicken, *162, 163*

Cornish Game Hens with Rice Stuffing, **48–50**, *49*

Creamy Chicken and Waffles, **138–39**

Creamy Chicken Pan Pie, **4–5**

Crunchy Chicken, **91**

Duck Gumbo, **165–66**

Granny's Tamale Pie, *6*, **7–8**

Home Ranch Chicken and Dumplings Casserole, *1*, **2–3**

Hunter's Chicken, **40**, *41*

International Dateline Chicken, **92**, *93*

Lorraine's Pork Chops and Corn, **95**

Mom's Chicken and Rice Dish, **137**

Oh My God Chicken (Chicken Fricassee with Heads of Garlic), **36–38**, *37*

Olive Martini Chicken, **94**

Pan-Fried Chicken with Milk Gravy, **32–33**

Pennsylvania Dutch Slippery Chicken Bott Bie, **160–61**

Pheasants in Wine Sauce, **46–47**

Roast Chicken with Orange Cream Gravy, **42**

WWII Chicken à la King, **136**

Main dishes (seafood)

Char's Maine Fish Chowder, **174**

Chesapeake Partan Bree, *152*, **172–73**

Grandma Taylor's Crab Cakes, **177**

Long Island Clam Pie, **175–76**

Mighty Good Shrimp Salad, **26**

Pivoto-Robinson Shrimp Creole, **170**, *171*

Salmon Loaf, **147**

Salmon Wiggle, **84**

Tuna-Tater Bake, **148**

Maine Blueberry Grunt, *190, 191*

Manicotti, Delicate, **120–21**

Martini Mac and Cheese, **24, 25**

Maryland Caramel Tomatoes, **72, 85**

Ma Sapp's Gingerbread, **187**

Meat

Louisiana Smothered Rabbit, **164**

Mock Chicken Legs, **79–81**, *80*

see also Beef; Lamb; Pork

Meatballs

Chili Balls, **68**

Little, Aunt Fanny's Pasta Soup with, *106*, **116**

Sunday Tomato Sauce with, **69**

Sweet and Sour, **70**

Meatloaf

Cornbread, **98, 99**

Hamburger Potato Roll, **76–77**

Mrs. Rockefeller's, **74–75**

Sicilian, *114, 115*

The, with the Frosting, **64–65**

Meat-za Pie, **145**

Mighty Good Shrimp Salad, **26**

Mock Chicken Legs, **79–81**, *80*

Mom's Chicken and Rice Dish, **137**

Mom's Hominy, **19**

Mrs. Rockefeller's Meatloaf, **74–75**

Mushrooms

Chesapeake Partan Bree, *152*, **172–73**

Chicken Tetrazzini (à la Aunt Leah), **9–10**, *11*

Funeral Potatoes with Ham, **17**

Meat-za Pie, **145**

Pheasants in Wine Sauce, **46–47**

Southern Braised Pork Chops 'n' Gravy, **96**

N

New England Boiled Dinner, **158**, *159*

Nonni's Pasta Mollica (Pasta with Bread Crumbs), **119**

Noodles

Bubie Alte's Lukshen Kugel, **126**

Easy Bird's Nest, **150**, *151*

Pennsylvania Dutch Slippery Chicken Bott Bie, **160–61**

Pot Roast Soup, **146**

Preacher's Delight, **12**

Screaming, **102**, *103*

Nuts. *See* Pecans

O

Oh My God Chicken (Chicken Fricassee with Heads of Garlic), **36–38**, *37*

Olive(s)

Chicken Tetrazzini (à la Aunt Leah), **9–10**, *11*

Martini Chicken, **94**

Martini Mac and Cheese, **24**, *25*

Mighty Good Shrimp Salad, **26**

One-Egg Cake, **185**

Orange(s)

Cream Gravy, Roasted Chicken with, **42**

International Dateline Chicken, **92**, *93*

Pork Chops, **52**

Outrageous Gulyás, **129**

P

Pan-Fried Chicken with Milk Gravy, **32–33**

Papa's Lasagna, **21–23**, *22*

Pasta

Chicken Tetrazzini (à la Aunt Leah), **9–10**, *11*

Delicate Manicotti, **120–21**

Glop, **100**

Johnny Marzetti, **78**

Martini Mac and Cheese, **24**, *25*

Mighty Good Shrimp Salad, **26**

Mollica, Nonni's (Pasta with Bread Crumbs), **119**

Papa's Lasagna, **21–23**, *22*

Shall's Classic Lasagna, **122–25**, *123*

Soup with Little Meatballs, Aunt Fanny's, *106*, **116**

see also Noodles

Peas

Chicken Vesuvio, **82**, *83*

Creamy Chicken Pan Pie, **4–5**

Home Ranch Chicken and Dumplings Casserole, *1*, **2–3**

Salmon Wiggle, **84**

Pecans

Boiled Cake, **186**

Fruitcake, **198–99**

Jefferson Davis Pie, **193**

Vanilla Wafer Cake, *182*, **184**

Pennsylvania Dutch Slippery Chicken Bott Bie, **160–61**

Pesto, Italian, Lamb, **132**, *133*

Pheasants in Wine Sauce, **46–47**

Pie Dough

fitting into pie plate, **194**

rolling out, **29**

Single-Crust, **194**

Pies

Chocolate, French Silk, **196**, *197*

Clam, Long Island, **175–76**

Corn, **27–29**, *28*

Creamy Chicken Pan, **4–5**

double-crust, preparing, **176**

Egg, **195**

Jefferson Davis, **193**

Tamale, Granny's, *6*, **7–8**

Pivoto-Robinson Shrimp Creole, **170**, *171*

Pork

Braciole with Neapolitan Sauce, **117–18**

Chili Balls, **68**

Chops, Apple and Sauerkraut, **51**

Chops, Orange, **52**

Chops and Corn, Lorraine's, **95**

Chop Scallop, **53**

Chops 'n' Gravy, Southern Braised, **96**

Crispy Iowa Skinnies, **156**

cutlets, preparing, **156**

Johnny Marzetti, **78**

The Meatloaf with the Frosting, **64–65**

Mock Chicken Legs, **79–81**, *80*

Mrs. Rockefeller's Meatloaf, **74–75**

Sunday Sugo, **66**, *67*

Sunday Tomato Sauce with Meatballs, **69**

see also Ham; Sausages

Potato(es)
    Beef, and Onions, Savory Strudel with, **111–12**
    Char's Maine Fish Chowder, **174**
    Chicken in a Pot, **43–45**, *44*
    Chicken Vesuvio, **82**, *83*
    Funeral, with Ham, **17**
    Hamburger Roll, **76–77**
    Home Ranch Chicken and Dumplings Casserole,
        1, **2–3**
    Horseradish Beef Stew, **59**
    Hot Dish, Snowed-In, **149**
    Kids' Favorite Shepherd's Pie, **97**
    Long Island Clam Pie, **175–76**
    The Meatloaf with the Frosting, **64–65**
    New England Boiled Dinner, **158**, *159*
    Outrageous Gulyás, **129**
    Pennsylvania Dutch Slippery Chicken Bott Bie, **160–61**
    Pork Chop Scallop, **53**
    Puff, Creamy, **104**
    Tia's Coffee Pot Roast, **57–58**
    Traditional Upper Peninsula Pasties, **108–10**, *109*
    Tuna-Tater Bake, **148**
    Yankee Pot Roast Supper, **157**
Pot Roast Soup, **146**
Poultry
    Cornish Game Hens with Rice Stuffing, **48–50**, *49*
    Duck Gumbo, **165–66**
    Glop, **100**
    Pheasants in Wine Sauce, **46–47**
    see also Chicken
Preacher's Delight, **12**
Prune Meat, **128**
Pudding, Rice, Grandma Newman's, **192**
Pudding Cake, Lemon, **188**, *189*

Q
Quilt-Top Country Ham, **154–55**

R
Rabbit, Louisiana Smothered, **164**
Raisins
    Baked Boston Brown Bread, **180**, *181*
    Boiled Cake, **186**
    Bubie Alte's Lukshen Kugel, **126**
    Fruitcake, **198–99**
    Jefferson Davis Pie, **193**

Rice
    and Chicken Dish, Mom's, **137**
    Chili Balls, **68**
    Green Mountain Surprise, **101**
    Hunter's Chicken, **40**, *41*
    Pudding, Grandma Newman's, **192**
    Salmagundi Bake, **13**
    Stuffing, Cornish Game Hens with, **48–50**, *49*
Roast Chicken with Orange Cream Gravy, **42**

S
Salad, Shrimp, Mighty Good, **26**
Salmagundi Bake, **13**
Salmon Loaf, **147**
Salmon Wiggle, **84**
Saltine Lasagna, **134**, **141**
Sandwiches
    Cheese Frenchees, **86**, *87*
    Crispy Iowa Skinnies, **156**
    Grandma Wooly's Beef Barbecue, **62**, *63*
Sauces
    Sunday Sugo, **66**, *67*
    Tomato, Sunday, with Meatballs, **69**
Saucy Mustard Beef Steak, **61**
Sauerkraut and Apple Pork Chops, **51**
Sausages
    Cornbread Meatloaf, **98**, *99*
    Johnny Marzetti, **78**
    Mrs. Rockefeller's Meatloaf, **74–75**
    Shall's Classic Lasagna, **122–25**, *123*
    Sicilian Meatloaf, *114*, **115**
    Sunday Sugo, **66**, *67*
Savory Strudel with Beef, Potatoes, and Onions, **111–12**
Screaming Noodles, **102**, *103*
Shall's Classic Lasagna, **122–25**, *123*
Shellfish
    Chesapeake Partan Bree, *152*, **172–73**
    Grandma Taylor's Crab Cakes, **177**
    Long Island Clam Pie, **175–76**
    Mighty Good Shrimp Salad, **26**
    Pivoto-Robinson Shrimp Creole, **170**, *171*
Shepherd's Pie, Kids' Favorite, **97**
Shrimp Creole, Pivoto-Robinson, **170**, *171*
Shrimp Salad, Mighty Good, **26**
Sicilian Meatloaf, *114*, **115**

Side dishes
    Aunt Nina's Breadballs and Sauce, **142–44**, *143*
    Blue Ridge Baked Bean Burgoo, **167**
    Bubie Alte's Lukshen Kugel, **126**
    "Candied" Apples in Cinnamon Syrup, **105**
    Corn Pie, **27–29**, *28*
    Creamy Potato Puff, **104**
    Great-Grandma's Corn Fritters, *178*, **179**
    Martini Mac and Cheese, **24, 25**
    Maryland Caramel Tomatoes, **72, 85**
    Mom's Hominy, **19**
    Nonni's Pasta Mollica (Pasta with Bread Crumbs), **119**
    Saltine Lasagna, *134*, **141**
    Screaming Noodles, **102**, *103*
    Snowed-In Potato Hot Dish, **149**
Single-Crust Pie Dough, **194**
Snowed-In Potato Hot Dish, **149**
Soups
    Char's Maine Fish Chowder, **174**
    Chesapeake Partan Bree, *152*, **172–73**
    Grandma's Borscht, **127**
    Pasta, with Little Meatballs, Aunt Fanny's, **106**, *116*
    Pennsylvania Dutch Slippery Chicken Bott Bie,
        160–61
    Pot Roast, **146**
    see also Stews
Southern Braised Pork Chops 'n' Gravy, **96**
Spinach
    Delicate Manicotti, **120–21**
    Green Mountain Surprise, **101**
    Screaming Noodles, **102**, *103*
    Shall's Classic Lasagna, **122–25**, *123*
Squash. *See* Zucchini
Stews
    Blue Ridge Baked Bean Burgoo, **167**
    Chicken 'n' Dumplings, **39**
    Chicken Paprikash, **130–31**
    Deviled Beef Tenders, **60**
    Horseradish Beef, **59**
    Outrageous Gulyás, **129**
    Prune Meat, **128**
Strudel, Savory, with Beef, Potatoes, and Onions, **111–12**
Sunday Sugo, **66, 67**
Sunday Tomato Sauce with Meatballs, **69**
Sweet and Sour Meatballs, **70**

T
Tamale Pie, Granny's, **6, 7–8**
Tia's Coffee Pot Roast, **57–58**
Tomato(es)
    Aunt Fanny's Pasta Soup with Little Meatballs,
        106, *116*
    Aunt Nina's Breadballs and Sauce, **142–44**, *143*
    Blue Ridge Baked Bean Burgoo, **167**
    Braciole with Neapolitan Sauce, **117–18**
    Chili Balls, **68**
    Delicate Manicotti, **120–21**
    Glop, **100**
    Granny's Tamale Pie, **6, 7–8**
    Johnny Marzetti, **78**
    Maryland Caramel, **72, 85**
    Papa's Lasagna, **21–23**, *22*
    peeling, **85**
    Pivoto-Robinson Shrimp Creole, **170**, *171*
    Sauce, Sunday, with Meatballs, **69**
    Sunday Sugo, **66, 67**
    Sweet and Sour Meatballs, **70**
Traditional Upper Peninsula Pasties, **108–10**, *109*
Tuna-Tater Bake, **148**
Turkey
    Glop, **100**

V
Vanilla Wafer Cake, *182*, **184**
Veal
    Mock Chicken Legs, **79–81**, *80*
Vegetables. *See specific vegetables*

W
Waffles, Creamy Chicken and, **138–39**
Whipped Cream, Bourbon, **193**
WWII Chicken à la King, **136**

Y
Yankee Pot Roast Supper, **157**

Z
Zucchini
    Saltine Lasagna, *134*, **141**

FROM THE KITCHEN OF

FROM THE KITCHEN OF